G000271315

Spain

Also by Robert Elms

In Search of the Crack

Spain

A Portrait after the General

ROBERT ELMS

HEINEMANN : LONDON

Para mi madre

Thank-you: Carlos, Iain, Ivan, Lorenzo and Sade.

Acknowledgements

There are certain books which have been invaluable in improving my understanding of Spain. Foremost among them is John Hooper's excellent study of Spanish history and society, *The Spaniards* (1986). As a general guide the most informative and entertaining that I have read is the *Cadogan Guide to Spain* (1987) by Dana Facaros and Michael Pauls. Two books on Spanish design were of particular help. Emma Dent Coad's *Spanish Design and Architecture* (1990) and *New Spanish Design* by Guy Julier (1991). And on the complex and much analysed subject of the Corrida nothing in English has yet come close to equalling the excellence of *Bull Fever* by Kenneth Tynan (1955). I would also at this point like to thank my editor Tom Weldon whose enthusiasm for a country which was new to him came as a constant source of support to a hardened Hispanophile.

William Heinemann Ltd
Michelin House, 81 Fulham Road, London SW3 6RB
LONDON   MELBOURNE   AUCKLAND

First published 1992
Copyright © Robert Elms 1992
Reprinted 1992

A CIP catalogue record for this book
is held by the British Library
ISBN 0 434 22824 9

Printed in Great Britain
by Clays Ltd, St. Ives plc

Introduction

The General and I were both dying when I first set foot on Spanish tarmac. He was a man in his eighties rotting inexorably in a Madrid palace; I was a fifteen-year-old boy on a school skiing trip to Andorra, clutching his new passport like a bible and wondering whether he would live to see the outside of Barcelona airport. Francisco Franco, the unflinching leader of the Civil War, would no doubt have sneered at the sight of a green English youth reduced to heaving over an airport toilet bowl, but airsickness can rarely have taken so virulent a hold on a first-time flyer. Nine months later though Franco was even closer to death and I was back at that airport with an expectant glow, bound for abandon on the Costa Brava, so I guess I had the last laugh. Spain has been laughing and living ever since that November night in 1975 when the great leader was finally led away. I'm glad I've been there to see some of it.

Franco's death, like that of Dali fourteen years later, was an epic and messy affair. Both spent months suffering whatever is the opposite of euthanasia, as they were kept alive mercilessly by people terrified of the vacuum that their demise would leave in its wake. To this day those who remember the former event with shining eyes tell a tale of opening the refrigerator door time and again to reach for the bottle of champagne that they had been waiting so long to drink, only to have their celebration quashed by news of yet another recovery.

When finally he was allowed to go, so runs an oft-told joke, a doctor, his body trembling with emotion, announced to the inner circle, 'The generalissimo is dead, who will tell the people?' The response was rapid and revealing: 'Sod the people, who will tell the generalissimo?' Such was the hold that Francisco Franco had exerted over his country for forty frozen years, such was the fear and, it must be said, the respect he generated.

Yet his departure led to the rolling back of a shroud which had suffocated and isolated the Spanish peoples since the Civil War. Breathing again, this large and brilliant land has forged a remarkable role in the new world that the old continent of Europe has been trying to create for itself. Spain has gone from being the pariah of the West, the last great bastion of the dictatorial days, to one of the most liberal states in the world; from a country where regional identities were violently suppressed to one where genuine local autonomy co-exists with real national harmony.

It is a true and telling testimony to the achievements of the Spanish peoples that when the collapsing countries of Eastern Europe recently began their own struggle from the shackles of dictatorship, the place they went to learn how to emerge from darkness and into democracy was Spain. There was no other contemporary example where the success had been so complete.

Spain has witnessed too an economic rebirth in which it has risen from being the poorest country in Western Europe, a land which knew real hunger, to one of the ten richest nations in the world, with the highest growth rate in the entire continent sustained for over a decade. It has jumped from being a pre-industrial to a post-industrial society and it has gone from being an exporter to an importer of people. Along the way it has also been transformed from a closed and separate land, standing haughtily apart from its neighbours, to an outward-looking, progressively European nation. Spain is not just back in Europe, right now it is at the very front of it. All of this has occurred in a time scale too short and too full to be credible.

2

Change has been both rapid and occasionally wrenching. But all in all the transformation has been achieved with an ease which is both remarkable and indicative of the desire within the Spanish to rid themselves of the worst of their recent past and to play a part in the real world. Yet they have not turned their back on the very traditions which have always made Spain so vividly attractive for the traveller. Instead, the past and the present, the conventional and the novel, have flowered and blended together in a fascinating synthesis.

It is this unique and powerful combination of the old and the new, the radical and the traditional, which has made Spain so special. Spain is so remarkable, so exciting today because it can draw on such a deep well from yesterday, a fund which was preserved, frozen by Francoism, to be unleashed as the warmth of freedom flowed from his death. As King Juan Carlos put it so incisively in a speech in 1986, 'The new Spain returns to her past, using the best of her traditions to build the future – a free, plural and tolerant Spain.'

None of this of course occurred to that teenager turning a violent shade of mildew as he experienced the thrill of descending from 20,000 feet for the first time. Neither did I realise that I would grow sick of Barcelona airport for very different reasons a dozen years later, as I spent endless, embittered hours waiting for dodgy and invariably delayed charter flights to ferry me back to London from my adopted city.

I didn't really notice Spain on my first visit there. For one thing, this was a skiing holiday and the impoverished Pyrenean resort where I learned to fall over in the snow-plough position bore little relation to anybody's image of Iberia. For another, I didn't look.

Six months later though I had a second chance to discover what I supposed was the real Spain, as I headed for a promised land of girls and barmen who both said yes. I was sixteen now, freed from the scrutiny of schoolmasters, travelling with two pals and by coincidence heading yet again for the Catalan capital. This time though it was simply a dropping-off point for somewhere far more important called Lloret del Mar and the cheapest week that the brochures could offer.

Lloret, which sits an hour or so's drive from Barcelona along the Costa Brava, was the very first resort on the Spanish coast to be colonised by British holiday-makers and stands today as a vivid, crumbling concrete testament to the achievements of package tour imperialism. The brochures describe this high-rise, low-rent collection of shanty skyscrapers as 'Bubbling with action twenty-four hours a day', or 'A simmering, young and lively resort'. And it is of course all very, very true. There are over six hundred bars in Lloret, every single one of them with at least one British kid throwing up outside. The front is a kind of lager-golden mile where the clubs have names like the Queen Vic (honest!) and Rockerfellers, and where the prosaic dreams of the massed ranks of the youth section of the British working classes come true night after night.

Lloret is the kind of resort that the Spanish are now trying to disown as canned holidays go out of fashion and the Spanish tourist industry tries to move up-market. But I thought then that it was the best place in the world and I still believe I wasn't entirely wrong.

It was there that I met that pre-fabricated, self-contained country where swimming pools mysteriously fill up with garden furniture overnight, buffet lunches fly through the air and discotheques stage grandiose mock battles nightly for the enjoyment of the tourists. In this surreal, juvenile principality where pink people rule, I managed to lie my way into bed with a dappled girl from Greenford whose father worked at London airport, and regularly drink myself into a stupor.

One morning though, shortly after dawn, woken by the kind of thirst which only drinking can create, I went in search of something, anything bar fetid tap water, to soothe my arid throat. My eyes, already raw through excess, were dazzled by a sunlight which seemed even more potent at so early an

4

hour and I stumbled on, driven by my coca-cola craving, like some cheap actor in a desert melodrama. Except that once outside the resort compound I wasn't in a wasteland, but another country.

Here in an ordinary, everyday Costa Brava village there were real people, including grown-ups, who were not taking part in some gaudy holiday masquerade, but waking up and living lives. It came as quite a shock to realise that women cleaned their steps and working men went off to work, that things were different here from the hotel Spain just a mile away. With a small church and a sandy square where old men sat, already seeking shade, it was a glimpse of a way of living. Everything was strangely normal in a foreign kind of way: not just recognisable but instantly, almost instinctively attractive.

Apart from armada sagas learnt by rote and old film of Real Madrid demolishing all-comers in European Cups, Spain had not impinged itself too deeply on my teenage consciousness. I guess I had a remote and romantic idea of the Civil War and of that general then just three months from death, but I had no notion that this was a real country, the first one I'd seen going about its everyday business. That was something else indeed.

The sun certainly played its part. Burning down, it made life look more intense, slowed it down like the dream sequences in corny films. The colours too, the dusty, ochre hues which touch all Spanish towns, no matter how lowly, were rich and romantic to a boy from the rain streaked greys of suburban London. Truth be told, these are all reasons I've added on since: I don't really know why, but I was touched. From that point on, deep down I knew that abroad for me meant Spain. And Spain was now somewhere exotic and tangible, somewhere I was meant to see.

Or so it seems now. I don't remember whether I located some liquid in a local shop on that scorching, thirsty morning or returned to the hotel still dry to devour the breakfast coffee before the morning bun-fight began. I don't suppose I spent the rest of the week musing on that sad southern land of blood and sand that they talk about in books. I got drunk again and failed to convince the girl whose father worked at Heathrow to repeat the rapid experience. But that day stayed with me.

Spain became, in the minor, nagging way that things do in adolescence, my other country. This adoption, coinciding with a burgeoning political awareness, led me to immerse myself sporadically in tales of the Civil War, of La Pasionaria, Guernica and the brave bereted men of the International Brigades. I discovered that a fellow sixth-former at Orange Hill Grammar School, Colin Paynter, was actually the son of Will Paynter, a Welsh miner who had been a leading British Brigadista. Will Paynter was still alive, still politically active and still filled with the passion that made young British men board boats for Spain. That made it all seem more tangible, more terrible, and even more romantic.

Then later at the LSE, where everybody still played student politics, I made friends with an English kid who had lived for years in Spain as a boy, and with a young, politically active Basque exile who gave us cryptic reports from the front line that usually involved flying bits of Guardia Civil commanders. In between studying, going out, dressing up and falling down, I kept half an eye on the democratic Spain that was emerging from the long sleep of autocracy. I think I only had half an eye on the television the day Lieutenant-Colonel Antonio Tejero made his début.

For young Spaniards, this caricature of a Guardia Civil commander plays the same role as that of President Kennedy's death in the lives of Americans. Everybody can remember what they were doing on the afternoon of 23 February 1981 when Tejero marched into a televised session of the Congress, raised a pistol and held the new democracy to ransom in the name of the king, the Church and the nation. I was sitting in my mum's living room in north London, eating dinner and watching the news, as this little man with the green uniform, droopy Zapata moustache and ominous tricorn hat strutted his ridiculous stuff with a group of frightened-looking young soldiers behind him.

I can remember being terrified too in case this meant that I was going to have a chance to live out all those Civil War fantasies for real, and it certainly came close. Valencia fell instantly to the tanks which took to the streets, Basque fishing ships readied themselves to start running guns again and the newly legalised Communist Party predictably told its supporters to do nothing but stay calm and organise.

I hadn't been back to Spain since that hazy week of teenage hedonism, and despite all my romantic delusions I can't honestly say that I fancied going off to die in some dusty field. I didn't even know where the Ebro was and I certainly wasn't eager to perish romantically defending it, no matter how good the clothes looked. So I was pretty relieved when a day later the news came through that the coup attempt had collapsed, the young king had sided with the good guys (some people still wonder though why it took him eight hours to make a statement supporting the fragile new constitution) and Tejero's moustache was behind bars. But I don't suppose I was as relieved as the mass of the peoples of Spain.

For two days after the military made their final (well not quite, but that story comes later), abortive effort to pickle the Spanish peoples in the bitter fluid of autocracy, those people turned out in their millions to show their support for the future against the past.

Any idea of a new Spain, any look at this incredible success story, really begins with the failure of that cartoon coup. Tejero may have been a profoundly ridiculous figure, but the forces manipulating him were serious indeed, and if they had succeeded in stifling the infant democracy, the dark ages could have fallen again south of the Pyrenees.

Instead Spain in the last decade, the Spain which has exerted such a powerful hold over me, has been a place of light. Not just the sun which seems to shine with a clarity and a brilliance more imposing than anywhere in Europe. But a sense of optimism and a feeling of weightlessness, a joy if

7

you like, which has radiated from the people themselves. This book is a look at them and a mobile and very personal portrait of a small part of the land they inhabit. It is also a look at my continuing love affair with this old and proud, this coming country.

I

It was a search for civilisation which led me back to Barcelona. I'd been, as so many do, to Ibiza to holiday, and anybody who has served time on the Island will know that sanity can seem a long way off. Ibiza is a place full of wild stories, many of them lies admittedly, but there's enough truth in the tales of mayhem to disrupt seriously the brains of an English boy. So with a head scrambled by far too many good nights and a few days of holiday left, I thought it a wise idea to board a boat and head for that place I'd heard about in whispers and read about in books. I was lucky to see the city from the sea.

The statue of Christopher Columbus, or Cristobal Colón as the Spanish call him, stares sternly out at new arrivals, reminding them that far greater men have pulled into this port. It's morning when the ferry arrives from Ibiza, hopefully a strong, azure morning like the one which met me as I awoke from that awful, tiring sleep that ships provide. Barcelona, framed by a crystal Mediterranean sky, looks like a serious city, a busy, noisy, seaside city. It is good to arrive by boat, because then you begin to understand.

Barcelona is above all a port. The city is built around the bay where rusting ships come to empty their bowels and the Catalan wealth is built on trade. Columbus is there, alongside a replica of the Santa Maria, because this is where he arrived when he sailed right back across the sea. And bell-bottomed sailors still swing along the quay, Americans with their wide-eyed, New World bravado and Spaniards with red pom-poms on their hats. The minute you step from the ferry to the land

9

you can feel that this is a happening town. It is good to arrive by boat, because then you begin at the beginning.

Barcelona is like one of those giant old trees that have been sliced through the middle to expose the rings that reveal its history. If you start with your back to the water and walk slowly towards Jesus, who stands arms outstretched, high on one of the hills in the distance, the story of how this town grew, of its great and its terrible days, is all laid out before you.

You soon understand that this is a town without ghosts, because nothing ever dies here. All of the pasts from the Gothic to the Francoist, the Catholic to the anarchist are still vividly and very noisily alive. The future is also being constructed at a remarkable rate but, when you've just arrived at the docks and need somewhere to stay, the past is more likely to present itself.

The road leading up from the port into the town is actually a series of roads strung together to form the Ramblas, the spinal thoroughfare around which the old part of Barcelona is constructed. And this Ramblas is like no other road I've ever travelled.

The nature of this unique street with its ornate modernist pharmacies and fancy Miró pavement changes as it progresses up town. It is by turns a market for flowers and caged animals, a political forum and a promenade, it is a boulevard lined with cafés, and a centre for museums and theatres, it is a centre for street theatre and street sex. Knots of old men gather at one end to argue, some of them refighting their civil war. While boys with the haughty air of the dark and arty do their best to convince themselves that they could be the next Dali. And through all of this and all the time, the Catalans stroll with the laconic, slightly indifferent gait that they invariably employ, and double-park to show their famed disrespect for authority.

Along the entire length of this gaudy, rollicking pantomime of a street there awaits an inferno of hawkers and bootblacks, pushers and buskers, prophets and cutpurses. According to the locals the Ramblas has more ways of taking your money than any street in the world, and when you arrive from a ship with your bag in hand the first people trying to separate you from your cash are the whores.

For a city with such a highly developed sense of aesthetics Barcelona has the ugliest prostitute population imaginable. At the very foot of the Ramblas they stand, all varicose veins protruding from plump, pallid legs, hair bleached into an orange bottle blonde, or dyed harsh raven black. The ones hanging on the left-hand side of the Ramblas, in the fetid alleys around the admirably named Euro-Sex Snack Bar, tend to be a little better looking. But then you'd better look closer because these are the transvestites. It is probably safer just to head for a hotel, the Ramblas has plenty of those too.

From the poorest of pensiones to hotels that have known real grandeur, the roads around the Ramblas offer a variety of places to unpack your bag. I learned later that the real good hotels, the modern places with conditioned air and staff who understand, are up and away from this fine madness. To everybody who spends more than a moment in this city, a time comes when they crave those cool marble floors and bars that make a good Martini. You need a refuge from the suffocating old town and all its high-pressure charms. Modern, successful, elegant Barcelona is a great city to live in, but for the first time it's perhaps best to be buried down in the riot.

I was armed that day with the name of a hotel adorned with mythologies. It came complete with a forlorn little escritorium, a writing room where Picasso once stuck stamps on letters and a dining room ceiling which fell regularly into my coffee. Another nearby has the most bizarre modernist fireplace in its tea-bar, and a dining room so ornate I thought I'd stumbled into some forgotten palace. The hotels around the Ramblas can be charming, atmospheric and cheap. But they certainly cannot be quiet.

The Ramblas and the warren of streets which lead off it are alive and lively for more hours than you could ever care to be awake. Barcelona really is the city that never lets you sleep, as it goes on so long and gets up so early that the two ends invariably meet in the middle, right outside your bedroom window. On that first visit, which now seems a long time ago, I was staying in my crumbling hotel and looking for civilisation through tired eyes. You have to counter this by mastering the rhythm of the place quickly.

The town rises to work before you are going to get up. Other Spaniards moan about the exaggerated work ethic of the Catalans (they also think they are indefensibly tight with money) and you would probably do the same if they decided to start working with pneumatic drills while you were attempting to get some sleep. They do though, like all good Iberians, observe the tradition of the siesta, so lunchtime goes on forever. Then in the early evening people often nap again to catch up on the sleep that they are about to miss. This I learnt is the way it must be. For the most remarkable aspect of life in any Spanish city, to someone from an early-to-bed Protestant society at least, is just how late everybody goes out and stays out. Dinner rarely starts before ten and often much later. Arrive at a nightclub at two and you are too early. Dawn is when the night logically ends for the Spanish, unless of course they really feel like going on. When I first landed in Barcelona, not knowing any of this, I wandered around with a kind of ship lag, gazing into closed shops and eating in empty restaurants. But still I wandered around in love.

Back then, before the selling job had been done so success-fully and Barcelona became a name again, the most remark-able thing about being there was that you seemed to be alone in the crowd. The word had been out of course, but was the gossip of no more than a few. So on that first excursion it felt like walking around some glorious modern-day and incredibly crowded Machu Picchu between the mountains and the Mediterranean.

Barcelona is divided very neatly into uptown and down by the pivotal Plaza de Cataluña. Up is modernist and then modern: an impressive, expansive metropolis where the well-to-do shop for fashion and furniture, and stop for coffee and gossip. Down is ancient and claustrophobic, dark with its crowded past and sometimes seedy present. Down is also bisected by the Ramblas into two distinctly different barrios, on one side the Gotico, on the other the Chino. These when you first arrive are the places you discover.

The barrio Gotico, or the Gothic quarter, is the dense heart of the ancient capital of the country of the Catalans. Here are the rich edifices of the local government, with buildings and a street pattern dating back to the thirteenth century. The alleys are so narrow that the light rarely enters, and the twists and turns so labyrinthine that you can easily find yourself lost in its cobbled folds. This is no bad place to be lost though.

In the area that sits clustered around the ominous, rather worrying black spikes of the cathedral, the Gotico is beautiful and gentrified. Its streets are full of dark and dusty antique shops that seem to be permanently shut, and the occasional strumming hippy, equally out to lunch. Inside the vast, rich church you can feel the awe that Catholicism created for so long, see perhaps why churches were burnt in Barcelona with such regularity during the fighting time. But you can also see the beauty, especially in the soft, dappled light of the cloisters where old women encased in mourning sit and stare at the twelve geese who live by the pond.

Near here is the Picasso museum, a handsome old court-yard house converted to hold many of the early works of the master. But here too is a bar name of Portillon which seems to have been dug from a cave and then singed to make it even darker. This was one of the homes of the wild anarchists who torched the churches and fought alongside Durruti in the Civil War. And to this day those who hate the state gather to eat tapas, drink cheap red wine from tumblers and talk of freedoms. The patrons of Portillon all seemed then to be outcasts, the lame and the infirm, many in wheelchairs, mixed with the anarchists and the artists and those who simply wanted a good soaking. I loved it instantly and love it still.

In this hypnotic neighbourhood there are dozens of small old shops staffed by small and implausibly old ladies, selling everything from hams to millinery. There are *churrerías*, the kiosks which sell the sweet, greasy and irresistible Spanish variant on the doughnut. Restaurants, bars and pensiones crowd together, fitting themselves into unlikely, uncomfortable gaps. The darkness is exaggerated by the washing which flaps like so many flags of proud poverty from the tiny apartments which hang over you. The barrio Gotico is what estate agents would describe as full of character. And many of those characters gather in the Spanish square of the Plaza Real.

A regular, perfectly balanced neo-classical square where the sun falls on fading yellow facades and palm trees sway just like they should, this plaza off the Ramblas looks, unlike its surrounding Gothic streets, like the Spain you expected. But when I first sat here drinking beer and thinking of food, I noticed that other darker faces of this country were beginning to appear.

For amid the tables, where shabbily white-coated waiters scurry for tourists, one of these sorry servants maybe dragging a club-foot, were the bruised and the beaten. Dark-skinned and thin, the *gitanos* in clothes too tight, watched for angles, looking expectantly for an edge. While the junkies, their eyes emptied, hung disconsolate, waiting perhaps for a man. The Plaza Real back then was a long way from gentrified, a long way even from the nearby streets of the barrio Gotico. The Plaza Real then was like an outpost of the Chino.

A few years later, when the process of cleaning up the downtown was well underway, and some of this was in danger of becoming history, I was to sit in a friend's apartment playing a kitsch and curious board game called El Chino. In this game you could either opt to be a hooker or a pusher, gangster or pimp, and you moved around the board collecting drugs and venereal diseases, money and condoms, buying, selling and generally conducting the business of the night. If you were a transvestite, you saved your ill-gotten for a sex-change operation. I thought that that game, with its cheerful amorality, said a lot about the changes which had taken place in this country since the end of Franco. But when I first walked into the real barrio Chino I never knew.

Over on the other side, the wild side, of the Ramblas, the barrio Chino is a mysteriously chineseless China town, a dripping tenderloin where things go on. Secreted behind the huge undercover food market, the Chino is just as maze-like as the Gothic quarter, though it lacks the beauty and the charm of that ancient district. It is a messy and undeniably dark district occasionally punctuated by quiet and quite beautiful little squares – except they tend to be made a little less attractive by the used needles lying on the floor. Still you can't help liking it, or at least I couldn't: despite being a true home of the lowest life this city has to offer, the barrio Chino, certainly during the day, has never felt like a particularly dangerous place to be – providing of course you watch your step. For in among its sometimes filthy streets there are some great treasures.

There is Casa Leopoldo, a classic and expensive, tiled Catalan restaurant which is up a text-book alley filled with boys who will be girls; Egipto, a cheap and fine young eaterie busy with the new designer bohemia of fashionable Barcelona. And down yet another near blind alley, the wonderful bull-fighting bar Pena Manolete. This rock-bottom bar covered in pictures of old toreros, smelling dense with cooking oil and coruscating tobacco smoke, is the place where expatriate Andalusians come to drink anise and talk of the Arena. Here the fat men in dark glasses and the skinny men who once longed to wear the suit of lights curse the bull breeders and managers and dream of the perfect corrida. I don't recall if I found these then or later. But I definitely met, down a street that starts with broken neon, bar Marseille.

I stumbled upon the bar Marseille on my first ignorant excursion into the barrio Chino on that first weekend in Barcelona. People have been stumbling out of there for years. A black and white television plays noiselessly in the corner of this large, scruffy, barely furnished bar. But then few people bar the huge barmaid are looking. Some are playing an animated game of cards or dominos in the corner, but most sit alone and stare hard at their drinks. For Marseille is an absinthe bar.

Absinthe is drunk with dreamy ceremony, a fork placed over the top of a glass with a sugar cube resting on its prongs, water is dripped slowly onto the sugar and the sweet solution runs into the dark green liquid. Despite all the romantic associations with Paris at its peak, the stuff is so toxic and absinthism is so virulent an addiction that the drink has been banned in most parts of the world, but not in the barrio Chino. Here even bad dreams are still allowed.

When I finally allowed myself to try absinthe I ended up losing a day which survives now only as shards, but which definitely included sitting with the working women of the barrio who I believe showed me a certain kindness. Later on, in a time not obscured by the green liquid, I discovered in the Chino, on a square lined with lumpy prostitutes, that there is a small plaque celebrating Alexander Fleming, such is the affection of this diseased place for the man who discovered penicillin. When you have discovered the great down of Barcelona, the only way to go is uptown.

Uptown starts at the Plaza de Cataluña, starts really at the bar Zurich where the young and posed start their day by looking at each other. There is (or at least there was then) a kind of apartheid operating in Barcelona between up- and downtown, with those whose lives take place in the neat streets north of the plaza rarely descending into the area of the Ramblas. Having spent some time buried in the hot and vivid Kowloon which winds towards the sea, I was certainly glad that there was somewhere else to go.

If the Ramblas represents the passion and the wildness that gave the anarchist stronghold of Barcelona its Civil War nickname, the 'Rose of Fire', then the Paseo de Gracia is its cool antidote, the other side of the Catalan character. Or maybe I should call it by its Catalan name, the Passeig de

Gracia. I guess this is a good time for a quick discussion of schizophrenia.

The most common piece of graffiti to be seen on the walls of Barcelona consists of a star with three lines beneath it and the scrawled inscription *En Catala*! This is probably the work of an earnest young man with a beard, who has spent an evening getting stoned in a local bar, and listening intently to stories (told in Catalan of course) about the barbarism of the Spanish. In response he has gone out and sprayed over the nearest piece of Castilian he can find, the symbol of the *Terra Llure* (free earth, the Catalan separatist movement), and the message, 'In Catalan'. This graffiti which appears with numbing regularity at least serves to remind you that you are, after all, in Catalonia.

That first time I certainly needed telling. I arrived with the notion that Catalan was something like Geordie, a northern dialect used only by footballers and TV script-writers. But you soon learn that it is a language, closest if anything to French, and as distinct from Castilian, the language of Madrid, as is, say, Italian. And because Catalan was suppressed by the General and because Madrid is the repository of all evil, it is an object of much pride among those who can speak it. And they do speak it. Describing Catalan as a dialect is still a good way of winding up earnest young Barcelonan men with beards though.

The town is now officially and genuinely bilingual with every street name, road sign and proclamation in both idioms, but any bits of stray Castilian which stand alone are bound to get the treatment. Since the many moves towards autonomy which have occurred in democratic Spain, the clamour for an independent Catalonia has largely died down. But there is no doubt that these Iberians with their hissing, sibilant tongue which looks like French and sounds somehow Eastern European, are different to their more southerly brothers. That difference, and the split personality which seems to be an essential part of the Catalan character, become obvious the moment you walk up the Paseo de Gracia.

For one thing there are the banks. Housed in buildings of which any potentate would be proud, the banks which fan out in huge numbers from the square look like some terribly tasteful festival of finance. Their hoardings and logos designed by the most renowned and respected of artists, they stand as a permanent exhibition of the business acumen and aesthetic sensibility of these people. Affluence and efficiency shout quietly and stylishly from all sides. This does not look like a land famous for *mañana*.

Then there is the contrast between the wide, gracious and almost perfectly beautiful boulevard before you, and its warped mirror image, the Ramblas. The chasm between these two streets divided by a few hundred metres is so great that it is difficult to believe that they belong in the same city – until, that is, you come to terms with the fact that the Catalans are themselves a very contradictory lot.

Two expressions in the Catalan language are said to express this split personality. One is *seny*, a word which roughly translates as common sense with a bit of business acumen thrown in. This is the characteristic which makes the Catalans such successful businessmen, such tolerant, rational people. But the other great word in the Catalan canon is *arrauxment*, a revelling in extremism, impetuousness, even violence. *Arrauxment* is said to account for the anarchism, the art and the architecture. Taken together the two words portray a people who are prepared to go to violent lengths to protect what they see as reasonable, a people for whom sweet liberalism is an extreme cause worth giving your all for. *Seny* and *arrauxment* just about sum them up.

But then so does the geography of their great town. Where the downtown is crazed and secretive, so the city from the Plaza de Cataluña up to the hills is a clean, open, airy grid of broad streets lined with refined shops and apartments. Here, even then, you could buy fine white china, or the latest chair from Paris or Milan. You could watch men with white hair and money stroll their wives to restaurants where the linen was as crisp as the wine. You could read the newspapers of the world, or just watch the young queuing in the united pastel colours of Benetton to see movies and make out. And from the tall, graceful buildings with their fancy, wrought-iron balconies you could see the three flags, of Spain, Catalonia and of Europe, flying next to each other, and see that they all made sense in this intensely European city.

The city around the Paseo de Gracia is known as Eixample and it is a striking testament, not only to the wealth, the power and the sophistication of the Barcelonans, but also to their powerful sense of order. I was told by a young friend, a chaotic poet prone to wild drinking fits, his chest swollen with civic pride, how town planners the world over are brought to Barcelona to see how to make a city work. This, you must never forget, is the place where it was the anarchists who made the trains run on time.

All of the Spanish are thoroughly urban people: even the smaller towns make like major cities with genuine street life. The people use the streets and the plazas as their theatres, places to congregate and to gossip, to show off and to hang out, so that urban life is a kind of perpetual public display. They are also intensely proud of their major cities and the culture which exists in them. The hard, often arid countryside is seen as the domain of the uncivilised; the building of great cities as the triumph of man over the bitter elements. For all their agricultural prowess, Spaniards congregate: even in the countryside the pattern is one of villages rather than isolated farms, and in the major centres they are crammed together. Barcelona for example is the fourth most densely populated city in the world. And walking that continental, cosmopolitan street with two names, drinking good coffee and seeing the people going seriously about their business in the sunshine, I realised just how good and great a city this is.

Once I struggled up from the addictive miasma downtown to the light, liberating Barcelona which lies beyond, I knew I'd found that civilisation I was looking for. And civilisation is a fine thing, especially when Antoní Gaudí was its architect.

When you look at those delirious buildings which Gaudí gave the city and the world, when you walk into those ornate, organic wombs, the most remarkable thing is not how they look, but how they ever let it happen. These are the most remarkable, the most ridiculous, and, in their way, the most sublime buildings ever constructed, with a beauty that can only be considered in terms of itself, because there really is nothing like this anywhere. And the good, steady bourgeois folk of this town allowed them, paid for them, to be made.

Modernismo, the startling Spanish variant on the theme of art nouveau, found a home in the bold, confident city that was Barcelona at the turn of the century. And it found in Antoní Gaudí a man who was prepared and able to make his fantastic private visions into public statements of the most radical intent.

Watching his bizarre unfinished masterpiece, the church of the Sagrada Familia, being slowly constructed is like watching a dinosaur being born. Here, in this city where the past is still present, they labour away on this mad, impossibly surreal carnival of a building that will still look futuristic way into the future. Even though Gaudí left no plans when he was run over by a tram (his death was just as eccentric as his life), workmen carry on piecing together this giant jigsaw. In Barcelona a building site is the biggest tourist attraction, and it all seems normal.

On the Paseo de Gracia the stamp of this undoubted, undoubting genius has turned a road that would have been graceful and elegant without him into one which sets the imagination flying. The two daring, thrilling edifices which he constructed as apartments and offices are kept not as museums, not in the kind of architectural aspic which Paris wraps around its great monuments, but as offices and apartments.

Gaudí and his masterful contemporary Domènech i Montaner, who have left their brilliant, individualist signature throughout the city, bequeathed not only a legacy of great buildings, but the idea of the fantastic, the remarkable, as commonplace. The everyday in Barcelona is a visual odyssey.

Modernismo found a home among the Catalans because they are a people, for all their nous and acumen, for all their sophistication and taste, with extremism in their soul. And the modern-day Catalans have continued that tradition in architecture and art, in interiors and graphics. Barcelona today is the most designed city in the world, but then it always has been. All of this I thought as I walked along the Paseo de Gracia. Though it may have been much later.

It may seem odd going to Barcelona as I did on the run from Ibiza to seek refuge from nightclubs, but you see nobody knew back then. I knew a name, or at least a phone number, and fancying a night out before returning to London, I rang to see if my contact minded being a guide. In such ways do terrible things begin.

Pino is a big man, a large-bearded, bear-hugging kind of man who promotes pop music and lives on a hill called Tibidabo up near Jesus. Pino is actually an Italian, but he came to settle, for reasons which remain mysterious, in Barcelona as a youth and has stayed there ever since, which is not really all that long as Pino is still a young man. But he's done a bit.

I seem to remember he said, 'Meet me at Universal at midnight.' It was also, as I recall, rather quiet walking up towards Universal, a bar which is right up out of historic Barcelona and into the more conventional, continental-looking new town where most people actually live. It may have been a Thursday: it certainly didn't feel like an especially big night and I had no great expectations of raving.

Universal, a large, good-looking bar spread over two floors, was perhaps a quarter full of the kind of people most European cities provide. Boys with sunglasses in their top pockets who probably came on scooters, men with brightly coloured pullovers draped just so, girls with short skirts and flat shoes leaning on bars and smoking. The music downstairs was loud and rocky, sounding a little dated to my élitist ears. Upstairs it was quieter so I settled there, bought a drink and waited for Pino.

When we left Universal a couple of hours later it was rammed and we were heading for another well-designed, well-attended bar, only now the streets had changed. They were not quiet, but buzzing with the young. Groups of kids hung, casting hopefully cool shapes, around dozens of little drinking centres. They were standing on the pavements, spilling into the road, leaning on cars and scooters, flirting gently, the boys performing for each other. People were drinking, but not raucous or rude, just easy and natural, and the more we walked the more there were. It was like a fiesta, only this was just a Thursday, an everyday Thursday night and the night was just beginning.

'Is it always like this?' I asked my new-found friend. 'Of course,' he said.

Two more bars took us way past three and the streets were getting, if anything, livelier. I assumed that home time must soon come, but instead it was club time. 'Let's just pop into Otto's,' suggested Pino.

Otto's is a space. A large, sparse New York-style dance space, a hip slate-coloured club designed to be a kind of hedonist HQ for the city. In a quiet street always noisy at night with revellers, Otto Zutz is a place where it seems everybody goes. We walked past the girl in Doctor Martens' holding the clipboard – nobody was paying, so it was straight to a bar for a drink, only we couldn't go straight anywhere.

The place was full and rocking, the body heat hitting as soon as we entered, the dancing torsos making a moving, rhythmic obstacle course as Pino led us upstairs. I could barely believe that a club could be this kicking at four o'clock on a Thursday morning, but it all seemed somehow natural here. The people too were good and cool and warm, not the desperadoes who inhabit the latest night in so many cities, but the shakers and makers of a city enjoying itself like none I'd seen.

I thought again about the odd contradictions contained

within these people and questioned a friend of Pino's who seemed to speak good English and good sense.

'How come the Catalans have a reputation for being so hard working and so enterprising and yet people go out so late and so strong?'

He seemed surprised at my question, as if swinging London was surely just like this.

'Going out late is not a problem if you organise yourself properly. We like to have a good time, but you have to work to get that. Deep down though I believe all Spaniards are addicted to *la marcha*.'

Here for the very first time I had heard the word, the new word, the buzz-word, the by-word for Spain today, a word I was to hear a thousand times. *La marcha* is a slang expression which has no exact translation in English, but comes close to the Irish term 'the crack', meaning a good time. Literally '*la marcha*' means 'at the head of the march': the place where things are really happening. According to one source it dates back to the Civil War and the wild anarchists of the Durruti column, who were always desperate to be at the very front of the march, where you could guarantee the action would be.

Whatever its origin, the term *la marcha* is constantly on the tongues of young Spaniards. It is used as a description of a place, as in: 'This club', or 'This city has *la marcha*.' It is used to described a time, as in: 'There was great *marcha* on Friday night.' But most of all it is used to describe a state of mind, a philosophy almost, that is shared by all those who want seriously to enjoy the pleasures and the possibilities which freedom is now offering.

That night which had now become *mañana* someone suggested that somewhere called KGB had *la marcha* now and that as it would be open until eight, we should go there. I thought I'd probably done enough travelling for one night so took my leave. Pino too was going home to get a couple of hours before work. In the streets outside Otto Zutz, the cabs lined up to take us home, a baker's sold croissants and *ensaimadas* to people who wanted breakfast before bed, and

Pino talked to me for a little about Spain. He spoke with the volume of an Italian and the fervour of a convert.

'This place is really good, you know. My country, this country, is the one to be in at the moment, things are happening, exciting things, this is the time for Spain.'

Even when that night had worn off, when I was back in a London that seemed hemmed down by low, grey horizons, and held back by a lack of *la marcha*, I believed he wasn't wrong.

2

The time I guess had come to go. I'd been back many times now to the city of the Catalans, spent time floating in the cool luxury of fine hotels wondering at the elegance of it all. I'd also dived again into the pit and revelled in the murky half-lights, singing the praises to all who would listen of this so rounded town. I thought in all my enthusiasm that somehow I now knew Spain, that I was at home. So Barcelona was the obvious place to go to write the book that was in my head. I wanted to be there so I bought a one-way ticket.

It actually comes as something of a shock to learn that a man called Angel can lie to you. After a couple of weeks back in my screeching, crumbling hotel off the Ramblas, pretending romantically to write in the escritorium, I knew that I had to get somewhere to live. But it came as a sad blow to my notions of straight-backed Spanish honour, to discover that estate agents there are just as dodgy as their slick northern counterparts, even if they do have celestial names.

After viewing a series of grotty modern apartments which Angel – who spoke English with a Californian accent, wore striped shirts and tassel loafers – had described as modernist palaces, I finally succumbed to a nondescript but serviceable flat in the dreary eastern sector of town which had the one dubious advantage of being near the airport. This apartment, which boasted ninety-three individually numbered knick-knacks, was owned by an evangelist bookseller who was pleased to let his home to me because I'd heard of his hero Cliff Richard. By now though I didn't care.

A friend from London, name of Lee Barrett, who was in exile from the taxman, offered to come over and share the place for a time, so I wasn't to be alone in my new country. He'd fallen equally in love with the city, and he already had a girlfriend, an English girl, who lived in town by teaching English to the employees of the Barcelona branch of Barclays Bank. These were my first compatriots, soon I had another.

On one strangely romantic night, sitting among the smack fiends, tattooed transvestites and slippery, oily men at a place aptly named the Drug Store which smelt of disinfectant, sold dirty books and muddy coffee, and stayed open twenty-four hours, I'd fallen in love with a half Catalan, half German girl named Inka Marti. She was a great beauty who had made a living modelling pretty young mummies in Spanish soap powder ads. But, as a linguist fluent in five languages (thankfully one of them was English as I still spoke no Spanish) and a graduate of Barelona University, she thought that grinning inanely over a packet of Spanish Daz was probably not stretching her talents.

So she had taken a TV job which entailed grinning inanely and presenting the prizes on one of the numerous Neanderthal game shows which made up the staple diet of popular Spanish TV. It was a beginning though, the kind of beginning which a twenty-two-year-old girl in still male-dominated Spain had to make.

I'd made a start too: I was now in love with a city and a girl and I had to get to know them both. Spain, the big country beyond the city walls, was still, truth be told, profoundly foreign, wrapped as it was in blood-red romance and Manichaean myths, but I knew that I would commence learning. The next important thing to do was acquire a cleaner.

Organised through an agency, a short but pretty girl called Pilar arrived at the apartment. Lee's girlfriend Lorraine ascertained that Pilar, who was in her early twenties, had recently moved to Barcelona with her husband from Murcia, and then left us to convey in a nervous sign language that we just

26

wanted the place kept more or less sanitary. It should have been easy.

Terrified that she might actually talk to us in her strong, strangled accent, or ask difficult questions about how the vacuum cleaner worked, Lee and I offered her a cup of coffee which was refused, and then went and hid in the back room to play a game of chess. She went about her business for a couple of hours, dodging all the useless ornaments and making the place perfectly habitable. We paid her the agreed fee. A week later Pilar came again, and trying not to look like the cold English fish of popular Spanish prejudice, we attempted clumsily to communicate for a while in the couple of Spanish words we'd mastered, and in the laboured Esperanto of gesticulation. Another cup of coffee was turned down before we gave in to our embarrassment and hid again for more chess. The next week no Pilar.

Three weeks passed with the apartment falling into a state of rancid decay before Lorraine was finally persuaded to telephone the agency. I could see from her flush and tell from the odd tones of her Spanish that something strange was being suggested on the other end of the telephone lines. When she had put down the phone and finally regained her composure a little she said, 'They told me that Pilar refuses to come here any more because she is in moral danger.'

'What?'

Lorraine already had a grin on her face. 'They said that Pilar refuses to come to this apartment ever again because you two offered her whiskey and made her dance on the tables.'

'What?'

Now obviously relishing our bafflement and embarrassment she continued, 'You're lucky her husband or her brothers didn't come round here with a shotgun, you know, you shouldn't have made her dance.'

'But we didn't do anything.'

'This is Spain, remember.'

We never did see Pilar again, never did get to know what we'd done wrong or why she should tell such a ridiculous story to the agents. I suppose she was nervous about spending time alone with two foreign men of mating age, unless of course she thought it was something other than chess which we were playing together. Our next cleaner was a tough old Barcelonan bird who you could never imagine dancing on anything, but the incident left me slightly nervous about talking to strange women and mightily confused about Spanish morality and attitudes towards sexuality. It's not surprising though, I think they're a little confused too.

When censorship finally vanished in Spain in the late seventies the first forbidden fruits which appeared on the newstands were pornography and *Das Kapital*. Today you don't see too much Marx on sale in the street, but pornography of every imaginable variety is available at every one of these green garden sheds which dispense the news in Spanish towns. Sex shops resplendent with rubber masks and private video booths showing such delights as *Zoofilia* (bestiality) and *Lluvia Dorada* (golden showers) opened in almost every town. Indeed some time later I was to live in an apartment above a sex shop called Eros, where a young cleaner brandished her mop in the stained *cabins privés* with no fears for her moral well-being.

Barcelona, which has long considered itself more advanced and sophisticated in these matters, has a thriving if rather unappetising sex industry. There is even a famous live sex 'cabaret' called Club Bagdad where they used to boast an act involving two girls and a donkey. This was finally stopped, not on grounds of indecency, but because the Spanish equivalent of the RSPCA (yes, there is such a thing) complained that it was cruel to the donkey. Club Bagdad still does a roaring trade though.

Yet despite such apparent liberalism towards sex in the current, pluralist climate, there is still a certain propriety about relations between the sexes. Young girls in Spanish cities now sunbathe topless on the beach at every available opportunity, dress in the tight, revealing clothes of the fashion magazines and go out just as ferociously late as the boys. Yet bars and nightclubs in Spain do not have the air of sexuality that you get in many other countries: there is little overt pulling, certainly no sense of a cattle market. Sex, as anything other than a visual tease or a long-term project, doesn't usually seem to be on the agenda. (I have sometimes thought that this could be why there are so many drugs, especially cocaine, consumed in Spanish nightclubs. If the aim of the night is not to go out and get sex, it seems to be to go out and get out of it – although the cocaine consumption could more simply be put down to the fact that nobody ever sleeps, and vice-versa.)

Most young single Spaniards still live at home with their parents, and there is a more elaborate sense of courtship, a more demure approach to affairs of the flesh than in much of Western Europe. This, combined with the deeply ingrained Spanish revulsion against overt public display, means for example that you rarely see kids necking. It explains too why the rowdy drunkenness of British tourists is so alien and so frowned upon. It is considered a terrible slight to the honour and masculinity of a Spanish man to make a fool of himself in public because he cannot hold his drink. A clown is one thing you must never be in the Spanish-speaking world, and so if a Spaniard does get drunk he goes home and does it quietly. It also explains the snogging bars of Barcelona.

For weeks I walked around the city, musing on the architectural elegance of it all, and wondering what lay behind the perpetually closed doors of the small, windowless bars which appeared every now and then on the more unpromising backstreets. One night Inka decided to show me. On pushing open the heavy door I saw, or rather didn't see, a profoundly dark room with a barely lit bar on one side and a large-screen TV flickering in the back. When my eyes grew more accustomed to the gloom I realised that there were a series of sofas spread around the room and that ensconced on some of them were couples deep in exploratory embrace.

For some reason, or more probably for no reason at all, the Talking Heads movie *Stop Making Sense* was playing on the large screen. But no one was watching David Byrne cavorting in his oversized suit. Glasses of whiskey and coca-cola or gin and tonic sat on low tables by the occupied sofas, but there was little drinking and no socialising going on. The business here was serious snogging, the kind of endless, breathless entwining which usually occurs in living rooms and bedsits. Except these people presumably had no living rooms or bedsits to go to and so they came to this darkened and discreet home from home.

What happens when all this foreplay goes too far, I thought, or is this a preamble without a dénouement? Well, probably usually, yes. But as Inka explained, if you can afford a room and you've got a car outside or you can whistle up a taxi, well, there's always the white house.

You cannot walk into the Casa Blanca. The only way to enter is to drive or be driven down a ramp that appears to lead to an underground car park. The building itself is a completely anonymous, once white, edifice with shuttered windows, and the reason that you cannot stroll up to the subterranean door of this remarkable hotel is that you may be seen going in. Nobody is allowed to know who's in residence at the white house.

When your car arrives at the door a curtain is drawn right around it to conceal the identity of all concerned. A lone, dinner-jacketed doorman emerges to lead you into the tiny foyer, at the same time asking you which of the specialist rooms you require. The room with the sunken bath, the one with the mirrored ceilings . . . ? You pay for the night up front – no cheques or credit cards accepted – so that you leave no trace, and only heterosexual twosomes allowed. Then the same man leads you up the corridor, turning lights off as he goes, to ensure continued secrecy until you arrive at your room. If you came in your own car it is parked for you while you go about your business.

Once inside the red-velvet and red-lit room – a small but perfectly formed impersonation of a classic New Orleans bordello – the door is closed and locked behind you. If you want room service – they only serve champagne – you have to ring a bell. When you want to leave, the same bell is rung, and the same elaborate process of turning off lights and pulling curtains is repeated in reverse, with a taxi called and waiting if necessary.

The Casa Blanca is obviously an anachronism, a rather sweet reminder of days of gentler sin. In the General's time it was rumoured to be much favoured by local governors and the like, carrying out their clandestine extra-maritals in the confidence of absolute anonymity. But it still points to an apparent contradiction which thrives in modern Spain between the openness of public sexual display and the more conservative mores of private, personal sexual behaviour.

Seeing lurid pictures of fornicating foreigners (much of the pornography is imported) daily doesn't mean that the average Spaniard believes he or she has to follow suit. Rejecting the rigid regimentation of the old mores has led to a huge freedom of choice, but not necessarily to the lessening of a deep, reflex, moral propriety.

Spanish history has often been portrayed as a perpetual and often violent struggle between the two sides of a deeply split national personality; between a wild, anarchic liberalism and a staunch, authoritarian conservatism. Today it's as if the two, weary of this continual, bloody war, have come to a compact which enables both to exist, not necessarily in harmony, but in a sometimes confusing acceptance of each other. The reason that no one these days seems to mind the sex cinema being in the same plaza as the church is because nobody is forcing you attend either of them or stopping you from doing so.

The man who wishes to attend live sex acts with donkeys is probably viewed by the majority of people in the same light as the man who wishes to don a Ku-Klux-Klan-style hood every Easter and whip himelf in the name of the Lord (he may of course be the same man). Extremism of every kind, political, religious, social and sexual, still exists in Spain today and is accepted as just that, the choice of each individual.

In Spanish there is a word for this, a word which is vital to the understanding of this complex, contrary society. Clumsily translated *desfase* means dis-phase, a gap between two logics, a sense of two things being out of step. Rather than being scorned or worried about, *desfase* is perversely celebrated in Spain in much the way that irony and understatement are in England. But to the outsider a society which seems to accept so many double standards, where so many ends are left fluttering, where the contrarieties are so celebrated, can be both fascinating and frustrating. After a while though I gave up trying to resolve the contradictions. I realised that in sex, as in so many other aspects of life, pluralism – which has become the by-word of the new, tolerant Spanish society – really means let the contradictions be, all of them.

3

Wherever you go in Barcelona you can see the son of God and I'm sure he can see you. With his arms outstretched, a giant statue of Jesus looks out from his place on the top of a mountain, casting a stony eye over the town and its sometimes wayward ways. And standing right up there alongside Jesus is a Ferris wheel.

On top of Tibidabo, the mountain which rises above the valley in which sits the city, the good folk of Barcelona built a pretty, chocolate-box church crowned with an imposing stone son of God to look out over the town. But they also built a permanent funfair right next to it, with a big wheel which carries you up to eyeball level with the deity. This guiltless juxtaposition of piety and pleasure is made even more perfect by the succession of restaurants and bars which climb the hill towards its heavenly summit. The people of this city are certainly going to have fun on the way to their maker.

Even the process of prayer in the church of Tibidabo is somehow part of the game. Like some ecclesiastical amusement arcade machine, you put a coin in the slot and an electric candle lights up to show your devotion. I was amazed by the kitsch-me-quick insincerity of it all, but no one I spoke to seemed to see the irony in this. They've lived for years with the overburdened imagery of Catholicism and it now takes its place alongside the fantastic extravagances of their architecture. They certainly don't let it stop them from having a good time.

Riding around town on a red scooter, like just about everybody else in Barcelona, I was having a time too. Work was usually accomplished between an outside breakfast of creamy *café con leche*, and a late lunch with a cold wine. So I had plenty of time for gazing out at sea, exploring corners and courtyards and reading graffiti.

The fringe politics of this town are laid out in elaborate multi-coloured murals and embittered but often eloquent scrawls. From the *España Puta* (Spain is a whore) of the separatists, the *Vota Aqui* (Vote here), spraycanned on the sides of municipal dustbins by young members of CNT FAI, the anarchist trade union, to the *Ni Yanqui, Ni Russo* (Neither Yankees nor Russians) of one of the myriad Trotskyite groups, there was always a certain colour in the bile and it definitely isn't green.

I was just as intrigued by my first sighting on the Gran Vía of the offices of the Falange. That their red and navy flag with its bundle-of-arrows insignia should still be draped from the first floor balcony of a nondescript office building seemed somehow wrong, like first meeting a man named Jesus. I stopped I remember to stare, believing that nothing had changed. I was wrong of course, everything has changed in Spain today, but nothing has passed away.

The Spanish seem strangely impervious to all this, they are good at not noticing things. Anachronisms flaunt themselves, and dichotomies glare at you, but not at them. There is a transvestite swimming baths in Barcelona which would surely raise a chuckle or an eyebrow anywhere in the world, but not here. They even have trouble spotting physical things: monuments lie decaying, rubbish dumps appear mysteriously, new buildings sprout without prior warning while old ones vanish. A heavy-metal bar will suddenly open where a baker's stood before and nobody will comment or seem to care — they probably haven't seen it. But there was plenty for me to see, and with Inka to tell me tales and drive her 2CV, which I'd named rather predictably Rocinante, down to the sea and up to the hills, I was very in love. I felt like I belonged, almost.

There were days too though when the place drove me mad. If you don't pay your electricity bills in Spain there are no reminders – seven days later darkness – because the electricity is cut off from a central switch. Other times, even when we had diligently passed our pesetas over the counter of the electricity showroom, the power would simply decide not to work in the whole block, or the lifts would go down and the phones would refuse to talk to England. Spain, for all its catching up, can feel decidedly backward on the bad days.

'No one speaks English and everything's broken.' It's a line from a Tom Waits song which I found myself singing when things went wrong and all Spain conspired against me. Days when you have no food, no water, no nothing, and without informing you first the authorities have decided that it is time for yet another infernal and seemingly eternal high and holy day. So nothing whatsoever is going to function, including you. Then even Catalonia, for all its efficiency and smart businessmen in those ubiquitous euro-check jackets, can feel very close to the third world.

But then on the days when words flowed and the breeze off the sea made the heat benign, when the town was at its most elegant and airy and I could sit sipping beer and watch it all work, then I knew why I fell.

It was that civilisation I'd been searching for. The thoroughly civilised attitude towards pleasure which stretches beyond the liberalism of 'let it be', to an entirely positive position of 'enable it to happen'. When the neighbourhood of bars and clubs around Universal and Otto Zutz was becoming congested and difficult for traffic to pass at night, because of people socialising in the street, the official response was not to limit the number of people in the road, or place restrictions on the clubs, but to redirect the traffic after midnight so that the scene could continue.

That attitude, which I believe lies deep in the psyche of these most sociable of peoples, also shows itself in an infrastructure of pleasure in Barcelona, and indeed in most Spanish cities, which often pre-dates the current liberal climate. That funfair at Tibidabo, for instance, with its trams and funiculars is only one of three Xanadus which serve the city.

The most famed and in its way the most fabulous of these dream parks is Gaudí's lovely, life-enriching park Guell. This is the other side of the man's undeniable genius from the dark and intense devotion of the macabre *Sagrada Familia* — a playful, almost childlike fantasy land of mosaic dragons and domed Wendy houses. Here Japanese tourists mix with the local kids playing dusty football in this sweet madness, and the whole thing amounts to one of the world's most remarkable monuments to possibility.

Montjuích to the west of the town has an even larger funfair than Tibidabo with a cable car swinging aimlessly out to the sea so that all can take in the view. Up on this rich green hill there is also a castle, abundant verdant parks and gardens where young couples come on the day of their wedding to be photographed amid the roses. There is the gleaming white modernist building, Fundación Miró, which houses the works of the city's favourite artistic son, a palace and a series of elaborate fountains which dance every Saturday night. It also has a stadium, which when I first saw it was no more than a wreck, and a famed architectural masterpiece which at that time was no more.

In 1929, when the city was in one of its most exuberant and turbulent phases Barcelona was the site for an international exhibition. Most of Montjuích is a bequest from that time, but in the ensuing years of civil war and stagnation, two of the most important and symbolic remnants of that era were allowed to fall into decay. The huge neo-classical stadium, built under orders of Franco's dictatorial predecessor, José Antonio Primo de Rivera, was crumbling and covered in weeds, used largely as an arena for kids to smash things in.

Another edifice of that era, the magnificent Mies van der Rohe pavilion, built as the German stand at the exhibition and the first home of the renowned Barcelona chair, had fared even worse. It had been pulled down when the neglect went too far, and existed only as a memory of one of modernism's finest moments. The resurrection of those two buildings in the time that I was there served as a concrete symbol for me of the rising fortunes of Barcelona and, in a way, of Spain.

I could feel that this city was stirring the first time I stepped off the boat. The energy level of the place was so high, work seemed to be going on everywhere, and perhaps most importantly the town had a powerful self-awareness, a sense of its own identity which was reinforced wherever you looked. *Barcelona Mes Que Mai* was the official slogan, in Catalan of course, that seemed to sprout from every lamp-post and shop front. 'Barcelona More Than Ever', with a bright graphic reminiscent of Miró, reminding all who saw it that this was a community on its way back, on its way to big things.

Living in the middle of these people I soon became aware that this was a town talking about itself. One of the many old Spanish traditions which was undergoing a revival in Barcelona at that time was that of the *tertulia*. Described by my dictionary as 'a social gathering in a café, a literary circle', it is a more or less formal gathering of people who meet on a regular basis over a bottle or two of wine to talk and drink and talk.

A little self-consciously perhaps, Inka and her friends instituted a *tertulia*. Many of them were writers or designers, artists and poets (I found it kind of touching that people here could still describe themselves as poets without feeling embarrassed) but in typical Catalan fashion many actually made money working in advertising, publishing or by owning bars. Their *tertulia* started in a café, but invariably ended up in a nightclub at dawn. Wherever they were though, no matter how loud the music or how strong the liquor, they talked, and often as not they talked about their town.

Certainly they aired the traditional anti-Madrid bias which is endemic in all Catalans. 'That shithole in the desert has been bleeding us for years,' is one of the more temperate comments that I recall from a *tertulia*. They also spent many

37

hours chasing themselves up the latest intellectual culs-de-sac as they attempted to define post-modernism or post-Marxism. It used to be said that where you get six Spaniards you get seven opinions, which, having spent long nights listening to that lot, I found still undeniably true. The difference today is that an argument doesn't instantly lead to a civil war. Though it may come close.

There was a certain consensus, though, on the way the city was going architecturally. Design has a place in the mind of young Catalans which is usually reserved for pop music or fashion elsewhere, and the subject of the city's architectural renaissance was a favourite. Young 'interior architects' like Samso and Arribas were stars who could cause a stir simply by walking into the bars they'd designed. Javier Mariscal was tipped by everybody as the most important artist the country had offered in many years. The *tertulias* argued endlessly about details of deconstructionism or the use of irony in architectural motifs. But they were all excited. Excited about the building of the new and the renovation of the old.

The name of Mayor Maragall was one which cropped up more than often. When they talked about the reconstruction of the Mies van der Rohe pavilion or about the bid to stage the 1992 Olympics or just about the exhortative posters which appeared everywhere, it was Maragall who got the blame. Most of this of course I received second-hand. I was still struggling to master the language (it didn't help that in a *tertulia* they would invariably speak a baffling amalgam of Castilian and Catalan) and felt like a dumb waiter, waiting, that is, to contribute when I could finally knot a coherent sentence together. I didn't need to be told about Pascual Maragall though.

As Ken Livingstone was to London at the time and Ed Koch to New York, so Mayor Maragall is to Barcelona. A member of PSOE – the ruling socialist party which is led nationally by Felipe Gonzalez – Maragall is a media mayor. He's a celebrity whose face appears on television and on posters, a man in his mid-forties who has somehow come to represent the spirit of his rapidly rejuvenating city.

The *Barcelona Mes Que Mai* campaign had come directly from his office, as the result of a collaboration with the cartoonist/designer Javier Mariscal whom everybody was singing about. Before that, though, he'd already run a successful campaign to turn the town around. 'Barcelona Looks to the Sea,' said the posters, which was a successful attempt to reverse the historical tide which had always carried the city away from the waves and up towards the mountains.

Wealthy people always lived as far away from the waterfront and therefore the old town as possible. As a result the docks area was abused and neglected and the beach and water foul. Realising that Barcelona's most important natural resource was being wasted, Maragall commenced his campaign, which involved a massive building programme to create a pleasant seaside promenade and a drive to clean up the water which was often coated with a layer of raw sewage. When the sea was officially declared clean for bathing, Maragall took his life in his hands by stripping to his swimming trunks for the TV cameras and diving into the Mediterranean. When he lived to tell the tale, others followed suit, and you could almost see the seafront becoming gentrified on a daily basis, as the hip young things headed downtown again.

Another great publicity coup, this time on an international scale, occurred when Maragall unveiled what was a tiny architectural project compared to the major renovation schemes going on throughout the city, but a vital one as a symbol of a born-again Barcelona. In front of a large and excitable international audience clad in the baggy suits and polo shirts of architects and designers, journalists and style junkies, many of them there on a local government-financed junket, Maragall revealed the wonderfully elegant little phoenix of Mies van der Rohe's pavilion, which had grown again at the foot of Montjuich.

Financed by private and public subscriptions, with much of the money coming from those powerful banks, this hypnotically calm construction with its deceptively simple interplay of marble and glass, water and steel, looked just as radical and just as wonderful as it must have done in 1929. By building it again from scratch, they displayed to the world that the city had lost none of its style, that the Catalans were prepared to pay for splendid buildings again, that Barcelona was once more staking its claim as a great European city. And dozens of journalists and commentators went home and said just that.

Inside this shrine to elegance and simplicity, the Barcelona chairs were back in place, chairs originally designed exclusively for the king to sit on. And now they were fit for the king again. The whole project somehow said, 'The terrible interregnum of the Franco times is over. And having rebuilt the past so successfully we can now move on to the future.' That's where winning the Olympics came in.

I was there in the Plaza de Cataluña on the day that the decision of the Olympic committee was announced, and Barcelona finally knew that the Olympic flame was definitely coming to the Rose of Fire. The thousands who gathered in the square, the scene of so many more bitter and violent demonstrations in the near past, weren't surprised. They knew by then, not only that their city had prepared the best bid, (I used to get embarrassed when people asked me what Birmingham is like; 'It's like a motorway service station,' I'd say), but that the world was now looking at Barcelona through different eyes. These were a proud and confident people and Pascual Maragall was their home-grown Olympic hero.

That night Barcelona had *la marcha*.

And as I kept sending back reports from the head of the march, I became increasingly aware of increased interest in my adopted town. Friends were anxious to come and visit, magazines demanding articles. One American journal of some note phoned up and asked me to write about 'the trendiest place in the world'. There were now many more British, French and American tourists in town (the Japanese had always come to pay homage to Gaudí) and the place felt even more like the cosmopolitan city it had always claimed to be.

Maragall seemed to encapsulate all this so I decided to try and interview him. That was when I learned that being an English writer in Spain still opens doors, even the heavy, carved fifteenth-century oak doors of the *ayuntamiento*.

I'd walked past the local government buildings many times. The Catalans claim to have invented democracy (but then the Catalans claim to have invented most things including champagne and crème brûlée which is on every local menu as *crema Catalana*), and the centre of that ancient democratic tradition is downtown in Plaza de Sant Jaume, deep in the barrio Gotico where the old parliament buildings stand.

With the rise of local autonomy the Plaza de Sant Jaume is rich once again with the standards and heraldry of Catalonia. The patron saint of Barcelona is Sant Jordi (Saint George — and they claim of course that he slayed the dragon somewhere on the outskirts of town), and his red and white flag flying outside the town hall made me feel at home. It is here, in a building slippery with black marble stairs and rich with delicate oils, that Mayor Maragall dreams up his slogans and polishes his TV manner. It was here that I was summonsed.

Somehow it seemed odd meeting an avowedly socialist mayor in such a sumptuous setting. Being conditioned to the English left and their habit of constructing ugly cloth-cap and roll-your-own environments out of the most palatial surroundings, I was unprepared for luxury. I should have known of course. Maragall is the kind of bespoke and manicure socialist which is common in southern Europe, the kind of suave Mr Efficiency that the PSOE likes to push as the reasonable, effective image of the new, ruling Spanish left.

Greeting me with a heavy handshake, and imparting curt but polite missives to a group of minions, who then left us alone, he made an instant impression: here is a man at ease in four languages and wood-panelled rooms with great masters on the walls. Dark-haired, mustachioed and attractive

41

without being good looking, Maragall, as I'd long suspected, is a style man.

I began the interview by asking him if he was aware of just how fashionable Barcelona had become. Do you know what it feels like to ask an important man a silly question?

'Do I know how fashionable Barcelona is?' He was laughing sardonically to himself a little. 'I am sorry to respond to your question with a question. But do you know how much time, money and effort we have invested in making that happen? It has taken years of intense planning and pushing to put the name of Barcelona back onto people's lips.' His smile was more kindly now. 'Yes, I am aware.'

I'd written and boasted and raved and ranted about Barcelona so often and so long that I felt personally responsible for its status as a town to go to. Maragall of course knew that there was more to it than that.

Obviously warming to the subject he began talking freely about the process of raising a city from the dead, while giving me a brief outline of his own personal rise. Born in Barcelona in the decade after the Civil War, he had taken on the political interests that were normal for a young Catalan at the time, and ended up as a student, active at a local level in the clandestine Socialist Party.

'Back then, in Franco days, people used to say Barcelona was like the *Titanic*, a great ship which had sunk. But I knew that was not true, that it was a submarine just waiting to resurface. When the time was right, I knew we could do just that.'

The process began with what Maragall called 'getting us back into the small print of international affairs'. That meant bombarding every industry with news of what the city had to offer, attracting conventions and shows, displaying that Barcelona had the infrastructure of a modern international city. This painstaking work was followed though by a far grander project which was obviously more to the taste of this mayor.

Reaching up to his bookshelves he produced the catalogue

for 'Homage To Barcelona', the exhibition which he had helped to compile, and which had shown in the great cultural capitals of the world, advertising the fact that Barcelona deserved to be among them. 'This was very important,' he said with obvious pride, 'and its success the first real sign that we were on the right path.'

The aim of the exhibition had been to show that Barcelona had been buried under the shroud of Francoism, paying dearly for its resistance. It reminded the world of the fact that this city had been one of the most creative and exciting in Europe sixty years before, the city of Dali, Miró and Picasso, of Gaudí and Domènech i Montaner. And it worked. But even before the great international drive began, Maragall explained, there was a job to do at home.

'The first stage in getting everyone to realise that Barcelona is a great town was to make Barcelonans realise that they live in a great town. So we had all those campaigns: "Barcelona Looks to the Sea", "Barcelona More Than Ever", which were to convince the people of this place.' (A while later Maragall unveiled yet another striking poster propaganda campaign which featured the slogan 'Barcelona Make Yourself Beautiful' where the features of a woman's face were made up of the new landmarks in the town like Norman Foster's telecommunications tower and Mariscal's giant lobster statues on the waterfront.)

'Opening up the waterfront was vital to that process of creating collective self-confidence. We had been looking inward for so long because of Franco that we had to open our horizons again, look to the world. Then I knew the world would begin to look here.'

The world was certainly looking now, especially since the Olympic decision. Wandering around town it was almost impossble not to bump into film crews and writers gazing up at the Gaudí, ogling the Ramblas and analysing the myriad new building projects around town. I wondered whether all the effort which had obviously gone into raising the profile of

43

the town had simply been done to secure four weeks of fame in 1992.

'No, that is the wrong way round. Getting the Olympics was not the point of all this effort, but the proof that it was working, a kind of celebration.'

At this point he reached up to the bookshelf again and brought down a lovingly photographed tome produced by the *ayuntamiento* to show the various urban rejuvenation projects which had been undertaken by the city. It was a record of young architects constructing bold modernist buildings, of artists and sculptors creating new parks and gardens. Since 1979 and the first of the socialist administrations there has been a quiet revolution occurring in terms of urban development in Barcelona.

Rejecting the conventional corporate approach of a grand, monolithic plan for the city, they have opted instead for a piecemeal approach with each neighbourhood responding differently and creating its own identity. Francoism with its lust for conformity and faceless modern construction imposed a corset of ring roads and dull apartment blocks around the city which threatened to sap its street life. The response of Maragall's administration with its over-abundance of intellectuals and architects was to build a dozen new parks and an incredible 150 new plazas, many of them out in the drear working-class suburbs and many complete with specially commissioned sculptures.

In this city of Dali, Miró and Picasso art has always played an exaggerated role, so it should not come as a surprise to learn that the city had ordered thirty-five monumental public works from such international luminaries as Richard Serra, Ellsworth Kelly, Anthony Caro, Antoní Tàpies, Roy Lichtenstein, Claes Oldenburg, Joan Miró and Eduardo Chillida. But it still comes as a revelation to hear architect and city servant Oriol Bohigas say, 'The sculptures were introduced to give dignity to these public spaces. This is a new type of public planning for a new democracy.'

Each sculptor is paid only £10,000, a sum way beneath

what they could normally command, but they are also given complete artistic freedom and all materials provided. The results have been stunning. The red tape that would usually stand in the way of such a bold idea is somehow cut through, and the money found. There is much talk of a 'disaster fund', a pot of public money used to undo all the architectural damage which Franco perpetrated. Maragall explained why aesthetic considerations are given such a high political priority.

'We have a tradition of radical architecture and design to live up to. I believe it is our duty to support exciting, excellent projects, to back talent. This is happening throughout Spain, but most acutely here in Barcelona we cannot just live on our past.'

The mention of Spain made me sit up. Here we were in the heart of autonomous Catalonia, and everything we had discussed seemed to apply only to Barcelona. I wondered what the relationship was between the city and the state.

'I am Catalan and I am Spanish, and anything which is good for Barcelona is good for Spain, there is no conflict. Other cities, Madrid and Seville for example, have their projects. I am the mayor of Barcelona so I talk about her, but this process is a national one.'

Getting a little carried away now, thinking that perhaps the man had all the answers, I asked just what all of this meant for the homeless, the addicts and the whores in the barrio Chino, what this new, smart version of Spanish socialism had to offer the thousands living in decaying housing estates on the edge of town? I think I honestly expected to hear an answer.

'I do not have a solution. Spain now has the same problems as every other country and we on the left especially have had to learn that there is no easy, blanket solution, you just have to keep plugging away. There is still much to be done, and I suspect there always will be.'

His handshake as I left was just as firm.

Thinking about that meeting later, I was still impressed by

the man, but a little chastened too. I realised that today, even in Barcelona, there can be no dreams of the perfect world, of the glorious millennium that her anarchists so confidently predicted. Just the reality of 1992.

4

I'd finally managed to exorcise my Angel. Lee's return to England had been a blow, but moving out of the evangelist's dull and ornament-laden apartment and into a true Barcelonan home with Inka was the very best thing. The book half written, I'd also spent some time back in England earning money. But as soon as I'd accrued enough I was anxious to return to work and to love and to the powerful pulls which the rhythms of Spain were exerting on me.

The new flat was in the centre of Eixample, the very heart of Barcelona. With mosaic floors, high ceilings, shuttered windows, a balcony encased in wrought iron and a terrace drowning in bougainvillaea, it was a small section of a huge, rambling old apartment which had been recently subdivided. Property prices and rents were shooting up in the city, especially for the grand old buildings which a few years before were considered to be beneath anybody with taste and money.

A faceless modern duplex in the hills is still the typical Barcelonan's dream home. But the process of renovation and gentrification, of cherishing the old and authentic, which had already occurred throughout most of Europe, was just happening in Spain. More and more people were realising that the magnificent old modernist apartments were actually wonderful places to live and available stocks were becoming rarer and dearer. So we felt lucky to get even a little bit of one. Trying to get a telephone was a different matter though.

The hole-in-the-wall, automatic banking machines in Spain are a paragon of technological excellence, the most advanced

47

in the world. They ask you which of six languages you wish to conduct your transaction in, and deduct money from your account bank home. Getting around this large country on aeroplanes is quick and easy. At Spanish airports you can buy a ticket for Iberia internal flights by simply running your credit card through a machine. Spain has taken to new technology with a passion, but old tech is not so easy. Try getting a telephone installed in your apartment and see just how efficient this polished new Spain is.

Nobody connected with the Spanish state telephone corporation would ever dream of telling you that they will do something *mañana*. Instead they say things like, 'We will give you more information in three months.' People have died lonely, isolated deaths waiting for news of their telephone line, and so what you have to do is try to find a string to pull. Watching Inka trying to short-circuit the tortuous process of getting us on speaking terms with the world was like a master class in the Byzantine ways of this warped country.

She applied, of course, in the normal form-filling manner but was realistic about the prospect of getting a telephone before her retirement, which was likely to be a serious impediment to her burgeoning career prospects. What she had to do was find a way of exerting some influence. Influence is a big word in Spain, and so is connections. If you have the right connections, you may have influence, and you may just end up getting a telephone.

Nepotism is big too – it's virtually enshrined in the Spanish constitution – so the first thing to do was speak to dad. Now dad had connections in the local government who thought they may be able to do something to help his little girl get a line. So Inka had to write a letter to the friend of her father who would then go and see someone at the telephone company who could perhaps have a word in the right ear, so that we could have words with whoever we pleased.

This process went on over a matter of weeks, involved clandestine meetings in coffee shops, numerous letters and telephone calls (made from nearby bars and other people's houses of course) and seemed to hinge on the argument that because Inka worked in television she was somehow a national asset and therefore had to have a telephone as a matter of urgency. The argument of course, even one as preposterous as that, was less important than the connections and the influence. And somehow at the end of the whole ridiculous, exhausting charade our somewhat less than splendid isolation was ended and we got a phone.

In doing this kind of business I learned that in Spain nothing is simple and little is straight. Inka was getting wound up about this too. She had progressed from game shows to talk shows and was suddenly becoming a name to know in the still small world of Spanish TV. Lots of offers of work were coming in, but every one seemed to involve intricate machinations and bitter and twisted politics. I got perpetually lost in the folds of it all, but apparently the independent Catalan TV station couldn't use her if she'd worked in Madrid, and Channel 1 would get funny about Channel 2. And everybody wanted her to dress like a forty-year-old woman with a severe identity crisis.

That could of course have been because the head of Spanish television at the time was in fact a woman of approximately that age: Pilar Miró. But then Pilar Miró was as fond of leather mini-skirts, the ultimate sartorial status symbol, as every other middle-aged Spanish woman. Her appointment had been one of the most controversial made by Felipe Gonzalez's socialist government. In the early eighties Pilar Miró had been something of a 'terrible child' film director, whose movie *El Crimen de Cuenca* had so offended the military that it was banned for a while even by the new democracy.

When she was later put in charge of cinematic affairs at the ministry of culture, and then made head of television, there was all the predictable gossip about love affairs with ministers, about connections and influence. Her main problem was probably that she was a woman in a society still dominated by macho men. Her other problem was that Spanish TV is terrible.

49

Spanish television has changed now, in that there is lots more of it, but it is not noticeably better than it was when there were just two state-run national channels and the new autonomous regional services for Catalonia, Galicia and the Basque lands. Sports coverage has always been good, but then this is a country obsessed by sport. Everything else seemed to consist of cheap game shows (*321* is Spain's only noticeable televisual export to the world, and they are mighty proud of that show), endless dreary talk shows and foreign programmes dubbed artlessly into Spanish.

Dubbing is endemic in Spain, both on TV and at the cinema. It was actually compulsory under Franco, in order to maintain censorship, and the habit of turning everything into Castilian remains. (Curiously every name is translated too, so Karl Marx becomes Carlos Marx and Prince Charles, El Príncipe Carlos.) So all the imported shows are dubbed and little drama is home produced for TV. Basically Spanish television is dreadful, amateurish and with no middle ground between the deadly serious and the plain silly.

All of which could explain why Pilar Miró was deposed in a rollicking scandal concerning millions of pesetas reputed to have been spent on her private wardrobe (lots of leather mini-skirts no doubt) instead of on programmes. The Spanish love a scandal like no other nation, and the delight they took from the Pilar Miró saga undoubtedly compensated for the many hours of awful TV they had to sit through when she was in charge. So we can probably expect a come-back.

I tell you all of this to point out the curious world which Inka was trying to penetrate. Also to show why I spent many hours tuned in to the World Service writing on the terrace amid the bougainvillaeas. Unfortunately though I managed to snap off the aerial of my radio a couple of days before the British general election. It still worked providing I held the aerial aloft in one hand while holding the radio in the other. The vision of myself on election night, sitting on a pitch dark terrace at four o'clock in the morning, pointing my antenna at England and wincing as the results came in, is one that will remain with me forever.

The other visions though are dearer: the skinny man of Extremadura delivering bottles of the cheapest, thickest red wine to our doorstep, and collecting the empties with his toothless grin; the chocolate shops with their elaborate fondants and sweetmeats; the restaurants where you sit in terraces after midnight and devour the rich *carajillo* – coffee and sweet anis – and the strong opinions of the people; or lunchtime down by the side of the sea, eating every slippery beast of the deep, as the conversations buzzed on all around until the sun turned everybody drowsy.

There were night-times spent in the company of desperate friends getting irredeemable – like the time Lee and I finished on Pino's roof with Juan Mark, an expert in sweet delight, drinking Catalan champagne, watching the morning rise gently over the hills after a night of unfathomable indulgence. Juan Mark surveyed the scene and with nary a hint of sarcasm said, 'It's the little things which make life liveable.'

Living in my Spain was perhaps best on a Sunday. That was the day for traditions, such as pastries in boxes tied with string, taken to the house of a friend as an adjunct to the saffron paella; then later on to the bulls, the brutal, beautiful ritual which bound me tightest to the heart of old Spain; and sometimes to the football which showed me the bruised face of Catalonia.

Barcelona football club is an institution unlike any other in the world. For the 120,000-capacity Nou Camp stadium, where nonpareils like Maradonna, Cruyf and Lineker have all cast their spells, is not so much a shrine to sport, as the high church of Catalan nationalism. The football team, known universally as Barca or the Bluegrens (Catalan for red and blue), is actually seen as the political and cultural representative of a people repressed for so many years by Madrid. The maroon and red stripes of FC Barcelona are as much the colours of Catalonia as the red and yellow stripes of the official flag. And what really matters most to the fanatical followers of the world's richest club is not that they win trophies or play the best football, but that they beat Real Madrid, Franco's team.

Even now Real are seen as representing the establishment, as the all-white embodiment of an ancient hierarchy. Every Catalan who has ever seen a football match is convinced that the rules are biased towards the Madrid team, that fixtures are rigged and competitions weighted. How else could you explain the fact that Real have been so much more successful than Barca, who have won the Spanish league only once in a dozen years? They are passionate and they are embittered to a degree which is sometimes painful to see.

The intensity with which football is followed in Barcelona is almost insufferable: there are three daily sports papers which do little other than analyse the minutiae of Barcelona FC. While I was living there an argument between their famous British manager Terry Venables and a star German mid-field player, Bernt Schuster, led to the publication of two hardback books on the subject. Going to see Barcelona play an ordinary Spanish league game is like going to a political rally. Going to see Barcelona play Real Madrid is like going to a war.

For the men in the famous all-white strip of Real represent not just that terrible town to the south, but the dictator who lived there and supported its leading team. And if, amid the burning flares and the huge flags, the screaming children and the praying women, Barcelona can beat them, then all those years of suffering are temporarily forgotten and the town lights up. Rockets literally illuminate the sky, car horns sing, bars do brilliant business and even fewer people sleep than usual. If they lose human sacrifices are made.

Going to watch FC Barcelona is not necessarily a pleasant experience: the stakes are too high, the tension too tight, it all matters too much, but it is certainly an experience. Securing the gold dust tickets and going finally to watch them play 'the big one' I actually found my favours swinging toward Real, the men in pure white with their more elegant, carefree skills. But I couldn't possibly admit that and retain friends. When they are rational the Catalans accept that they are part of a Spain which has Madrid as its capital. When they are at football they see that place as the sworn enemy.

The relationship between the two great modern cities of Spain is perhaps best summed up by the Catalans' derogatory quip that Madrileños are 'half African', and the equally snide Madrileño response: 'It is better to be half African than half French.' The antipathy between the two is playful but real. And after too long of knowing only one half of the story I was about to find out what the reality was. I was off at last to the belly of the beast, to Madrid the capital of all the Spanish.

5

She is a puffed up, ugly old tart. Like its *Dallas*-infatuated women with their quarterback shoulderpads and theatrical slap, the city itself looks overdressed and overdone. I guess it is the pressure of being the capital of a country with so many beautiful towns which makes Madrid try so hard. That, coupled with the collective historical desire for architectural grandeur, as physical proof of dominion over the quarrelsome provinces, has left Madrid heavy jowled, burdened with a kind of faceless monumentalism as one grand but bland square follows another. Every portal in this town, whether it leads anywhere or not, is twenty feet high; every arch positively and pointlessly triumphal. Madrid, it must be said, is not an elegant city, but there's certainly some life in the girl.

With all my second-hand Catalan prejudices packed neatly in a Globetrotter suitcase, my first taste of the centre of Spain lived nicely down to expectations. Flying for just half an hour on the remarkably efficient hourly shuttle known as the Flying Bridge, I found the change from that light, stylish city by the sea too dramatic to take in properly. And stepping off a plane and into this steaming, southern soup of a town is a bit of a shock. The long, relentless journey south from the Costa Brava by car or train gives you a better idea of Madrid's physical handicap, time to understand how location has shaped the place.

For Madrid is a kind of sixteenth-century Iberian Brasilia, a contrived capital built at the whim of a king and stuck in the middle of a flat, parched central plateau known as the *meseta*, the table-land, whose topography is unchanging and whose austerity is tangible. Miles from the sea, and with a only a dirty little river and a dozen dreary fountains for negative ions, Madrid is instantly recognisable as a hard town. It is also a very Spanish town.

Inka had to come to Madrid to see about an important job presenting a big daytime chat show. I wanted to see some English friends who were living there. It was also San Isidro, the week of Madrid's patron saint, the week of her *feria* and consequently of the best bulls the capital would see all season. I was excited about all of that, but also about finally experiencing the heartland of this country whose second city I'd lived in for a year; about meeting the devil herself.

The cab drivers who push their white Seat taxis around town are certainly all convinced that diabolical things await you. 'This is a dangerous town, you must be careful, the drug problems are terrible, junkies [in Spanish it is pronounced "yunkies"] leave their dirty needles everywhere, the gypsies will rob you, nobody has any respect, be careful where you go at night.' This melancholy mantra of foreboding, which seems to come from the mouth of every Madrid *taxista* the moment he realises you are not a local, took me by surprise the first time I heard it, the first time in the capital. Being driven slowly to the house in the nice middle-class district where Inka and I were going to stay, I was suitably shaken by the ominous tones and worried about what my week was likely to hold. It took me a while to recognise the glee which accompanies this sorry soliloquy. It was during another ride on another visit, when an oily overweight driver with a tendency to punch his horn, and a Spanish flag in the back of his cab, complete with the old imperial eagle of Franco days, described his city as 'a jungle' that I knew where I'd heard that tune before.

For Madrileños in general and their cab drivers in particular take a positively Manhattanite pleasure in telling you just how terrible their town is. They are powerfully proud of how hard and hot, how noisy, dirty and dangerous their city is.

You can see the satisfaction in their eyes when they tell you yet again how everything is getting worse. If their over-wrought, overweight, overheated home cannot be the pret-tiest on the peninsula then it is sure as hell going to be the toughest. That Falangist cab driver undoubtedly loves his job really.

And deep down I believe they all even love the heat. San Isidro sensibly takes place in early summer, before the place really starts to burn, but even then you can feel how powerful a role the sun plays in this town. For just as knowing its geography helps to understand the city, so feeling its scorch-ing high-summer sun eat into you day after day is essential to a real appreciation of the place and its remarkable people.

All along the preposterously wide boulevards which lacer-ate the centre of town there are digital display units showing the time of day followed by the temperature in centigrade. Only in a city as perversely pleased with itself as Madrid could modern technology have been used to create such a masochistic civic torture. For throughout the summer months, once the clock flicks past midday, the thermometer regularly rises way above forty centigrade. And when the air feels like a battery of celestial hair-dryers aimed directly at your face, you really do not need reminding of just how hot it is. But then, as I said, Madrileños love to broadcast how bad everything has become. The prospect of global warming is secretly seen as a great boon here.

Madrileños love talking about the weather almost as much as the English. But commenting on the killer heat is different from going out in it, and the hours of the midday sun really are left to mad dogs and Americans. The locals dive instead into air-conditioned restaurants or darkened apartments to hide until it cools down a little. In Barcelona you will always find some people working in the middle of the day, always see some signs of economic life. But when I first arrived in Madrid at midday it really was a ghost town. I thought that the place was not only ugly, but dead. You can be very wrong when you don't know.

For apart from the sacred, baking hours of the siesta, this is a city where things go on. Behind the Brobdingnagian boulevards every narrow back street smells of a dozen soiled intrigues and every plaza is thick with the hint of things happening, probably unspeakable things. As soon as the people of this fetid, swirling town realised in the late seventies that Franco was really dead they breathed out and showed their true, brazen colours again. And they've been exhaling noisily ever since.

This re-awakening was known as the *movida* which roughly translated means the movement, the commotion, the scene. Madrid was the centre of the *movida* and it is still a place of perpetual agitation and crazed events. One of the most famous products of the *movida* Madrileña is movie director Pedro Almodóvar, and as soon as you spend a little time there you realise that his fantastic, funny/tragic films with their twisted tales of incestuous, drug-fiend, sex-change nuns, make absolute sense here. They could be everyday sagas of this tumultuous, voluble town. When in *Women on the Verge of a Nervous Breakdown*, his leading lady Carmen Maura says, 'The strangest things can happen suddenly', she is simply repeating a truism of Madrid life.

All of this, of course, took me some time to discover – about eight hours.

When the bulk of the day is a no-go zone, then the night comes as sweet release, the time to leave your shelters and live. So at an hour when most of Europe is removing its clothes to go to bed the people of Madrid, almost all the people, are getting dressed up to go out. When the digital clocks tell you that it is officially tomorrow and the thermometers have slipped back to, say, twenty-five then those streets, both the broad and the narrow, begin to fill up. Madrid at night makes New York seem positively narcoleptic.

Old señoras sit out on the streets in long feminine rows, sewing and shaking their heads while their daughters gossip about missing men. Old affluent *hombres* with leathery skin, dark glasses and silk shirts, park their Mercedes and stroll the streets with their spangled consorts, on their way no doubt to the same suffocating restaurants they've dined in since the Civil War. Young couples drag their tiny, overdressed children to cafés where they run silently amok. And through all this you walk.

In the working-class barrios families move their entire lives out onto the streets and into the tiny neighbourhood bars. There is said to be one bar for every ninety-six inhabitants of Madrid and they all still seem to be full. *Gitanos* sing warbling flamenco and young toughs in tight jeans and bad haircuts hang out on every available corner with a kind of lazy intent in their eyes. Others just sit around – sitting around is very big in Madrid. You continue walking, probably to a terrace.

The first night in Madrid in San Isidro I could not believe the life of the *terrazas*, I still have problems. These are not just the idling street cafés of all southern Europe, but swarming testaments to the powerful sociability of these nocturnal people. And from almost every speaker Phil Collins fills the night with one of his euro-dirges. Even the most ardent advocates of Madrid do not claim that it has good taste.

Some *terrazas* do have an air of elegance and charm, where arty *tertulias* have made their home. Others see serious business deals discussed and clinched and are said to have a vital role in oiling the wheels of Spanish business. This is a country with a passion for intrigue and indiscretion, for trysts and assignations, where everything has to be settled over a drink and a whisper and the terraces are perfect for such plotting. But still more *terrazas* turn into vast pavement raves where the business of flirting, drinking and finding your man goes on before you go on to a nightclub.

It has become the greatest cliché of the Spanish capital to say that Madrid is the only city in the world where there are traffic jams at four o'clock in the morning. But it was more like five on that first swimming night, when in the company of old English and new Spanish friends I sat in the back of a taxi, cursing in my best Castilian, because we were lodged in a mass of treble-packed cars and revellers in transit. I mean we had a club to go to too.

This period is known in Spanish as the *madrugada*, the early hours, the time between night and day, the time that Madrid feels most at home. Except that home is precisely where nobody seems to be. For the *madrugada* is a time of great movement in the city. This is when the Madrileños earn their nickname *los gatos* (the cats) because they stalk the streets in vast numbers: some strolling and driving round before sneaking back finally to steal some sleep; just as many heading to one of the numerous after-hours clubs which carry on and on.

The *madrugada* is said to be a time when business deals are done, projects begun, love affairs finalised and finished. During the long Madrid summers *madrugada* is the time of *la fresca*, the cool. Cool is a very rare commodity in this town.

The ebony Africans lounging along the Gran Vía certainly try to exude some cool as they attempt half-heartedly to sell you a gram or a girl. The 'Great Way' used to be Madrid's most important and prestigious artery, but these days it makes like 42nd Street, revelling in its own decay and hiding the cracks behind a barrage of burning neon. In the tangled streets behind the Gran Vía, though, nobody is hiding anything.

The lucky ones who've managed to shoot away the pain nod off on benches or sit and sip from a bottle of beer. Those still waiting for the necessary pesetas or a pusher huddle in doorways or fidget along the streets looking for an angle. Here you really do have to be careful (just like your cab driver told you) to avoid the needles and, some say, the knives of desperate users.

Madrid in particular and Spain in general has an awful heroin problem which has taken hold from the upper levels of *alta sociedad* to the poorest southern peasant. In this traditional vice-zone, male and female prostitutes walk these streets to pay for their all too visible habits. The eyes here are empty, emotionless, but the arms weep from open sores. Madrid certainly can be a tough town, not least for the hordes of dark-skinned poor, who've travelled up from the deep south in their many thousands.

Whether or not they are really gypsies and whether or not they have anything to do with the heroin trade, it is generally the *gitanos* who get the blame for all the very public drug problems. Many of them live in the *chabolas*, the shanty settlements which ring the city like a nasty stain around a bath, and where some of the heavy selling undoubtedly does go on. The *chabolas*, which first appeared around every major Spanish city during the *años de hambre* the hungry years after the war, are supposed to have disappeared since the advent of the economic miracle and the socialist government. But try telling that to the twelve-year-old kids dealing smack amid the broken refrigerators and anorexic dogs.

This was not the Madrid I met on my first visit though. A glutinous, tricky town, it will get you lost many times in its swamps, and reveal its various faces gradually. But during San Isidro all of the Madrids are partying.

There are Pijo parties and Chulo parties, Moderno parties and Jet parties and dozens of chattering arty parties. Pijos are spoilt rich kids, except they're not so much rich as middle class, and at times it is possible to believe that every kid in Spain with with a sweater wrapped Italian-style round his or her waist is a Pijo. Unless of course they're Modernos. Almost anybody who has been for a weekend's shopping trip to London or Paris could qualify as a Moderno, which basically means they wear bits of black and like the music of black America, just like every other euro-hipster. Chulos are the street toughs of Madrid, the machos who suck air noisily between their teeth and try to convince themselves that cap-sleeved T-shirts are coming back. The Jet, well everybody knows the Jet.

Every week *¡Hola!* which is the bible of Spanish bad taste read by millions, devotes dozens of pages to gory pictures of the wealthy avoiding work. *¡Hola!* is dedicated to ensuring that the rich stay famous and the famous stay rich, because it pays them large sums for the privilege of printing their holiday snaps. Marbella, or rather Puerto Banus, is the true home of the Jet (short of course for Jet Set), where the chosen few can be seen in the flesh, the invariably burnt and gilt-encrusted flesh. But in Madrid thousands aspire to such depths.

In a land over-burdened with petty aristos and landless gentry, and still extremely impressed by cheap stardom, the capital has a huge population of people with airs and few graces who set the tone for what is desirable in this town. Gold is definitely good here and less just means less. So the more you can look like you may just have been one of Princess Stephanie's unsuitable lovers or Julio Iglesias' conquests, the better you will be respected. Budgie-blue eye shadow is still big in Madrid and shoulder pads are even bigger, Texas-size.

But there is no doubt that the terrible taste of those who would be Jet adds to the colour of this primary town. And during San Isidro, their week of saint's days and sinners' nights, this old-fashioned in-crowd goes to the bulls at six-thirty, to dine at midnight and to party at every possible opportunity. I find it very difficult not to enjoy the sheer tastelessness of the Madrid Jet Set side-show.

Over in my more natural constituency with the Modernos, I began to see the differences between the two cities of Spain.

In Barcelona every bar is a designer fantasy and every nightclub a lesson in post-modern theory; in Madrid the venues are far less fancy and the crowd doesn't really care. In Barcelona they are likely to have been to a chic Japanese or nouvelle restaurant first; in Madrid good foreign food is hard to find and most meals consist of a huge lump of meat and lots of oil. In Barcelona the revellers are going to be Catalan or English, French or American; in Madrid they are likely to be Asturian or Gallegan, Andalusian or Balearic – this is a thoroughly Spanish city. In Barcelona, though people are out late, they will probably have jobs in offices, interior-designed offices with furniture by such luminaries as Jorge Pensi or Alberto Lievore, but offices none the less; whereas in Madrid the far smaller fashion crowd either works in one of two clothes shops or it doesn't really work. In Barcelona they don't get to sleep until very late. In Madrid they don't get to sleep at all.

Madrid is a very foreign city, certainly. The English people I was visiting were Sade, the singer, and the three boys from her band. She was there because of a love affair with Spain and a Spanish man; they were there because she was there. They were writing a new album, and they were all taking a year out from British tax. Songwriter and saxman Stuart Matthewman was full of thoughts about his new town.

'We could be living anywhere in the world, so we chose a city where the phones don't work, where the electricity doesn't work, where nobody works for more than about two hours a day, where you can't get anything done and where you can't get fresh milk or decent records. They don't even serve vegetables with your food. You ask me if I like Madrid. The nightlife is good, too good – I'm likely to die here.'

Sade was a little more relaxed about the lifestyle. 'I love Spain because I've always had trouble getting up in the mornings. In a city where everybody goes back to sleep at lunchtime they might not notice that I'm just getting up for the first time.'

Inka of course was going bananas because of the political intrigue that surrounded her new job and because, well, because this was Madrid. 'It's so bloody primitive here.'

One evening though, after a day at the *corrida* which had been blessed by good bulls and a moment or two of greatness with the cape, this group of English joined a few Spaniards to sit and eat and talk. In a restaurant that specialised like most in large, unadorned lumps of meat, and was graced as so many are by pictures of Hemingway and Ordonez, we did all the corny things and they weren't corny.

Here with grand old Riojas, their taste steeped in wood and soil, the conversation ranged and rolled from bulls to music and back. You often hear in Spain today how the traditions of hospitality and courtesy have vanished under a deluge of hamburgers and motor scooters. But that powerful combination of sociability and reserve which has always made these people so attractive still survives. Or at least it did on that night in Madrid.

Confident, attractive, open, the young Spaniards gathered around that plentiful table were polite without ever being mannered, moved by the chances their future offered, but full too of a past which was still thriving, a past from which they had never been severed. And listening to them, arguing about the deep song of the gypsies or the correct footwork for a particular pass with the crimson cape, listening to them living a folk tradition of intensity and beauty with no self-consciousness filled me with culture. It was there and then I believe that this book really began.

6

It was inevitably in a bar in Madrid that I received the first politics lesson I'd had since leaving university. My teacher was José Luis, a journalist in his late thirties whom I'd met at a party and who had convinced me that he knew everything about Spain's political parties. He reminded me of the kind of serious East Coast American who always wears a shirt and tie and actually liked Michael Dukakis. José Luis is neat and clever and understands politics as a rational, everyday process of power, manipulation and marketing. The very fact that he exists seemed to me to be a sign of the leaps Spain has made – the whole idea of politics is new here – and yet you get a type of knowledgeable, almost cynical, political sophisticate like José Luis.

'The first and perhaps most important thing to understand is that politics does not matter very much here any more. At the end of the dictatorship everything was politics, but very quickly that settled down. Most people are now pretty much apolitical: they moan a little about the government of course and especially about income tax which was almost unheard of here and is considered a terrible imposition on the individual. But there is no great fervour, which must be a good sign, that surely is how it is in most properly functioning countries.'

This reminded me of the reasoning of a Catalan friend, Susanna, who had once said to me, 'We have had to learn to calm down, to join the world that everybody else lives in. It is a little dull, but being bored is better than killing each other.'

I told José Luis about this and he smiled, 'It is true, the young in particular don't even bother to vote and sometimes that saddens me a little, they do not know how much suffering went into attaining that privilege.'

I could see how it might be seen as good that politics in Spain has lost its passion and its romance; romance is traditionally very dangerous for these fervent, intense people, safer certainly to leave it to the men in check suits. But that loss seems to be belied by the apparently healthy state of political life at the fringes. Certainly if its health is to be judged by abundance and proliferation then the walls of Spain testify to a vigorous political debate going on. The tangle of spraycanned initials is like some preposterously entwined Alphabeti Spaghetti where the letter 'p' for *partido* is most popular.

'This is true, but it doesn't mean too much. Partly it occurs because of the tradition of underground politics which were necessary in the old days. Then what you did was go out and write on walls because it was all that you could do. Also it is because of the fact that we have so many parties because of the autonomous regions. As well as the Spanish communists there are the Catalan communists, the Gallegan communists etc, so there is much repetition and then there is the far right and the separatists. Even in an area like Andalusia which does not have its own language there is a separatist movement and all of these groups feel that they have to go out and write on walls. But they are very small and unimportant in reality.'

The exceptions to this seemed to me to be the Mili No movement which had certainly impinged itself on my consciousness as the only graffiti gang without a 'p' to its name. That is because Mili No is not a political party but a single-issue group who are attracting a lot of support, especially from young men who do not want their hair cut off. Their issue is military conscription which is still compulsory for all males in Spain. In a land where the army is viewed with intense suspicion and seen as the natural enemy of democracy,

65

it is not surprising that conscription should be laced with even more dread than, say, it is in neighbouring France.

'Yes the anti-conscription movement is quite strong and very noisy, I also think they will succeed and that we will sooon opt for a purely professional army like in Britain. But that is not really a political movement, if anything it is anarchist led and a reminder that the anarchist tradition still exists here. But all of this is so far outside the real running of things as to be irrelevant. What really matters is PSOE and who will one day challenge them.'

PSOE stands for the Socialist Workers Party of Spain, but bears no resemblance to the British street-corner Trots of the same name. The PSOE is the ruling party of Spain and has been since 1982, the year of the third post-Franco general election and the first where a real political system had sorted itself out. The PSOE is in many ways the only political party in Spain and that, according to José Luis, is where the trouble lies.

'Many political analysts said that the great test of Spanish democracy was passed when the army allowed the Socialists to take over in nineteen-eighty-two without trying to stop them, and of course this is true. But for me there is an even bigger test awaiting us when the time comes for the Socialists to relinquish power. At the moment we are a *de facto* one party state.'

This was not exactly a new theory to me, even Felipe Gonzalez had commented publicly on the lack of a coherent opposition to his ruling party and the fact that this was detrimental to the creation of truly democratic debate in Spain. He had not of course said that this made the PSOE dictatorial and secretive, nepotistic and self-satisfied, unable to accept criticism and unwilling to listen to arguments. Nor had he said that the process of government in Spain consisted largely of a series of dictates handed down from Gonzalez and a group of his old Sevillian comrades who made up the inner sanctum of the PSOE, that parliament was there simply to ratify and the judiciary to coalesce. Everyone else was saying that, and José Luis was saying it with a cynical smirk on his face.

'It is true and they do it rather well. Our country is basically run by a small club of men in their late forties who all made names for themselves at the end of Franco days. Gonzalez was a lawyer, a good-looking, intelligent young man who managed to gain control of the still illegal Socialist Party from its old exiled leadership and forge it into a party capable of governing by the early eighties. He made them drop their Marxism and pledge exactly the kind of moderate centre-left socialism which was undoubedly what most Spaniards wanted. He is a very efficient administrator, he has done an excellent job. But there is nobody and no party challenging him, so inevitably abuses creep in. It's not his fault that the others are all so useless, but I accept that it is a problem for Spain.'

I wondered, though, why there was no coherent opposition: Gonzalez couldn't be the only clever man in all Spain, and the PSOE surely isn't the party of all the talents.

'In many ways, in terms of national politics, it is. In the autonomous regions there was more of a tradition of sustained opposition, so in Catalonia you have a conservative Catalan administration and the right wing are in control in Galicia. But, basically, for forty years Franco alone made all the nation's important decisions so there was no way of learning to be a politician. The only real exception to that was in the clandestine political parties, which by the end were really quite well organised, but obviously they came almost exclusively from the left, and most notably from the PSOE. The far left, the communists, were also quite active, but they are too much of a reminder of the past, of the Civil War. As of course are the right who also suffer from the fact that Franco never exactly encouraged great minds to compete with him even from his own side. What we really need is a new generation of politicians from the right, from Alianza Popular or Partido Popular, who are completely free from the past.'

I was about to interject but José Luis was really in his stride now.

'The only problem of course is that as a nation we have such a deep-seated fear now of conflict, such a desire for calm and consensus, that people do not really want to see opposition. Instead of checks and balances we have scandal and rumour which is much more in our character anyway. When we can replace that with a truly democratic system of opposition and a smooth change of power, then I will know that we have really made the transformation to a democratic state and a democratic people.'

When will that happen then, José Luis?

'You asked me "when" not "if"? It probably is when, if we want it to be. But I do not think we will want that until a generation also asks questions, perhaps not until a new generation of Spaniards has to ask the biggest question of all which is: "Who was General Franco?"'

7

They stood in the bar most of the time, cradling large shots of brandy in hands heavy with oversized rings, smoking like old-fashioned film stars. One wore a red suit, a poppy-red three-piece, with wide lapels on a jacket fitted tight into the waist and trousers climbing to his rib cage and flaring just enough to break perfectly over the snub-nosed, stack-heeled boots. Beneath the waistcoat his shirt was open, but only a little gold showed. They talked and drank and smoked in groups of three or four, strident, vivid, perfumed huddles apart. Another wore lime green.

They were not bothered about Paco, all that jazz stuff and film scores. Paco's good sure – many say he's technically the best there is – but that's not enough to leave a bar for, not when you know you look as fine as this. The real reason they didn't leave their drinks to listen was because Paco de Lucia isn't one of them, isn't a *gitano*. Camarón is though, Camarón de la Isla is the man from the province of Cádiz, whose voice captures the spirit of these dark men in bright suits. And when he came on they went in, and the whole place watched.

Madrid's large featureless sports palace is not the best place to see flamenco. But a bill that includes Paco de Lucia and Camarón is big business: they are stars. Flamenco has grown immensely popular throughout Spain recently. Like most of the folkloric forms which play such a part in the picture-book conception of Spain, its death was prematurely announced in the swinging seventies (things happened later here), when everybody wanted to be the Beatles.

For a while flamenco looked like going the sorry way of most Western European folk music. But then in the deep south it was revived through a series of competitions and festivals which were organised to keep the faith alive, and are now as much a part of the Andalusian calendar as the bullfighting *ferias*. Today you can hardly walk across a plaza or through a park without hearing young kids trying to perfect their rapid rhythmic clapping or a drunk trying desperately to warble his way through a sorry song.

What was once the exclusive property of those *gitanos* and sombre Andalusian musicologists has spread so that you hear flamenco constantly on popular radio stations. You can hear *cante jondo* deep song, the pure, oriental, and profoundly soulful music of voice and guitar. This is a music of the ages which tells of the loss of many mothers and the ruin of so many sons on the long gypsy journey from their original home in Northern India. It is a difficult, sober music, yet one which people are singing and listening to again.

As with so many aspects of Spanish life, the fading of Francoism was a factor: it took away the stigma of national-ism which had attached itself to all the distinctly 'Spanish' cultural forms. Young people who would once have been embarrassed to enjoy flamenco or bullfighting because of their conservative, traditionalist overtones could now see them as living parts of their culture. In flamenco there was also a new breed of performers: the young men from the towns and villages of the south who look and live like rock stars, but sing and play a music still drenched in that moving darkness. Of these Camarón is undeniably the king.

That is why there were huge, tank-like Mercedes lined up in the street outside the sports hall on the night when Camarón sang, why the affluent, flash young *gitanos* had pulled on their best suits. I'd seen Paco de Lucia before and loved his flowing, daring guitar playing. But it was the prospect of catching the wild one, de la Isla, the man of the island, which made me pay way over the odds for a ticket to a shifty Madrileño scalper. It could have been a risky investment though.

Camarón is a man with very bad habits. Unpredictable, often ill, prone to disappearing for long black periods of excess, he loses himself deep in the *gitano* sub-culture of caravans and *chabolas*. And they love him for it. Camarón wears his problems like a badge, and like some latter-day Spanish Billie Holiday his voice has the cracked, fragile tones that can turn the suffering into somthing sublime.

Standing on stage that night in a billowing white shirt he sang fierce and soft, sang of all the usual themes, of all the loss. The men from the bar stood in the hall in groups still, shouting their occasional support, letting loose soft and strong *olés* in the trance-like gaps between the sounds. They closed their eyes those men, tapping, occasionally clapping softly to the rhythms, throwing back their heads when Camarón roared. Flamenco music means gypsy music, and this defiant, self-destructive singer was the essence of flamenco that night. To the strident *hombres* from the bar Camarón's very existence is a statement of their outsideness, their difference, a 'fuck you' as loud and proud as their suits. To me he was a great singer.

Which is more than can be said of most Spanish crooners. The incessant, ubiquitous Phil Collins and Tina Turner records which ricochet round every bar and boutique in the country come as a pleasant treat if you've been subjected to a selection of Spanish pop.

'Black is Black' by Los Bravos, an awful 1970s band who had one international hit, is the high point of Spanish rock music thus far, and you still occasionally hear that terrible, heavy-handed tune seeping from radios in taxis. The *movida* threw up a couple of punky curios like Alaska, who had black boots, dyed hair and lots of rude songs, and Radio Futura, a band who would dearly love to be the Clash and almost manage to achieve rocking mundaneness. But it was all years too late, and tended like so much in popular Spanish music to have a terrible leaning towards humour.

Songs about bullfighters wearing glasses and fat women farting are the standard stuff of Spanish rock. In common with the French they also suffer from the Johnny Halliday syndrome whereby anybody who has his hair in a quiff and his collar turned up is instantly given a recording contract and adored for life.

A distinctly separate youth culture is an extremely new idea in Spain. The strength of Catholic family ties, the lack of teenage affluence, the fact that most young Spaniards have never felt the need to reject the adult ways, has meant that there is not the same concept of a generation gap. Even today old and young mix naturally together in a way that feels so foreign and so refreshing to an Englishman used to the pointless apartheid of the ages. It also means though that pop music has had no real world of its own in which to develop: few pop shows on TV or radio, no real room or reason for pop culture to evolve its own identity, few record shops even. So most of it is either depressingly derivative of Britain and America, or else it slides into that cabaret slot.

Miguel Bose was born to be a cabaret star. The son of a highly lauded union between a famous torero and an actress, he has pretty, waif-like good looks and a nice smile, and because of that is being groomed as the new Julio. But he insists on wearing ripped up jeans and leather jackets on television (and Miguel Bose is on television almost every night) as he warbles away feebly and camps it up deplorably on yet another variety show presented by a girl with big tits and a man with a tuxedo. Sometimes I despair for Spanish pop which seriously believes it is in the middle of some kind of golden age and yet consistently fails to produce anything which would merit a second listen outside of Spain. Even the Gypsy Kings who have cracked international success with their rocked up, party-down flamenco are actually French *gitanes*, singing in Spanish but living in the Camargue.

The big hope for some serious Spanish input to the world of modern music was *rock con raíces*, rock with roots, where bands like Pata Negra from the south, Mondragon from

Catalonia and Duncan Dhu from the Basque lands mixed rock with their traditional regional musical styles. But all too often it produced an ugly synthesis that flattered neither. Paco de Lucia who played on the same bill as Camarón that night has managed to colour flamenco with jazz and create some marvellous music in the process, but Pata Negra and the other Spanish flamenco/rock bands like Los Gitanos have yet to make the idea really work. Mondragon ended up as a kind of Catalan comedy group singing silly parody songs about fat people.

Fat singers of course have a special place in Spanish music. Tenors Plácido Domingo, Antonio Ordonez and José Carreras and soloist Montserrat Caballé are national heroes and seen as international ambassadors for the Spanish classical music tradition, stars almost in the Julio class (not quite of course because the Spanish are convinced that there is no star in the world who is quite the equal of the former Real Madrid reserve goalkeeper). But in Spain classical music, opera and ballet all have to compete with the true classic performance art of Spain: flamenco.

The dance of the *gitanos* was never as endangered as their song. Even in the tacky tourist flamenco tableaux, there is a fair degree of authenticity of step and costume. These tourist shows are usually staffed by girls from the dance academies working to pay their way through school. And in the south at least the movements of flamenco are such a strong and vital part of the popular culture of all Andalusians that it was always danced at *ferias* and weddings. But in the eighties it underwent a huge boom.

Ballet Español, the blend of flamenco with classical ballet which the magnetic Antonio Gades made so famous, was largely responsible for this. His company became hugely popular both at home and abroad through the movies they made with director Carlos Saura: *Blood Wedding* and *Carmen*. By turning two of the most renowned tales of Andalusian pride and passion (*Blood Wedding* is Lorca's most

73

famous play) into highly stylised and thoroughly modern movies they made flamenco improbably chic.

Going to see flamenco dancers became a society affair, and so too did attempting to do it. Pijo girls who would never dream of dating a *gitano* got themselves togged up in elaborate flamenco gowns and paid for private tuition. *¡Hola!* was full of pretty, petty *aristas* who suddenly discovered distant Andalusian ancestry and wore the get-up to prove it.

Throughout the country a rash of more plebeian flamenco classes also appeared. In truth these were a kind of Spanish equivalent of aerobics sessions, where flamenco replaced disco as a medium for losing a few pounds and toning a few thighs. In Barcelona, which is about as far removed from Andalusia as you can get and remain Iberian, every other office girl and shop assistant bought a pair of flamenco shoes and castanets and tried to convince hereslf that she had gypsy blood somewhere in her veins. Even Inka, half Catalan and half German, came home one day with a pair of clumpy shoes and castanets, had one lesson, realised just how difficult it is and consigned them to a drawer.

Fans, one of the other potent symbols of fiery southern femininity, started turning up in discos, frequently waved by gay men while doing elaborate mock flamenco dance routines. I wanted to see the authentic stuff first hand.

The outskirts of Barcelona, like those of most large Spanish towns, consist mostly of ugly, neglected estates of dilapidated concrete apartment blocks. Invariably dusty, dreamily depressing places, they are full of ragged-arsed kids and dog shit. Much of the population of these disconsolate suburbs is Andalusian in origin, a legacy of the hungry years when the peasants left the south to live in *chabolas* around the big cities. The shanties have gone from Barcelona now, flattened in a show of civic redevelopment in the seventies, but the flatblocks which have replaced them are not really much of an improvement.

We travelled one night to one of these estates to the north east of the city, a fairly typical suburb about half an hour's drive out. Although it is not one of the violent, drug-ridden estates which make up the nightmares and inform the prejudices of so many Spaniards, this is not the sort of place that life would normally take me. But on a Friday night Inka and I, accompanied by three friends, crowded into the back of Rocinante and headed that way. One of those friends, Miguel the shameless poet, knew a man named Manolo who ran a bar there and he was expecting us.

Manolo is not a gypsy, but he is Andalusian and when we arrived at his bar in the main street of this plain, poor community he gave Miguel a huge southern hug. He then did the same with each of us before pouring out five glasses of cold Jerez for us to drink. With the green and white flag of Andalusia prominently displayed, pictures of matadors and footballers on the walls, and a large number of men playing noisy games of cards, Manolo's bar was clearly a kind of informal Andalusian social club.

But the business of the evening, the reason we'd driven out, was to go to a club of a different kind. A *pena* in Spanish is kind of a fan club. There are *penas* for bullfighters and *penas* for football teams, which have a particular bar as their headquarters. And here was the *pena* Fosfolita, the club in honour of one of the greatest *gitano* singers of them all. This was a place of flamenco.

On the short walk to the *pena* Fosfolita Monolo went through an intricate sales pitch on a battered 1970s Volvo which he had parked round the corner from his bar. None of us was in the market for a car and we made that clear, but that didn't stop Manolo, a large man with an even larger gut and a pair of trousers at least two sizes too small, from singing the praises of this *magnífico coche* as he called it, insisting that Miguel sit in the driver's seat 'to feel how safe it is'. We only just escaped having to take it for a test drive. Time was getting on and things were already happening at the *pena*.

Housed in an anonymous-looking bar by a drear, dank apartment block, the *pena* Fosfolita has a picture of the great singer on the back wall, a scattering of plastic tables and chairs, and a tiny raised wooden platform which serves as a stage. Manolo led us inside, introducing each of us formally and individually to the owner, and collectively to the thirty or so people who were sitting in the club. He then left to return to his bar, demanding that we all come back to see him soon and reminding us of just how good a car his Volvo was.

There was a certain scepticism in some of the dark eyes, not exactly animosity, but an unconvinced surprise perhaps, that these five young outsiders, clearly well off, were coming to their *pena*. We sat down at a table and ordered some food and some beers, and kept the kind of quiet that the watched keep.

A man with an acoustic guitar had taken up a position sitting on one of the plastic chairs on the small wooden stage. He began playing, softly at first, with a deft touch, but really just doodling, stopping to tune his guitar and to get a bottle of Jerez which was placed by his chair.

Our food arrived, a selection of strong tapas in the southern style, including a wonderful, thick rough *chorizo* oozing oil and taste. As we ate I looked gingerly round. Most of the customers were adults dressed in a kind of Friday-night best, certainly not the glamour clothes of the men in the Madrid sports hall – this was a poor community – but sporting the best they could offer. Despite the obvious racial differences, they looked to me like the crowds I knew so well from the rollicking Irish pubs of my native North London on a Friday night.

And as the music began to flow from the man bent over his guitar, and it became clear that we were there simply to listen, so some of the same kind of warmth that is generated in those vast gin palaces off the Edgware Road began to fill that small hall.

The guitar-playing had that hypnotic, rhythmic power which makes flamenco so compelling, and its circular, propelling dynamic was already producing positive responses. Then one of the men sitting drinking at a table with his family, a man in his mid-life, stepped up onto the stage, draped his vivid check jacket over the back of the chair and sat down.

For a while he sat just cracking the heel of his boot down into the stage in time to the guitar. Then he took to clapping, his hands held close by his bowed head, as if he were struggling to hear the rhythms that his softly colliding palms were producing. His powerful silence was matched by the audience who seemed to be respecting some shared, almost religious ritual.

Then, still sitting and with his eyes shut as if searching deep inside himself for something, he let out a soft moan. This swelled into a lyric, which was dragged and bent into a wail. He was perfectly in sync with the complex guitar patterns now and between them they were weaving a magic. There was something both ecstatic and strangely puritan, introspective and exclamatory, about this deeply disciplined music with its ululating tones sounding so like the muezzin who calls the faithful to prayer from the Muslim minarets.

'*Eso es cante moro*' – 'That's Moorish singing,' proclaimed the old man sitting at the next table, half to us, half to the man who was making it. '*Ole*,' sighed another.

The singer was lost in his soul now, his face racked as he expelled demons which came out as song, vibrato, grainy flamenco song, gypsy song and the gypsy audience were all responding to his experience made music.

The word *duende* was used by one of the congregation, a word I knew well, but still do not know how to translate well. In bullfighting – that other art touched by the gypsy – certain matadors can create moments which raise those watching to heights of excitement, which can enable you to transcend the bloody spectacle to a point of spirituality. For that transient moment they have *duende*, presence, charisma, that indescribable something which we all know when we are in its presence.

Duende is a vital word in the flamenco canon: it expresses the transcendent, cathartic nature of the music, the way in which the spirit is revealed, sometimes to soar. Camarón de la Isla undoubtedly has *duende*. And this man singing now, who lives his weeks in this grim suburb, perhaps unemployed, surely poor, had left all that on this Friday night in the *pena* Fosfolita to rise, so that he had *duende* too. And we all shared it.

When he had finished his song there was applause all round and a hug from a man at the table closest to the stage. The singer picked up his jacket and returned to his family sitting at a plastic table and drank a glass of Jerez. He sent a smile over to us, and we felt welcome.

The next to climb up was a little older, a skinny man whose features, despite the trenches that life had dug into his face, were so obviously Indian that he could still be living in the sub-continent. Where the last singer had performed a mournful gypsy blues, this one's aim was to move us in a different way. After communicating with the guitarist in the rapid, nasal accent of Andalusia, where words seem to stick to the palate, the hunched player skipped his fingers across the strings to a faster, more joyous beat, slapping his hands onto the sonorous wood of the soundboard.

The old man, standing cocksure and smiling, sang a tune, uninhibited, lusty, that pulled a woman from another table to the stage. There she danced, her back straight, the tails of her dress, a normal cheap dress of man-made fibre, raised and flicked in a gesture of open sexuality. This woman, as old as the man singing, circled the dais, keeping her eyes theatrically on his, acting out a kind of rhythmic ritual courtship. The place was laughing now, cheering as she grew more expressive, stamping her heels, clicking her fingers as her arms swept in an arc above her head, sweeping back her once dark hair. Finally she kissed the old man before returning to her table with a skip.

Half a dozen of the people in that place sang that night, although none for me came close to the first with his *duende*. Another carried his guitar onto the stage to indulge in an elaborate, racy duet-cum-duel. A couple more danced, including one man who used a walking stick to pound out more sounds than his heels alone could create. The tone of the music varied from the sombre to the gay, though the overriding colour was definitely dark with melancholy; but once revealed in song there was a spirit, a life, even in this suffering, which lighted and lifted us all. So that we felt not brought down but raised up.

It was a good night at the *pena* Fosfolita.

The life of the gypsies in Spain is not romantic. Too many know prison cells and prejudice, too many live in squalid, no-chance housing estates on the outskirts of Barcelona, Madrid or Seville. In the real *gitano* areas of Almería and Cádiz the levels of literacy are by far the lowest in Spain and among the lowest in Europe, the standard of living below the bottom of the graph, health care almost non-existent, religious manipulation rife at the hands of the zealot priests. Yet to spend a night in the company of the gypsies of the *pena* Fosfolito was to see a culture still in touch with its essence, a culture perhaps as it was at the beginning. It was to see a people who have not gone under.

8

I knew straight away what it was. I'd heard that sound before, many years before in London, on one of those dying days which we've grown so used to in our city under sporadic attack. That time I had been out shopping when I heard the rumble, followed by the silence, followed by the sirens, been maybe half a mile away from the insanity. This time I was further away, but out again strolling and talking aimlessly with Inka, enjoying the cool of a Friday evening in early summer, when that same big, slow hollow sound rolled into the air. 'That's a bomb,' I said straight away.

'It can't be,' said Inka looking puzzled, staring at the sky to search for some lightning which would prove me wrong.

'It is, I'm sure of it. It's certainly an explosion of some kind.' Then, as if to back me up, the siren wailed its hysterical epitaph.

When we got home the radio told us that there had indeed been an explosion out in the northern suburb of Sant Andreu, apparently in a supermarket full of families shopping. There were few details yet, but it seemed that there were definitely some people dead and that it was obviously a bomb.

Inka's reaction was one of bewilderment, 'Why here?'

In England the shock of being bombed by the IRA has gone, and the logic of the attacks, although evil, is clear. But on that night everybody seemed personally battered and severely baffled too. Was this the work of ETA, the Basque terrorist group, who were still waging a bloody war against Spain? They were the most likely perpetrators, but why would they blow up working-class Catalans out shopping for the week-end? In the days when Franco represented the common enemy, the people of Barcelona had been the strongest allies of the Basques in the struggle against the generals of Castile. To kill these people didn't even seem to make twisted terrorist sense.

Or could it be some hazy terror group from the half-light of extremist Spanish politics, trying perhaps to destabilise the democracy via a grisly Barcelonan equivalent of the Bologna bombings? Nobody knew who and nobody knew why. They shook their heads in bars and throughout the night the death toll rose.

The next morning Inka turned on the radio to learn that seventeen people were dead, including numerous women and children, blown away as they wheeled their trolleys between the aisles of the Hipercor Supermarket, buying maybe the products she'd promoted. Many more were injured, bleeding now in hospital. I don't think she cried, but her sense of loss was tangible, more to be honest than I could really feel or even quite comprehend.

Opening the shutters in the living room to let in the early daylight I looked out at the apartment block opposite and saw that the striped red and yellow flag of Catalonia was draped over the balcony and that a black rosette had been pinned in one corner. Looking down the street I saw the same flag with the same universal emblem of mourning obscuring the pretty, wrought iron railings of almost every other apartment. A whole Calle was spontaneously showing its respect and its revulsion, showing its powerful, personal sadness in a display which more that just moved me: it amazed me.

Throughout the weekend Barcelona was a subdued, dis-gusted, sorrowful city. Disembodied voices from San Sebas-tian, the cultural and criminal capital of the Basque lands, had claimed responsibility for the attack in the name of ETA. Eighteen people were now dead, and without them necess-arily articulating it, I could feel a community saying, 'We will not accept this.'

On the Sunday afternoon, in a move unprecedented for the silent, violent men of ETA, an official apology was published which talked about a 'serious error', but which went on predictably to blame the Spanish government. No one in Catalonia was blaming Spain this time though, and no one was willing to take this shoddy sorry.

That evening a demonstration in Sant Andreu was the largest ever seen in that traditionally left-wing, working-class suburb. Led by Mayor Maragall the people of the district turned out in their many thousands to parade quietly through the streets, ending up outside the scene of the carnage, where wreaths were laid, tears shed and a minute's absolute silence observed. Afterwards cries of 'ETA get out', in Catalan of course, rose from within the crowd.

The next day, a lovely summer Monday, another demonstration had been called, this time for the centre of town, for the whole town. At the appointed time of six o'clock, Inka and I walked the short walk from Calle Aribau to Paseo de Gracia. As we moved closer we were joined at every turn by people coming out of offices, apartments and shops, until we were part of a mass of people too large even to make it onto Paseo de Gracia.

Finally, inching our way onto that street which is so emblematic of Catalanism, we could see that the turn-out was such as to pack that widest of boulevards right to its end at the Plaza de Cataluña, with more arriving every moment. More people carrying outrage, sadness and pride.

Youngsters in the bright colours of an Iberian summer, mothers wheeling young children in push-chairs, office workers in their shirts and ties, factory workers in their overalls who had arrived from the Seat plant on the edge of town. All moved together, slowly, touched by a terrible loss. Many bore the Catalan flag with that rosette of black which had become the symbol of this tragedy. Remarkably, too, I saw a few carrying the broad-banded flag of Spain, also draped in mourning. The cry again of 'ETA get out' punctuated the silence at intervals.

When the demonstration, estimated later at 350,000 people, could condense itself no more it came to a halt. Every balcony, including those on the Gaudís and the other great edifices of *Modernismo*, was crowded with people. The extravagant wrought iron lamp-posts which the great architect has bequeathed to the city were draped with youngsters hanging off to get a better view of this solemn lake of mourners. And throughout it all, the dignity and discipline of this huge crowd was maintained magnificently.

The minute's silence was flawless, every head bowed, every heart I am sure as heavy as mine, the outsider's, felt. After a time of just standing and showing, of demonstrating by their sheer presence, their will as a community, a speech condemning all acts of terrorism was read by a famous Catalan actress Nuria Espert, and broadcast to the length of the demonstration by loudspeakers. I couldn't understand the language but I could feel the emotion and the immense humanity of these people who had responded with such stirring solidarity to what they saw as an attack upon them all.

London, for all its guts and its stirring history has, I suspect, lost the collective ability to respond with such unity to an attack upon its own. That made me feel prouder still of my new place, on that moving, enriching evening when a whole town stood still.

Then, as the magnificent, sorry event was fading and everybody was turning back to the private domain, there was nearly an incident to blur the dignity.

Down a side-street near where Inka and I were positioned a group of Spanish riot police were stationed in case of any trouble, a sight usually guaranteed to send hot young Catalan heads crazy. Indeed a tiny group of kids – many of them in the tight jeans and long hair of the 'kinkys', the local amalgam of punk and heavy metal – began chanting anti-Spanish slogans in a kind of automata response. The crowd instantly rounded on them, shutting them up and showing them how stupid they looked. All of Spain had been appalled by the bombing and today all Spain was in mourning, and these Catalans were part of that Spain.

It seemed to me, thinking about it later that night, that ETA had managed, by an act of gross and foul barbarism, virtually to put paid to violent separatism in Catalonia. (They had also severely damaged their own credibility in the Basque lands, a blow from which they have never really recovered.) Inka could remember being taken on demonstrations as a kid, where the rubber bullets and the tear gas flew and Madrid, the generals and Spain were the obvious enemy. But the largest demonstration in the city since the Civil War had been one against violence, against extremism, against a separatist movement.

The people of the wealthiest region, with the second largest city, with the longest established grudge against centralism, were now coming to terms with the fact that so many things had changed. In that time of the bomb, a time of loss and a heightened sense of community, there was no talk of better times to come in an independent Catalonia where all the men would have beards and every girl would be called Montserrat. Instead they talked about a new Spain in which all the regions could play their part, a new Spain rid of its demons and ready to contribute with all its deep talents.

It was a Spain I knew I had to know.

9

It didn't end in the sun in Spain. The winter in Madrid, a drizzling, sullen affair, didn't help, Inka didn't want to be living there and I couldn't fly too often from London. She was now a TV star based in the capital and I was back home with a finished novel and a need to earn some money as a journalist again. That was where and why it really ended.

The telephone can be a vicious tool, but it really told us only what we both already knew: a relationship between two people with different lives in different cities wasn't going to work. It had been a fine thing, teaching both of us I hope, me certainly, about so much. But now, without our even seeing each other's faces, it came to an end. The other love affair, though, was just beginning.

Living in this dynamic and charismatic country had served only to further the urge, the drive to locate the spirit of this insistent place and people. The idea was firmly fixed in my mind now: as soon as I could sort out the details I would return to Spain to research and write a book, a book about the country and about my relationship with it. This would not, I assured myself, be an act of catharsis but of discovery, a way of finding out more, of delving deeper, travelling further, of answering the so many questions that remained in my own mind.

The first stage of this process meant trying to make my already improving Spanish good enough to do the job in. So I bought all the usual cassette courses and grammar books, sat on the tube and in the bath talking to myself moronically. I also hired a private tutor, a girl from Valencia called Pilar who lived in Golders Green and would turn up at my apartment in Bloomsbury with two bottles of San Miguel and a copy of the latest *¡Hola!* for me to dissect. I realised then that I had actually learned more Spanish than I had let myself speak while I was living there. And on the day that I found myself arguing with Pilar about the concept of guilt in Catholic societies I realised that I was probably getting close.

The next stage was to get back to Spain. Despite my deep affection for Barcelona I knew I would have to base myself in Madrid. The plan was to talk to as many people as possible who were somehow indicative of the new Spain I'd watched emerge with such fascination, to people who could help me put that country in context, who could explain where Spain stands now in relation to the continent over the Pyrenees and to the hard and beautiful Iberia of old. And there was no doubt that most of those people would be living and working in the capital. Besides, being right in the centre, Madrid was a good vantage point for the other aspect of the research, which was to travel out to some of those parts of this wildly varied peninsula which I didn't already know.

But I did know by now (as anybody who has ever tried to drive from one end to the other will surely attest) that Spain is a very big land indeed. So I had to accept that I could only cover a tiny fraction, and besides this book of mine was not meant to be a guide – there are plenty of those about. Instead the aim was to provide an overall picture of the state of the nation through a series of almost random snapshots of people and places.

There was a method, though, in the wanderings which were to follow. I knew for example that I wanted to visit the other two autonomous regions with their own languages. I didn't want to go anywhere near the Costas which have been so ravaged by the gang gropings of international tourism and which have little or nothing to do with the realities of the real Spain. The Balearic Islands seemed to me to be a different matter, though; I certainly had a soft spot for Ibiza as do many

Spaniards, so I thought I'd probably go back there. But before I could actually accomplish any of these journeys, which were already being travelled in my head in London in the winter, I had to sort out somewhere to live in Madrid.

'Mi casa es su casa' is a common Spanish expression, it means 'my house is your house' and is invariably uttered at the end of long alcoholically sentimental evenings. As I was going to be travelling to the various corners of the country, it wasn't practical for me to rent a place (truth be told I was too tight) and so I was about to find out if 'mi casa es su casa' was actually genuine or not.

In this case the casa in question was an apartment and the person who lived there, a film-director friend called Carlos, had obviously been sincere in his offer. For he had no problems with the idea of an odd Englishman staying in his spare room that summer. The next task for me was to begin to arrange the interviews which would be central to the book, and it was with some trepidation that I sent off the first begging letter asking not for money but an hour or so of somebody's time.

Before any of this, though, before the campaign really began I decided to enter Madrid from the south. My previous visit to Andalusia had left me mesmerised by that most powerfully atmospheric of lands and it seemed to me that the best way to begin this odyssey was to dive into the mythic Spain of the imagination.

IO

Ronda is built around its bullring, a pretty, ornate plaza which rings silently with the echoes of so many red soaked afternoons. It is famous too for that bullring, the oldest in Spain and still one of the most revered, a taurine shrine in a kept and beautiful town which straddles a ravine. A once austere Andalusian town turned a little flabby perhaps by the oohs and aahs of too many travellers in search of the authentic, Ronda is now on all the itineraries. It was here that I began the journey through the land of Andalusia. It was past midnight when we arrived, tired but awake from the long hard drive high into the Sierras.

'We' was myself and Hattie my new English girlfriend, about to experience her first taste of Spain, and my old Barcelonan flatmate Lee and his lover. We were hungry, hungry beyond the reach of hotel sandwiches, so we threw our bags into the rooms with a view and headed for the centre of town, four English still amazed that town would still be functioning so late on an ordinary Sunday night in early spring. Chancing upon a restaurant in the main street, near the bullring, we parked the hired Seat and were glad to see that we were not alone, as a group of locals slowly finished a rambling meal. And no one seemed to mind, either, as one bottle of wine became two and Sunday went deep into Monday. They even suggested that if we wished to take another drink there was a bar just down the road which was sure to be open still.

Strolling through this quiet night-time I became romantic

88

no doubt about the bulls in this mountain-top town which as close as any could claim to be the birthplace of the *corrida*. For those who know a love of Spain, Andalusia is at the core of that love, and to be in this most Andalusian of places was bound to produce a tired monologue about the great metaphor of man versus nature; the wine probably didn't help. It was then I guess that Lee suggested that we hurry to the bar for that drink.

The bar was a typical small-town affair, with a silent video of *Gremlins* playing in one corner and an armless, push-button bandit collecting pesetas in the other. The young crowd though was perhaps a little too large and lively for an ordinary Sunday night in early April in this summer tourist town high in the Sierras. We ordered beers with brandy chasers and I set to boring my companions again. I was probably at the part where I drone on about a man creating a ballet of shapes while staring death in the face, when Lee, desperate no doubt to change the subject, said, 'They're all doing drugs.'

'What?' said we three, amazed at such a suggestion. 'Don't be ridiculous, Lee, this is a small town in Andalusia on an ordinary Sunday night in early spring. They won't be doing drugs, that's preposterous.'

Lee, bolstered no doubt by the amount we had now drunk, and a stubborn man at the best of times, was adamant. 'They're far too animated, and they keep going to the toilets. I bet you the price of a good lunch tomorrow they are all doing coke.'

'It's the sort of bet you make when you're drunk, and the sort of bet I accept. It is also the sort of silly bet you cannot possibly prove. I mean you can't exactly go and ask them can you?'

'¿*Hay coca aquí señor?*'

I couldn't believe it: Lee was leaning across the bar and doing just that. He was asking the barman whether they were taking coke. And I knew from the tone of the answer that I was right on both counts. No, they weren't doing coke, and no, Lee should not have asked.

'*No señor, ciertamente no.*'

The barman looked genuinely aggrieved at having been asked such a question by a group of drunken English, and Lee made hasty apologies both to him and to us, as we all headed as rapidly as possible for the exit. No one tried to stop us, but I could tell from the hum which filled the place that word of our indiscretion was flying around the bar.

Rather than hang around to see if we had upset anybody we clambered straight into the Seat and headed for our hotel and a much needed sleep. As we pulled into the drive I breathed out, realising that if we had seriously impugned the honour of an Andalusian anything could have happened. And then it did.

I don't know if it was drunkenness, nervousness or tiredness which had stopped us from seeing the car following us, but as we pulled up so did it, with a screech of brakes. This, I thought at the time, is the way that bad dreams and good movies begin.

As two burly-looking men emerged from the car now stopped right behind us, all of the options ran through my mind. The first one was that it was the Guardia Civil. I couldn't see any uniform but the remnants of Franco's militia were now famously bored since they had nobody really to repress, and the chance to hassle a few tourists who were talking about drugs would be too good to miss. It could of course be one of the other numerous kinds of police who look for something to do on a nothing-happening Sunday night. Or else it could be a friend of the barman who was coming to make sure we realised what a stupid question we had asked. None of the options was very nice.

As one of the two men approached the car I could see that he was definitely not wearing a uniform, but that didn't mean too much: they could easily have been off duty and having a late drink in the bar. I definitely had it in my mind now that they were police. But still we hadn't done anything illegal, so

I wasn't too worried. Then, as he leaned forward and made the international sign language for 'wind your window down you bastards, you're bang to rights', I realised that Lee at least had certainly committed a crime.

Drink-driving is not normally considered too great a problem in Spain. Unless you actually kill somebody important while swigging from a bottle behind the wheel, there is no real likelihood of you being stopped. But it is nonetheless technically a crime and one that a stroppy copper could pursue a long way if he so desired, and this guy looked like he desired. Lee looked like he'd also realised all of this and began apologising even before the man leaned his head in the window.

Then just as he leaned forward his hand went to his inside breast pocket and my life flashed before my eyes. Then I prayed that he was a policeman because the alternative was too horrible to contemplate. So I contemplated it anyway. He wasn't a copper at all but a bad man who was somehow worried that we were spying on him, and the gun that he was about to produce from his pocket was going to make sure that we didn't talk to anybody.

The time that it took him to remove his hand from inside his jacket was in real heart-pounding, palms-sweating, slow motion. I just froze and waited for the worst, but the object in his hand when it finally emerged was considerably smaller than gun-sized.

On that late and ordinary Sunday night in a kept and beautiful town high in the sierras, a town famous for its bullring, the man finally spoke.

'You want a gram?'

Lunch next day was good indeed, even if I was paying.

I I

I've always thought you can tell a lot about a town from its graffiti, and it doesn't take long to tell that Córdoba is a town where feelings still run deep. On a section of the old city wall, where the mists rise up from the Guadalquivir and deposit a layer of soporific melancholy which hangs heavy over the old town, stands the legend, YOU SOCIALISTS HAVE YOUR POWER BUT WE DON'T HAVE OUR UTOPIA. Then, a little further into the whitewashed warren you see, in the same red paint and undoubtedly the same hand, PSOE ABSOLUTE POWER – ABSOLUTE CORRUPTION.

Córdoba is still deepest red, a town with a communist administration and mayor and a reputation for producing firebrands. The third piece of graffiti though tells most. For here the vitriol against the socialists has been tampered with, the letters PSOE have been crossed out and the letters I.U. added. I.U. stands for Izquierda Unida, the United Left, the very communists who rule the town. And you can almost see the disillusionment and the anger in the eyes of the young activist as he worked. Córdoba feels like a town which is deep down unhappy with its lot.

This could of course come from the knowledge that this is a city which has fallen from grace with the world. For there was a time when this was the most marvellous and marvelled-at urban centre of them all, a place which ruled and enthralled the knowing world. When this region was the glittering Moorish caliphate of Al Andalus, Córdoba was a vast metropolis of learning and science, of palaces and potentates, a city whose stature was acknowledged by the largest and most magnificent mosque in the world. The mosque is still there, and still a marvel. But it is a centre now for tourists and phantoms, a place of lost power, a little perhaps like Córdoba.

Lorca called it 'Córdoba far away and along', giving a sense of the distant, ethereal atmosphere which pervades the place, but also 'Córdoba to die in'. And death is celebrated here like nowhere else in Spain. Manolete, a Cordoban and the most famous matador of them all, has numerous statues and his own museum, which contains not only his sarcophagus, but the hide of the bull that put him there. But the death which is really celebrated and mourned in this city is that of the great Arabic civilisation itself. For seven hundred years this was a Muslim town, in many ways the greatest Muslim town of them all. Now it is a sleepy, distant, but disturbed back-water, electing communists when all around are rejecting theirs, stubbornly flying the red flag and grumbling.

My cab driver was moaning about the perpetual road works which have become a sign of the communist adminstration's drive towards civic improvement. When I asked him what should be done I did not expect quite this vehemence.

'They should be shot like they were during the war. They talk all the time of freedom, but what does this mean, the freedom to talk like a communist that is all. Everything now is worse.'

Bad blood still runs deep. You also get the impression that it could still flow freely given an excuse.

Not that Córdoba is a particularly poor or turbulent city. I was now making my way alone through Andalusia intending to take in the triumvirate of towns, Córdoba, Granada and Seville, which are the greatest monuments to Moorish rule. Sitting in a half-hearted bar in the barrio around the mosque I realised that the old town lives well, if rather lazily, on the constant tourist trade while the modern city appears affluent and well run; the streets which aren't being dug up are clean and tidy. The only real excitement I saw there was an agitated teenage hustle outside a sportswear store which marked the arrival of a new consignment of Nike training shoes. A certain poverty of stature hangs over Córdoba, as if it can't accept that it is really an inconsequential Andalusian town, overshadowed by its nearest neighbour Seville. Another popular theory about all the roadworks is that the communist administration decided to dig everything up in order to keep up with the Joneses. Socialist Seville is undergoing a huge facelift for the Expo in 1992, and so communist Córdoba got the builders in too.

The last great and pointless piece of building work perpetrated on the city came in the sixteenth century when a group of stroppy priests convinced the Catholic king to construct an ugly church inside the giant mosque, doing much to obscure its unique beauty. But it is a lasting testament to the affection that the Cordobans felt for their Muslim ancestry, that despite the fact that the Inquisition was based here for three hundred years, the monument is still known as La Mezquita, the mosque rather than the cathedral that it officially became. Every statue in town that isn't of Manolete is of a learned and revered Arab man looking serious and holy. Christianity did Córdoba few favours, so perhaps it shouldn't have come as any great suprise to see Yama'a Islamica De Al Andalus, but it did.

The area where history hangs most heavily in Córdoba is the old and still ungentrified, one-time Christian ghetto which winds maze-like away from the mosque. This is a place of impressive and moving white silence where the Middle Ages could still seem pretty modern. It was here on a soporifically sunny afternoon that I stumbled upon Yama'a Islamica De Al Andalus. And I'm still trying to work out what it really means.

In the shadow of the great mosque it came as a real jolt to see a heavy wooden door framed by bold Islamic calligraphy, like some kind of time-travel doorway, or long-overlooked last bastion. For this was the Islamic centre of Al Andalus, a place offering prayer mats, halal meals, numerous infusions and a very strange vision of a future through the past. This

94

was the new centre for Muslim Andalusians. Could, I wondered, one of Spain's greatest collective nightmares really be beginning just here? Here in Córdoba I felt it might almost be welcomed.

The idea that one day the Moors would return to reclaim their most illustrious kingdom has played a strong part in the demonology of Spain ever since the Reconquista. Today, with areas of the Costa del Sol permanently occupied by the playboy sons of sheiks, and poor North Africans beginning to cross the tiny channel that separates the continents in search of new-found Spanish affluence, those fears have resurfaced. And here, a few metres from the greatest Muslim monument in all Spain, was a group dedicated to the re-Islamification of Andalusia.

The boy I met when I entered Yama'a Islamica introduced himself as Yusef, but it soon came clear that this was his chosen name. His Spanish was clearly natural and his looks, despite the neatly trimmed beard, were those of the locals. But when I asked if he was an Andalusian, he responded with a quiet and powerful politeness, 'No, friend, I am not Andalusian I am Al Andalus.'

Inviting me to remove my shoes and sit down on the scatter cushions to share a mint tea, he explained the aims of the group, a few of whom were hovering silently around the room. The long-term goal was to get all of the mosques converted back to their original purposes as places of worship of Allah. They were also building a new mosque near Granada which would act as a centre both for converts like himself and for the increasing (although still very small) number of immigrants. When I asked him why he, surely once a good Catholic, became involved in this strange spiritual odyssey his languorous manner became almost animated.

'People here now claim to be Catholics, my family included, but nobody really cares any more: few people are really devout. This is a secular land now, where drugs and possessions are more important than spirituality. Through my conversion I have learned the truth: that Christianity was

95

imposed upon my people; that Islam is our true heritage and that it shall be restored.'

When he asked me if I wished to go upstairs and pray I felt like a *News of The World* reporter as I made my excuses and left.

Here I believe was the same passion which had led the young disenchanted communist to go out and vent his spleen on the walls of the city. What both were suffering from was the fading of the fire. Andalusia was famous for zealots, both political and religious, but in the rational, reasonable new Spain there is little role left for the extremist, for the true believer.

The reality of the Yama'a Islamica De Al Andalus is that little will come of it. Like some punchy old pugilist trying to make a comeback long after his time has gone, Islam will never again flower in the ochre earth of Andalusia. But in the sleepy backstreets of Córdoba you can see why it may seem like a glorious or terrible proposition to some.

Walk a few streets further though and you can see the true faith in operation. The lottery, which is an obsession throughout Spain, is a dangerous addiction in Córdoba, and the plangent cries of the sellers floating through the heat sound oriental and hypnotic, like the muezzin calling the faithful to bet.

12

Jerez de la Frontera is another place entirely. In a lengthy, drowsy flatland yellow with sunflowers or green with grapes, it is a city you don't see coming. There are some signs, though: the agro-business becomes uglier as it becomes less agriculture and more business and plant replaces plants, but there is no hovering skyline, no ancient Moorish monuments. Jerez is a working town, but you can only work very slowly when the heat boils your breath away. Still, here it's a microbe which does the most important job.

A quirk of climate and geology has meant that in this region alone a particular type of yeast develops on top of the local wine as it ferments in wooden casks, a yeast which gives that wine a flavour unlike any other. And as a result of this freak of nature there is a corner of Spain which was forever more English than England. The English cannot pronounce the Moorish word Jerez, so they call it sherry. They can drink it though and over the years their prodigious taste for this peculiar, aromatic tipple has twisted the social history of this somnambulant corner of south western Andalusia. Jerez and its hinterland were a time-warp parody of an Albion long gone, but even that is going.

'In the great estate houses around here the people from the sherry families, the Domecqs and the Gonzalez' will be taking tea at five o'clock this afternoon, and taking it in immaculate English before going off to exercise the polo ponies, but there are very few left.'

The man talking to me, in immaculate English, is a

member of one of those families, a man known as Bartolome Vergara. Unusually tall for a Spaniard, upright even in the tough heat, he has the kind of easy but imposing presence and perfect, almost courtly manners once assumed to be the sole domain of the English upper classes. He also has a twenties' Rolex, a wonderful diamond tie-pin and no socks. An invitation to lunch in his company came about because he is the director of public relations for the Jerez appellation and I am an English writer, a writer who may be able to convince people back in the real England to drink real sherry again. This corner of not-quite England is in trouble because its spiritual motherland is turning its back on a forgotten unfashionable colony.

'We have a problem because people in England are drinking less sherry, and because they are drinking imitation sherry. We are over-dependent on England, we have to expand our market, but we also have to re-educate people back there: the ties between the two are too important to be severed.'

The reason why those ties were tied in the first place is buried in the confused and usually violent history of the two countries, but it goes something like this. After the prohibition of the Islamic years, wine production in this region grew with the Reconquista, and that coincided with a brief period of dalliance with the English. Henry VII married his son to the Spanish Catherine of Aragon, and when the Jews were expelled from Spain in 1492 they were replaced in this region largely by English merchants, many of whom began setting up bodegas to produce wine which they shipped home. That is how the English taste for Jerez, or sherry, began and over the years the links between English immigrants and their homeland grew.

Most of the great sherry houses were actually formed by Anglo-Spanish families in the eighteenth century, based on shipping much of their product to Bristol (hence Bristol Cream) and shipping clerks and administrators in the other direction. Names such as Mackenzie and Terry, Williams and Humbert, Harvey and Gordon became a kind of sherry aristocracy, marrying with their Spanish equivalents, so that the great maternal twentieth-century dame of Jerez could acquire a name like Margarita Gonzalez Gilbey (the English gin family). The atmosphere was a kind of Spanish raj with English spoken in the bodegas as a matter of pride, lawns manicured, dogs bred and habits like taking tea and playing polo practised religiously.

The vestiges of that strange cultural cross-pollination remain, but in recent years huge changes have occurred. The many small family bodegas have disappeared as a few large conglomerates came to dominate. The largest of those is Harvey's which grew by swallowing loads of little traditional concerns including that of the Vergara family, which brings me back to the man whose job is now to sell the whole idea of sherry to the world, and England.

Lunch is in a cool, casually expensive restaurant where a priest straight out of central casting comes over to talk to us as we sit sipping a glass of chilled fino. An overweight, smiling kind of priest in a full-length cassock, in a seemingly sumptuous middle age, he knows Sr Vergara, but then everyone in this town knows Sr Vergara. Jerez is not just dominated by the production of wine, it is its sole reason for being, everything here is sherry, including the drink in the pastor's hand. A brief conversation about the health of the industry follows before the priest tells me, in slightly scruffy English, how he once served a congregation in Buckinghamshire.

'It all came very easily,' he said. 'It reminded me so much of here.'

Sr Vergara smiles at that timely confirmation of the point he has been making about the Englishness of the region, as if God had sent his agent especially to prove that my host was telling the truth.

Bartolome Vergara is not the kind of man you would ever doubt, but his opinions are sometimes unusual. He is certainly not quite the cliché figure of the landed Andalusian aristocrat. His father, despite being an influential bodega owner, was a staunch republican who spent seven years in

99

Franco's jails after the Civil War, and that family radicalism is clearly still intact. When, in the wake of the portly priest's intervention, the conversation shifts to religion he says, 'I feel a little sorry for the priesthood in Spain now as they have no real role any more.' In an area famed for its arcane and sometimes macabre displays of religious fanaticism this seems an odd statement. But he follows it up by saying, 'Superstition is strong here masquerading as religion, people like to dress up and go on parades, but I am not sure we have ever really been very Catholic. We leave that to the Italians and the Irish.'

The real deity of the region though is obvious: they worship the wine that provides all. Well over three quarters of all people in the area are employed in some way or other in the production of Jerez, and the job of ensuring that their prosperity continues in the modern world is one that Sr Vergara takes very seriously. The big problem they have is that Jerez in Jerez and sherry in England are two very different drinks. If that priest had been back in Buckinghamshire chances are he would have been imbibing a sweet, blended drink, probably from a bottle kept in a sideboard for the last three years. Sherry in the English context is about as unfashionable as a drink can get, and probably isn't even real sherry anyhow. For reasons that remain buried in the entrails of EEC bureaucracy sherry is not a recognised and exclusive name, and so any blend can be sold as sherry. The stuff that winos, vicars and maiden aunts swig so profusely could come from anywhere. Fino comes only from Jerez.

There are various different types of Jerez, but the one which seems to pervade every aspect, almost very moment of Andalusian existence is fino, and my growing affection for that particular pale wine was part of the reason why my wanderings had pulled me to this otherwise sleepy corner of Spain. Fino is the young, fragrant, light and extremely dry wine which is served chilled and fresh and drunk all the time and everywhere. It is an omnipresent aperitif: it is the standard accompaniment to tapas; it is the drink of young and old.

And now that Andalusia is fashionable in the rest of Spain, so is fino. But it isn't in the homeland, England isn't in the know.

That's why Sr Vergara commissioned that glam and glossy TV advert which has been shown so often in Britain, selling sherry on the back of a beautiful girl on the back of a beautiful white horse; why images of an idealised and extremely hip-looking Andalusia are employed to sell a wine. The plan here is the one which Spain has used time and again to flog its born-again self to a sceptical world: a combination of potent and sumptuous traditionalist imagery which stresses the uniqueness and somehow the authenticity of Spanish culture, with the very latest in graphic design, photography and in this case cinematography.

'What we are promoting here certainly is one of the world's great wines. But in many ways it is more than that, we are selling a taste of Andalusia, and an image of Andalusia. This could be one of the wealthiest regions in Europe, we can turn the climate from a curse to a blessing by producing two crops a year and becoming one of the biggest suppliers of food stuffs for the entire continent. This is a vital time for us, we have to get it right and I believe we are getting it right, so we should tell people.'

Driving away from Jerez I passed countless construction projects, each of them seemingly backed by some EEC body or other and flying the starry flag. The new caliphs of all Spain, Felipe Gonzalez and many of the high-ups of PSOE, are sons of this soil and they have smiled upon their homeland. Huge investment programmes are opening the area up and bringing a new-found affluence and influence to what was once the poorest sister of a poor country.

The road I was travelling on is part of a vast new motorway network which criss-crosses the region. Tarmacked surfaces seem to appear overnight, and soon the dust, the red dust which stings your eyes and clogs your throat as you walk along, the dust which was so synonymous with Andalusia, will all but disappear. Switch on the car radio though as you travel these dust-free highways and the sinuous sound of *cante jondo*, the deep dark song of the gypsies, seeps out. This is still a different place.

13

She was fat enough to stop an opera with a hum. An unrelenting diet of oil and sugar regularly combines to turn the matriachs of the deep south into full-blown barrage balloons. In the Albaicín, the famed gypsy quarter of that sad and dark town, Granada, there are countless caricature fat women waddling stridently up and down the steep terraces of the mythic hill, trailing skinny-legged little men in their wake. The obesity of so many poor southern women is a dreadful indictment of the malnutrition of an area which still fits many of the clichés, but the obesity of this woman of Zahara, whose cheap jewellery clanked as she moved like some voluptuous battleship, was a remarkable and terrible twist of fate. To be that large and to live in a town which sits like an eagle's nest on the top of a high needle of rock, a town which you feel you could fall off if you put a foot wrong, cannot make for an easy life.

It was though sort of right for Zahara. The interior of Andalusia is made up of a chain of small, whitewashed towns clinging to the rocks which rise out of the difficult, undulating valley. These picturesque settlements, many of them built around the buttresses of an old crusader castle, are the living remnants of the dying grounds, the vestiges of the never-ending wars to drive the heathen Moors from God's own country.

If they're lucky, like Arcos, a few arid kilometres from Zahara, their redundant fortress has been turned into a *parador* and a few intrepid tourists, travelling most probably like me on towards Seville, spend their pesetas on enjoying a quick feel of ancient exotica. Then the kids of the town can earn the price of a pack of Ducados by guarding cars like so many menacing young Liverpool scallies at football matches on Merseyside back in England. They come running, these urchins, anxious to be first to imply the slight threat that if they are not paid the car might not fare too well. The fact that almost every car is a hire-car probably keeps their earnings down, but I don't suppose too many tourists who make it as far as Arcos begrudge them a few pesetas. In Zahara, though, nobody runs.

It would be difficult to imagine a place where less goes on and more slowly. If you wanted to take somebody to a small, rural community in southern Spain to show them that little has changed since the end of the war (the one against the Nazrid Kings), then Zahara could well be your spot. The constant battle continues here, the daily one against the sun, where whitewash is the main defensive weapon against the power of the rays and the human combatants surrender every lunch-time. The one against boredom which even the young seem to have given up as not worth the struggle. The battle to earn a living is still a fairly tough one too.

As in most of rural Spain those who work on the land but don't actually own large chunks of it band together in small towns rather than live out there in the wilderness. Antonio lives in Zahara and works on a nearby farm where olives are the main crop. He long ago gave up dreams of football or bulls and has pretty much stopped making the long journey into Seville for fun. Instead he sits in the one bar in town, smokes slow cigarettes, plays the old football machine and watches the world stay the same. 'Nothing much happens here,' he says with an almost English sense of understatement before lighting up another cigarette and ordering a fairy cake. I could not imagine anything more wildly out of place in this down-to-earth community high up a hill.

As we are half-talking, a sentence seeming to come every few minutes, a pace which is entirely in keeping with the town, a Guardia Civil car rolls past exuding a kind of empty, pointless menace, looking for God knows what. An old woman sweeping away the dust from her porch, the dust which will return tomorrow, stares at them hard for a second and goes back inside her darkened, undoubtedly neat little house. It is difficult to doubt Antonio when he says, 'They talk about changes in Andalusia, but I don't see them.'

Yet there is also no doubt that those changes have already occurred. Travelling those dust-free new motorways you sometimes see an old man or woman hunched over a field, wielding a scythe or leading a goat, still see the toothless old and the penniless old. But it is hard to imagine their grand-children living that way. Pull into another little town, a more affluent one perhaps, and you realise that the young are rapidly turning Italian.

Stop for a beer, as I did so many times on this journey, in a plaza as the evening begins to cool and you will be surrounded like a group of wagon train pioneers by gangs of boys circling you on scooters and motorbikes. Teenage boys with no socks and even less shame will rev up for all to hear and flirt speedily with girls with short skirts. Other boys in long Bermuda shorts will lounge a lot looking tanned and healthy, posing to some dance-pop emanating from a beat box or a bar, occasionally ordering a coke or a sandwich. These healthy-looking, cheery kids, who seem to have been allotted the early night as their time, are as much part of the face of Andalusia now as Antonio and his desultory days in Zahara.

Travelling further still the road towards the great city of Seville I came quite unexpectedly upon a funfair. In the middle of nowhere some nothing-town was having its day, and celebrating that fact with a fair which was to go on way into the night. As I wandered into this field with its big wheel and its *churros* stands, its cheap gambling games and gypsy women selling superstitions, the divides and the paradoxes of Andalusia past and future seemed to me to be summed up by two rides standing almost side by side, two rides which embody perfectly the concept of *desfase*. One was a sorry merry-go-round where the rides were provided by real ponies, threadbare and dying. These tiny horses walked a constant dreary circle to nowhere with small children on their backs, walked a sad, round furrow into the sand. The other was a state-of-the-art, highest of high-tec bumper-car ride imported recently from Japan where the polished and pristine toy cars were made by Toyota, controlled by computer and looked like they could cruise down a motorway at ninety with no trouble.

That both of these can still exist in the same field made me think about the state of Andalusia today, a place where I felt, more than any other in Spain, more truly at the core of this country of my obsession. Also though I knew that if I were to return to this lonely little fair in five years' time, one of them would no longer be there.

14

Just as every dog has its day, so every Spanish town, no matter how mangy, has its *feria*. That sudden fair on the roadside was a sign that the local town was 'in' feria, the almost pathological state of partying which is adopted *en masse* by the inhabitants when the appointed day for them and their saint arrives. Where the dog-towns have a day so the great cities have a week of boastful abandon, of pomp and preening and parades, of bulls and meals and endless night. Seville, which long ago appointed itself Spain's most charming and festive city, has the *feria* which is known as *the feria*.

And now it has the Fair too, and because this is Seville where all is extravagance, it has the World's Fair. In a land of grand gestures it has been decided that the landmark year of 1992 will be celebrated in extravagant style. Barcelona has its Olympics, Madrid, so as not to be left out, is the European City of Culture, and Seville has Expo '92. This is a vast trade fair designed to show the extent of man's achievements, and perhaps most importantly the extent of Spain's and Seville's achievements. But grand gestures are also seen as a way of accomplishing something here, and Expo is being used as an excuse to kick this most traditional of towns into the next century. The *feria* is designed to do exactly the opposite, so it's no surprise that there's a little tension between the two.

'There are attacks upon us almost every day in the local press, because there is a power struggle going on. The social leaders, the gentlemen farmers who have always ruled this town, can see power slipping away from them as things change. Expo is a huge symbol of this change and they see it as a threat'.

I had planned my arrival in Seville, a town I had already fallen for, the town that I probably consider to be my favourite in the world, to coincide with the *feria* and to see how the fair was progressing. The man talking to me was Sr Antonio Quijano who was in the middle of a vast building site, (defined in a wonderful piece of contemporary international signpost- ing as 'ten Disneylands' big), a slowly and sometimes pain- fully emerging futurescape, where monorails and cable cars will zip between international pavilions and theme-parks, where the heat is controlled by a botanical micro-climate and the security by lasers and computers. He is trying with great skill to make the mess of girders and diggers look like a wonderland to come. He is also trying to explain the complex internal politics of the Andalusian capital. A young Madri- leño, fluent in lots of languages, including the complex tongue of PR, Antonio Quijano is a glowing example of the new Spain.

While he was speaking, over in the old town the women were preparing their flamenco frocks and the men were grooming the horses. Tomorrow was to be the first day of *feria*, then even the fair stops.

'It is hard to explain to foreign journalists and businessmen, especially to Scandinavians, why absolutely everything stops for a week, why it is impossible to do any work. I just say it is the *feria*, if you come you will understand.'

It would be difficult to understand Seville without seeing her in her fancy.

The Andalusian love of dressing up and showing off which the sherry man, Sr Vergara, spoke of is displayed most potently in her capital, Seville, in two great communal events which occur every spring. Holy Week is the one which photographers photograph to show that Spain is still some kind of primitive, mystical mad-land. Then, to celebrate the fact that Jesus rose from the dead, local members of the mysteriously named 57 Brotherhoods don Ku-Klux-Klan gear, lug heavy wooden crosses about and parade overwrought icons on monstrous floats for hours on end. There is lots of moaning involved, plenty of fasting, a fair amount of flaying and the occasional trance-like state. From Palm Sunday to Easter Sunday pious Seville loves the Virgin Mary and the holy purple, loves to pray and pay penance. Then comes *feria*.

Restraint and excess, the two halves of the national contradiction, the two warring traits which have shaped the history of these peoples are enshrined in the remarkable backflip which Seville performs every spring. The same city which wears pointy hoods and starves itself to show its devotion, then pulls on its party gear and stays awake for a week to celebrate the fact that the sap is rising. It is a week like no other.

Seville is a *brio* city of monuments and manners. Its fortune was made from trade with the New World and spent on grace and charm, on sumptuous architecture and arch fashion. This is a staggeringly beautiful and almost painfully vain city which is convinced that the rest of Spain is jealous of its undoubted delights. And when in early April the time comes for the city to have its week, it shows off like the very worst stage-school brat. But what a show this is.

Restraint and excess are also apparent in the structure of the *feria* itself. This is a week of abandon and licence where everybody dresses up, groups of people dance and sing spontaneously in the streets, where drinking is non-stop and work unthinkable. Yet it is also a week ruled by the most exacting mores, the most formal codes, the most arcane and powerful web of correctness.

The *feria* itself takes place in a large open space just outside the centre of the town and consists of the obligatory funfair, but most importantly of a massive temporary settlement of marquees known as *casetas*. A few of these are open to the public, but most are private party spaces owned by families, companies, clubs, banks, political parties. And for the week they act as a home from home where you can drink and eat and dance and drink some more until six o'clock every morning.

Originally *feria* was a horse fair where the farmers from the countryside came to trade in steeds, and the equine nature of the event is still intact. But it has grown over the years to become a huge celebration of Sevilleness, a ritual display by this peacock town where the rules of the ritual must be obeyed. *Feria* is wildly hierarchical, rigidly formal and great fun. Everyone goes to *feria*, but *feria* is not the same for everyone. Status is what's really on parade in Seville in *feria*.

Felipe and Candela are the son and daughter of status, of precisely the kind of gentleman farmer that Antonio Quijano was talking about. The family owns a large *finca* in the countryside and a large apartment in the most fashionable part of town. Felipe, in his early twenties, is finishing his studies and will take over the running of the farm, while Candela, his elder by a few years, teaches a little English and looks beautiful. Tonight they are having a party in the apartment before going out to the *feria*.

Beginning a party at midnight is not unusual in Seville, but the gathering at this one was unusually privileged. I'd been invited at second-hand by an American writer, a member of the Bullfight Club of New York who had lived in the city in order to research a book about the bulls. His work had led him into the kind of wealthy Andalusian circles who controlled the *corrida* and he had led me here.

The boys were all early twenties going on early fifties, identical tall and elegant young men, every single one of them wrapped in the same dark blazers, the same slightly loud ties and the same rather quiet ideas. The girls were either dark and demure Spaniards of a similar caste to Candela, or blonde and boastful young Americans studying at the local university and clearly invited for the entertainment of the boys (many of whom seemed to have spent a year studying at American universities themselves). Fino was served in fine crystal, music was traditional *sevillana*, and the talk was of horses and bulls, hectares and banks.

When the time came to move from the apartment to the *feria* everybody crowded into one of the many large cars parked outside. I found myself wedged in the boot of an estate car with half a dozen barathea'd boys discussing in minute details the merits (or in this case mainly the demerits) of the *corridas* which had thus far passed. Every single one of them spoke with authority and knowledge and all of them were going to the bulls every day. When we spilled out into the real world it had gone very crazy.

Thousands and thousands of people moving like shoals of deranged fish in all directions around an illuminated and overdressed area which stretched as far as the eye could see. Girls and women of all ages and classes in the flouncy, frilled layered dresses, the *traje de feria*, flowers in their hair, many of them dancing in spontaneous circles, the *sevillana*, the arms arcing, feet stamping, dresses billowing, dance of the city. Boys, some in their finery, many more in everyday clothes, joining in or standing clapping and singing their encouragement, everybody drinking, everybody tuned to a logic which the outsider simply cannot see. Through all of this our band of privilege moved.

Our destination was the family *caseta* the tent which is stocked and staffed for a week of entertaining friends of the family. Most of the wealthy young Spaniards in our group had families which had *casetas*, each of them costing thousands of pounds for the duration of the *feria*. Most of the people who live in the city will have access to a *caseta* through their employers, or a club maybe, and the rest can always attend the few large public *casetas* where the food and drink is for sale.

But the point of the private, family *casetas* is that they are just that, open only to those whose social standing can gain them access. And the more important your family is in the region, the more elaborate and exclusive your *caseta* is. The best ones like that owned by Felipe's and Candela's father, whose sherry was lubricating my evening nicely, have live bands playing and feasts of food. The women are all dressed in *trajes* which cost thousands of pounds, and the men, no matter what their age, in uniform, deeply conservative attire. The whole thing is about flaunting your wealth but in such a manner that only those who need to see do so. The larger *casetas* are guarded and closed, completely inaccessible and the show going on is completely invisible to the many thousands of ordinary Andalusians spinning around outside. They will never gain access and don't seem to mind: that is the order of things.

Feria is like a kind of Henley Regatta taking place in the middle of the Notting Hill carnival, a raging, roaring street party where everybody knows their place. All night long these constant private parties go on with a perpetual movement along rigid class tramlines between *casetas* and bars. But then tomorrow for the likes of Candela and Felipe the show, the reminder to all concerned, really begins.

Mañana means both tomorrow and it means morning, but when during *feria* somebody says, 'I will see you *mañana*', you do not have to work out which they mean. When nothing ends before dawn, nothing starts before midday, then it really starts.

If the *casetas* are a closed-off show of wealth and station, then the parade of the *caballos* knows no such reticence. This is when the rural, horse-trading history of the *feria* really shows itself and when the past really comes back, not to haunt so much as to taunt. For in the early afternoon those who own the farms where the horses are bred (or those who have a £300-a-night room in the fabulous Alfonso XIII hotel where a horse can be arranged by the doorman) don their very best nineteenth-century costumes and ride into town to impress the poor, pedestrian masses.

The daily parade of the horses is one of the most remarkable and magnificent free shows in Spain. In wonderful old open coaches come the families with father driving, mother posing, small overdressed children looking too cute. On palaminos and greys, on dark arabic horses and beautiful white horses from Jerez come the young things. The men are immaculately

112

dressed in the *traje corte*, the short bolero jacket and high trousers with the broad flat-brimmed Cordoban hat, tie-less white shirt and brown, snub-nosed boots. The women riding side-saddle behind, sisters or lovers, are in their full *traje de feria* topped by a mantilla and long veil, like every classic Spanish beauty in a cheap and torrid movie.

Through the old town they ride, these dandies, clattering up cobbled alleys, past the sun-drenched, flower-dripping patios of the barrio, stopping probably for a glass of fino before heading out to the *feria*. Here they parade among the *casetas*, displaying all the while their horseflesh and their horsemanship, their overpowering sartorial elegance and above all their social standing. They sit still too, outside their chosen *case-tas*, lounging straight-backed and casual upon those magnificent horses, receiving drinks and compliments, lines of young people representing old money and old power for all to gaze upon and marvel at. You cannot fail to be impressed and that is exactly what you are supposed to be.

If a member of one of the fine families is away in another place or land it is considered their duty to return to take their place in *feria*. This great ritual shows all those who really need reminding just who really rules this town and this Andalusia. This is a potent annual reaffirmation of the hierarchy, where all are free to join in, but some play a more exalted role. To the technocrats and the businessmen, the Madrileños and the Catalans ('The Danes' to those who really harbour southern pride and prejudice) labouring away over at the Expo, it is a vivid reminder that there is another fair, another Seville. When the parade of the *caballos* is over and all eyes have seen the glory it is time for lunch, then the Maestranza.

The fine restaurants of this debonair town at lunchtime during *feria* are a great farce of code and mode, hectic beyond sanity, bursting with people of all classes trying to show off. Podgy *gitanos* splashing out on raven-haired consorts in stone-washed denim, foreign *aficionados* speaking their studied taurine Spanish, and the likes of Candela and Felipe and their families exuding easy class for all they are worth — which is probably quite a lot. Lunch is traditionally the big meal of the day in the south, and in *feria* it becomes a massive performance, a display of affluence and endurance which extends right up until the time for the bulls and the next great show.

Those who really want to rub it in arrive at the Maestranza, the great bullring by the Guadalquivir, in their carriages or on their horses as if this really were one hundred years ago. Certainly they don't look out of place beside the picture-book baroque of the great Plaza de Toros, the most beautiful and most revered ring in the world. Many more though are walking from the bars around, the lucky ones clutching tickets, the nervous ones looking for scalpers and hoping that the hysteria hasn't driven the prices crazy.

The *corrida* is one of the few art forms where you can be recognised as a prophet only in your own land, so what they like in Seville is matadors from Seville or at least from close enough to be able to claim them as their own. They also like *arte*, straight backs and noble gestures; so if one of the local *arte* toreros is appearing in *feria*, the expectation can be enormous and the extortion from those with tickets to sell terrible to witness. The atmosphere around the ring on those days is tangible, the buzz audible from streets away as you approach.

All of this is why the foreign *aficionados* come in such numbers to Seville for the *feria*. The French, some of them brought up with bulls in Provence and the Camargue (and many more from Paris driven wild by the style of it all), drive down in droves. The Americans, would-be Hemingways from Miami, East Coast intellectuals like my writer friend, and Chicago *machistas* in cowboy boots, also make their presence felt, talking too loud so as to be heard over their clothes. The Swedes come — or at least the Swede, Lars — who seems to spend most of the time drunk. The British are always there, perhaps twenty or so members of the 150-strong The Club

Taurino de Londres (of which I am one) with their/our innate belief that they/we know more than most.

You go to Seville in *feria* because it is most like the Spain of your romance. Here now with a book to write I realised that Seville is actually the perfect lover, one who allows you to project onto her whatever fantasies you like and plays a willing part in them. It is the perfect backdrop, and a day at the bulls the finest romantic theatre.

Candela and Felipe go to bulls because that is what their family does. The class division of *sol y sombra* is more apparent and more rigid in Seville than any other ring: a good *abono*, or season ticket, for the shaded section of the Maestranza is as much a banner of breeding as a *caseta* at the *feria*, and those going to the good seats do so in high style. When one of the great dons of bull breeding, a *ganadero* like don Eduardo Miura or don Victorino Martin, enters the ring the crowd will stand and applaud such standing. Candela also has a role to play.

As a daughter of the *alta nobilidad*, she is one of the beauties of the Seville *feria*, a dozen girls from the highest of society chosen to sit in full regalia in the seats around the president, who is himself a local dignitary. Her role is simply to impress yet again how little has changed, how the formal fashions, mores and codes of this most tradition-bound town are still intact, still there for all to see. Candela's friend Jaima, despite her looks and her social standing, could never be chosen to sit alongside the president at the Maestranza and will never even allow herself to wear the *traje de feria*. That's because she is from Badajoz, not Seville, and so to wear those clothes would not, she believes, be right. In Seville being right is mighty important, and things can get pretty complex. Make a noise at the wrong time in the Maestranza, clap an undeserving torero in this most serious plaza and you realise just how complex.

Once you've had a few drinks though, to toast a great triumph or curse a disappointment (probably the latter), it really doesn't matter. Every evening the party begins again.

And when the party's over, when hangover Monday, the last day of the *feria*, has passed, you see why the grandees are so intent upon making their annual grand gesture of the old order, why the *feria* gets bigger and more traditional every year. It's because Seville, fragile, exquisite Seville, is a town turning.

'We're spending 10,000 million US dollars on this. We're not stupid, you don't spend all that money for six months of Expo, we are taking this city from the third world to the first in five years. The process was already underway, but Expo has meant a huge acceleration and given us a definite deadline. Nineteen-ninety-two is a big deadline for all Spain.'

Antonio Quijano is explaining to me what Expo actually means for Seville, which is basically an entire new infrastructure. The new train station and railway line to Madrid will cut the journey to the capital from seven hours to two hours and forty-five minutes. They have constructed seven new bridges across the Guadalquivir, where they only managed five in the preceding thousand years. A new airport, motorway and ring road, new telecommunications, a dozen new hotels, and a complete face-lift for the city of La Giralda, and the Torre del Oro, of Carmen and Don Juan. No wonder the traditional power brokers are nervous, but they aren't the only ones.

Those from outside who like their Spain frozen are pulling sour faces. There is a particular type of Hispanophile, usually a nice middle-class traveller from the safe northlands, often a nice middle-class travel-writer from the safe northlands, who wants Spain to be a tragic, bleeding place. So they go to Seville now and write bad words.

The city, they say, is too modern, too much a part of the world. Seville they say, is a fashion city and therefore it has lost its soul and they tell us all to head for some forsaken town where the people are still poor enough to be authentic. Those who like their Spain covered in dust and blood and shrouded in authentic noble ignorance don't like what is happening to Seville or to the country.

116

For me the real glory of Seville, the most powerfully attractive thing about the place which I feel every time I walk its historic, redolent streets, is that it is once again a fashionable, affluent, efficient city, a city of graces. Seville is on its uppers and strutting, just as it had done when those marvellous old monuments were new. It is an industrious and decidedly trendy town again, and so it should be. But it is also one which can celebrate its uniqueness and its history with great gusto every April and in this particular April I was glad that I was there to see it.

Expo, following directly on from the *feria* in 1992, is the great celebration of the new-found confidence of a marvellous old city which had lived in the lea of its former triumphs for too long. It is also the symbol of how far it has come. I don't have any doubts that both the Sevilles, although they may argue every now and then, will survive side by side; the contradiction will thrive in all its delight.

The place where I spoke to Antonio Quijano, the site of Expo '92, is the island of La Cartuja. this is a vast disused strip of land in the Guadalquivir, where the sole vestige of greater days is a derelict monastery where Christopher Columbus stayed before his voyage of discovery and where he was briefly buried after it. The 500th anniversary of the discovery of the Americas is one of the reasons for, and themes of, Expo '92, but the significance of that anniversary goes far deeper than that. Throughout Spain there are ceremonies planned to mark that great event, ceremonies which are in reality a single act of communal catharsis.

The golden age of discovery was the last time that Spain was truly a great world power, and the weight of that era has acted to drag her down ever since. Wherever you go in Spain, and nowhere more than in Seville which owes so much to the New World, you are taunted by remnants and monuments of that time of empire, as if to make the decline which followed even more bitter, as if to inflame the wounds. but now that Spain can feel herself rising again, she is ready to lay those ghosts, to get rid of the onerous historical burden of

Colombus and his legacy once and for all. In Seville they are doing that by throwing the biggest party the city has ever seen, and this city knows how to party. Now that my party was over for a year it was time to travel north, to Madrid and some serious work.

15

'When I was at school in the fifties they used to teach us these things about Spain.

'One: "Spain is a poor country." Spain is no longer a poor country, we are one of the ten richest nations in the world.

'Two: "Spain is a Catholic country". Spain was a Catholic country. Ninety-nine per cent was the figure they gave to us then, now it is no more than twenty per cent, we are simply not a Catholic country any more.

'Three: "Spain is an agricultural country." We still have a strong agricultural sector which is producing for the EEC and becoming more efficient all the time, but we are the sixth largest producer of motor cars, the fifth largest exporter. You could never have imagined that.

'Four: "Spain is the country where family comes first." We now have the lowest rate of population growth in Europe, lower than Britain or Germany. That is another incredible change.

'Five: "Spain is separate and different." We were traditionally isolated from Europe. We stood with our backs to the continent, looking instead to Africa and South America, but we are now the most enthusiastic and committed Europeans of them all.

'All of the great truths that were supposed to sum up Spain when I was a kid have gone now, the face of this country has changed completely from the way it was twenty or thirty years ago. Now it is so much better.'

The man speaking has been called 'the most influential in

all Spain', which may be exaggerating a little, but only a little. I've also heard him described as 'the new dictator' which is certainly unfair, a little. Juan Luis Cebrian is the man whose name sits at the top of a newspaper called *El País*. These days he is officially described as the advisory represent-ative which in English is roughly equivalent to the post of consulting editor, because after fifteen years at the masthead he has decided to move to a more background capacity. But from its inception in 1976 Juan Luis Cebrian was the figure-head of this new newspaper and this newspaper was the symbol of the new democracy. His office seemed like a good place to begin.

Having been to Rupert Murdoch's imposing fortress Wap-ping, home of the News International titles, in London's East End, it didn't come as such a shock to see electronic gates, barbed wire and burly security guards at a newspaper plant. But then the *Sunday Times*, for all its troubles, has never really been under threat from men who mean death. In the sixteen years of its existence *El País* has managed to upset some serious people. In the early days it was the rightists who threatened to blow away the democracy and its most powerful mouthpiece. Now it is the separatists who use Semtex to settle scores and destabilise the status quo. *El País* is now unavoidably (and, for a campaigning, liberal paper, occasion-ally uncomfortably) part of that status quo, and as such has to take precautions. It was still a reminder on a balmy Madrid day though that Spain is not that far removed from its shadows.

In the process of exorcising those evil spirits *El País* has been undeniably important. Under Franco the press was both state controlled and in many cases state owned, with no real dissenting voices permitted. Newspapers then turned out unreadable drivel which nobody read. The idea of a democrat-ically inclined newspaper, with no majority shareholder and no fixed ideology, was first mooted in the early seventies. There was a tacit realisation from those involved that there had to be a paper to step into the vacuum when the General finally died, but before that happened they were denied the necessary licence to publish.

So those who were to be involved – and they came from both right and left, Catholic and communist, conservative and liberal – had a paper waiting to go as soon as the doctors gave the word. As a result on 4 May 1976, just six months after the end, and before political parties had been legalised, El País hit the streets. Its editor was a thirty-one-year-old whizz-kid journalist named Juan Luis Cebrian.

Like most of his journalistic generation Cebrian was a graduate of the Faculties of Information Science, the state-run institute set up to ensure political indoctrination in writers and broadcasters. Like so many of the institutions of Francoism though it had atrophied long before his death and ceased to function in an ideological sense in all but name. A whole generation of liberal writers emerged from its class-rooms to man the free press as soon as it emerged.

Cebrian was certainly never going to lead a servile ship, and from its very inception El País became a kind of daily symbol of the new democracy. Its parent company PRISA (it stands for Information Promotion Limited) also became one of the most advanced and most successful in the country, not just adopting but promoting new communications technology at a time when most Spanish homes barely had black and white TVs. The success of El País, both financially and intellectually, was instant.

Folklore now has it that, if, in those tumultuous and precipitous times in the early days of the democracy, you were seen reading a copy of El País (it simply means The Country), that was taken as a sign of which side you were on, a kind of badge of allegiance. In the intrigue ridden cafés of Madrid, which were at their most voluble in the late seventies, it is said that if you were reading a copy of El País, people would come up to you and start talking politics. The assumption was that if you took that paper then you took the view that the political future rather than the authoritarian past was the right way. From its very inception the life of El País was seen as directly analogous with the life of the new Spain. As Sr Cebrian puts it now.

'The success of the political transition was very much linked in the minds and dreams of the people with the success of the paper. Even when we had trouble and the democracy looked fragile people would say, "As long as we have *El País* then we have the country."'

The most notorious of those troubles was of course the night of the long moustache in 1981. It was then that *El País* and its young editor really assured their place in Spanish society. In his tidy, almost chic office Juan Luis has a large, bound volume entitled *300 Primeras Paginas*. This contains the front pages of the first three hundred issues of *El País*, including the most famous of them all, the one with the 48 point banner headline which read *EL PAÍS, CON LA CONSTITUCIÓN*.

At nine o'clock in the evening, three hours after Tejero walked into the Cortes, a special edition of *El País* appeared on the streets bearing that headline in support of the young and endangered democracy. This was followed by an editorial simply entitled *Viva La Constitución*. No other paper appeared, the radio was silent and television screens were blank, and so it was an act of some courage and great importance for *El País* to step into that dangerous void on the side of the good guys. When you ask him about it now it is still possible to see a light of excitement in his small dark eyes,.

'That night I felt like a newspaperman, an editor who had a duty to inform his readers. I thought, I have a paper, no guns or anything to defend us, but I do have a paper. It was our duty, the duty of self-defence for the paper itself, we had to take a stand. Because at that moment the coup was winning, and I knew that if the coup succeeded we would be finished, I certainly would be, so there was no real argument. We gave our opinion, we took a side, we published. That was a very important night for us.'

Just as King Juan Carlos is today eternally popular because

he stood by the democracy against all the odds, so *El País* created for itself a unique position in the mind and soul of the new Spain on that night.

With 350,000 copies per day and 190,000 on Sundays it is by far the best selling daily in a country where reading a newspaper at all is a notoriously élitist affair. The news kiosks which stand on the corner of every major street in Spain are miraculous affairs, overflowing green tardises abundant with every kind of publication. Yet the reading public is a small one — in the case of newspapers an intellectual, university-educated élite who also exclusively write them. There is no real popular press in Spain, no equivalent of the British tabloids, and even the more recent downmarket titles like *El Periodico* and *Diario 16* are full of intense political and economic news. There are numerous daily sporting papers, but even they take their subject matter very seriously.

Despite or maybe because of all this, though, newspapers are extremely influential in Spain and *El País* is by far the most influential of them all. It is considered by many to have been the best newspaper in Europe in the eighties. Crisply designed, scrupulously researched and powerfully independent. It breaks scandals and makes political careers.

One of its most celebrated and disturbing scoops was the revelation that the socialist government were in fact behind a mysterious, underground anti-terrorist, terrorist group who were responsible for killing members of ETA in the Basque lands. The repercussions of that story are still raging in Spain today, fostering as they did the notion that politics had not really left the murky swamp of the clandestine and the violent.

In 1991 on the tenth anniversary of the attempted coup, *El País* broke another story which stated that the army had planned to kill the king at a parade for Armed Forces day in 1985. At a speech in Corunna in Galicia a bomb was to be planted under the platform where the king was to speak and this was only prevented when the secret service discovered the plot at the last moment. The role that a now defunct right-wing paper *El Alcazar* played in the plot was also highlighted. But this incredible story, along with revelations about other abortive coups by the military in the early eighties, actually caused remarkably little upset when it appeared. A sign perhaps of the increasing confidence of the people in the solidity of their democracy, and the desire to consign such intrigues to the distant past. It was also perhaps an indication of the decreasing influence of *El País* now that Spain is a more normal country.

But it would be difficult to overestimate the power which *El País* wielded during Sr Cebrian's reign, and there for some lies the problem. For just as you hear complaints about the Socialists being a *de facto* one-party state because of the practical inability of the other parties ever to win power, so *El País* was the sole media voice of any clout. As a result its editor wielded a power far beyond that of normal newspaper-men. As a result the gossip and the slurs fly. Some say that for a democratic paper it was run on very authoritarian lines; others that Cebrian's influence was sometimes arbitrary and malign. 'If he takes against you, you have no chance,' said one disgruntled young man. Whatever the truth of the stories though there is little doubt that the paper he edited has been a powerful force for preserving a true democratic spirit. And for that Spain continues to be thankful and continues to buy the paper.

Although he no longer runs *El País* on a daily basis he does keep an office at the top of the building and it was there amid the modern art and the Tizio lamps that he kept me waiting three-quarters of an hour for the interview. Actually three-quarters of an hour is not too bad at all by Madrid time and there is no doubt that he is a busy man. As well as being the overseer of *El País*, he is a novelist and now the head of a radio and television group whose Canal + is the most up-market of the new Spanish television franchises.

Now in his mid-forties he has the clean-cut, almost preppy image which marks out the successful of his generation. His mind is also just as sharp as the creases in his charcoal, flannel trousers. I mean, I almost believed him when he said, 'The Spanish people are the most hard working in Europe, much more so than in, say, France and of course more than in England.'

This was when I'd been living in Madrid for a couple of weeks and had yet to see anybody go to bed before four o'clock in the morning. Juan Luis of course had an answer for this too, and he didn't even mention *desfase*.

'As well as hard-working, we are also very hedonistic so we spend a lot of time on pleasure and leisure, but we manage to combine that with hard work, believe me it is true, those people who are up all night go to work too, how do you think that the economic changes have occurred? The thing we do not do is sleep, nobody here sleeps, we work and play instead, except for Sundays. On Sundays now people sleep twenty-four hours to make up for the rest of the week.'

The almost obsessional late nights of the Spanish people are rapidly becoming their most marked contemporary national characteristic. Not going to bed, until as late as possible, surviving with very little sleep, is seen as a sign of machismo, as a way of sorting the men from the boys, like some nightly endurance test. The Spaniards are proud of a kind of toughness which they see as marking them out from other less hedonistic souls. If there is *marcha* to be had it is almost your patriotic duty to be there.

Some of the older traits though, the passion and the pride, the intemperance and intolerance, which seemed to make Spain so different and so romantically attractive to more pallid northern souls, are undoubtedly declining if not disappearing. Gabriel García Márquez, the great Colombian writer, recently caused something of a fuss by stating that he felt Spain was losing its soul, becoming too European and somehow too affluent and too ordinary. The response to that criticism from most Spaniards I spoke to was, 'Ask the average Colombian if it is much fun to be poor and fascinating', and 'Why does passion have to come from pain?' Juan Luis Cebrian analysed this in greater detail.

'Belonging to the generation that has created this new Spain, we are aware of just how much the country has changed. As far as being attractive in a folkloric or anthropological sense there are deep roots and deep rivers of our culture which will not disappear, they are not that superficial. But the Civil War had a profound effect on us all and still exerts a strong influence. I was born in nineteen-forty-four, but the Civil War has been an everyday part of my life because Franco and his people needed to keep it that way. All the time it was on the TV, in the papers, in school books, in the family. Franco kept the war alive because it was his way of maintaining power, his reason for existing. But equally this made people aware of the horrors of war and extremism, it gave them the will to make sure that never happened again at any price.

'That experience gave us a kind of pragmatism which is very important in your understanding of Spain today, it also gave us a great ambition to somehow become normal Europeans. My generation suffered a terrible inferiority complex about not being normal Europeans, we were determined to overcome this, that is why people have worked so hard. There has been an explosion of enthusiasm for democracy because economic growth seemed to be linked to that, and so did our very existence, there has been a real and quite remarkable consensus here considering the degree of change that has occurred.'

That consensus had been troubling me a little. One of the tasks in writing this book was to look for both sides, not only for those who had benefited from the new Spain, but also those who had lost or at least who felt that Spain had lost. Inevitably my life brought me more in contact with the young and the liberal and I was yet to hear any real dissenting voices, or any great enthusiasm for the old days and the old ways. Sr Cebrian doubted that I would find many.

'You have to go back to the last few years of Franco to really understand this. That man and his world were very, very boring at the end, unbelievably stifling. The whole country was waiting for a change, even the Francoists I am sure were waiting to start a new life, even they knew it had played itself out long ago. Of course, added to that, economic growth has been immense, almost everybody is better off economically.'

When I mentioned Spain's unemployment figures which run as high as sixteen per cent and are among the worst in Europe I was surprised by the response of this leading liberal.

'Unemployment, not at all, that is a myth. I would say that we have a situation of full employment: we now import Moroccan and Portugese and even Polish workers because there are jobs today that Spanish people will not do, that is an incredible turn-around. You must understand that we have a huge underground economy, at least twenty-five per cent of our GNP is clandestine and illegal work. We are very like the Italians in this sense.'

But what about the *chabolas*, the homeless, the junkies, the people begging on the Madrid underground? Are these not signs that the imbalances and inequalities which so marked Spanish society are still prevalent?

'No, not really, we have problems today certainly, but they are different problems, they are essentially the same as those in New York and London, they are problems of urban margin-alisation. In the fifties and sixties it was mass migration from the poor and rural south, that no longer exists. Our big housing problem now is that house prices have risen too high. We are seeing people commuting for the first time, being forced to move out of town into suburbs, that threatens to change our way of life and our habits hugely. But these if anything are problems of affluence and success.'

A Spain peopled by commuting surburbanites is indeed a chilling thought. If you have to drive an hour to get home you cannot really take a siesta, cannot sit in the squares or bars after work, cannot live the kind of communal street life which makes Spanish cities so vivid. Perhaps these were the kind of things which Márquez was remarking on?

'Of course, in every change you lose something and in

many respects I and my generation feel closer to the old than the new. The role of money and mass affluence is new here: it has altered the values of society, we now have conspicuous consumption, people showing off their wealth which is very alien to the Spain of old. We are undoubtedly becoming more Americanised too, there are fast-food joints along the Gran Vía, but the tapas bars will not disappear, and besides that is a small price to pay. Thirty years ago we had a problem of malnutrition in Andalusia, we sent two and a half million of our people away to work in terrible conditions abroad, now they go on holidays and people come here to work.'

It isn't only poor resident workers who have been coming to live in Spain. Throughout the south in particular you see blue-eyed, blond-haired kids playing football in the plazas and talking in deep Andalusian accents. Thousands of families from the cold and constricted northlands have upped and moved to Spain in recent years and they aren't all British villains. With the introduction of multi-national corporations, Spain has become one of the best postings in Europe. Dread the thought, but the expression 'the California of Europe' has become one that some Spaniards (the ones who have never been to Los Angeles presumably) have begun to apply to themselves.

Sr Cebrian avoided such crass comparisons, but he spoke of the Mediterranean as the most energetic and attractive section of the continent, spoke of a thriving, arriving Mediterranean culture. 'We are playing the climate card – the same is true of many parts of Italy – the way of life on offer is a very good one, people have realised that this is a very enjoyable part of Europe to live in, and in Europe today many people have that option.'

Talk of Europe led us on to the subject that Juan Luis Cebrian was most enthusiastic about. *El País* has established a reputation as one of the Continent's finest newspapers and one which he is convinced can continue to play an increasing continent-wide role. But it no longer has the heroic position that it did in creating the democracy: it is a great newspaper now, like *The Times* or *Le Monde*, and that one senses is why Sr Cebrian has stepped down.

Spanish film is witnessing a major resurgence and as a serious film buff he is about to take a serious interest by setting up a production company. Spanish television still has a long way to go, but Canal +, the station with which Cebrian is involved, is in the forefront of ensuring that they get there. He is now at the head of a genuine international communications group and that in itself speaks volumes about the changes Spain has undergone since the launch of *El País*.

Pan-European communications is the future now for the man from The Country, and when I asked him what Spain's greatest contribution to a converging Europe could be, I expected something along those lines.

'The most important thing that Spain can bring to Europe is our will to be European, a will like nowhere else. In Britain you are divided. France believes in Europe as far as Europe means France. Germans of course are sure that they are Europe and nobody else is etc, etc. But the idea of a real Europe without these chauvinistic conceits has found a real home in Spain, we have lost all national chauvinism because of Franco.

'The idea that Spain is different and better was drummed into us. We learnt these slogans at school like "There is only one Spain", "I am Spanish or I am nothing", "The best in the world is Spain". For years we had to repeat these silly phrases and as a result nobody believes in that rubbish. We like Spain, but patriotism has been so close to the idea of Francoism, to the winners of the Civil War, that it is no longer an important force here.'

Certainly the lack of popular enthusiasm for the trappings of nationalism is striking when you spend any time in Spain. Club football for example takes on spiritual proportions here, but the national team is poorly supported: watching a World Cup in Spain is almost eerie in the lack of patriotic passion it arouses. I had always put this down to the fact that the sense of nationalism is so fractured by regional differences. The

129

country is clearly deeply divided by its language groups with many Basques, Catalans and Gallegans feeling little affection for the centre. That is true even in Andalusia or Extremadura, where despite not possessing a separate language they are still intensely proud of their regional identity. While accepting that is part of the reason for the lack of popular Spanish patriotism Sr Cebrian insisted that it runs deeper than that.

'Basically we realise that we are Spanish by an accident of birth, and that accident makes us no better than anybody else. Certainly the Catalans and Basques are nationalistic, but they are also pro-European because they believe that is the best way to distance themselves from the "oppression of Madrid". So one way or another the whole of Spain is pro-European. Essentially we believe in a united Europe because being so far from Europe has been very bad for us. For five centuries we have turned our backs on the Continent, like you English we spoke of Europe as a foreign place. They were five centuries of decadence and loss of power. It has been a dream of all of us to return to Europe and so now we are ready to take our place and flourish.'

That Juan Luis Cebrian will play a vital part in that is in no doubt whatsoever, but I do wonder whether any form of contemporary Spanish media will ever come close to ¡Hola!

Every Thursday morning the publication of ¡Hola! brings with it one of the most remarkable rituals of contemporary Spanish society. For it is then that everybody from the countess to the shop steward rushes out to buy his or her copy of the most bland, the most sycophantic, the most predictable and the most addictive journal in the world.

Over three-quarters of a million people buy ¡Hola! each week, with three times that many reading it, and as many again reading one of the many competitors it has spawned. 'The press of the heart' is the suitably corny name given to such titles as *Diez Minutos*, *Pronto* and *Semana* and they play a unique role in Spanish life.

¡Hola! has been feeding the huge popular desire to see celebrity in action since 1944. Then it was the occasional visiting film star, the top torero and the landed and lauded gentry. And to this day it is still anachronistically full of the many overdressed and underworked aristos at home and at play. But it also has the full gamut of new Spanish aristocrats such as Julio Iglesias, Miguel Bose and Severiano Ballesteros, as well as seriously overexposed euro-trash like the princesses of Monaco and England. There is also a double dose of the Spanish Royal family every week.

Yet for what is essentially a glossy gossip column ¡Hola! never says anything remotely nasty or even suggestive about its subjects. The newer titles like Diez Minutos can be a little more scurrilous (though never about the holy Julio), but basically they are still remarkably nice about everybody. So for a long time I could not understand why anybody bought these magazines, and certainly not why everybody bought them. Then I began to realise.

First off it was obvious that every middle-aged woman in Spain uses ¡Hola! as a fashion bible, rushing out instantly to buy a cheap and nasty copy of some star or other's expensive and nasty outfit. Both sexes use it for erotic stimulation, with all those bikini- and brief-clad beauties, but most of all, like some cheap Victorian melodrama, the real appeal of ¡Hola! is that it allows you to read between the lines. And there can be few people as adept at that as the Spanish. Through years of censorship these essentially racy and scandal-loving people had to create their own steam as one bland publication followed another. So now, despite having a huge plethora of porn to choose from, most prefer to take ¡Hola! and then invent their own scenarios from the characters provided. ¡Hola! is essentially a photo-love story where you make up the stories.

I realised this when I discovered that every Spaniard is convinced that our own ¡Hola! lovely, Lady Di (it's pronounced Laddy Dee in Spanish), is secretly in love with their King Juan Carlos. Pictures of both appear almost every week, (on separate pages of course but that is all part of the game) so the scandal-mongers have plenty of ammunition. Then every summer there is a real splurge of gossip as Charles and Diana spend a week's holiday on Majorca with Juan Carlos and his rather plain wife Sofia.

Then *¡Hola!* and the other 'press of the heart' overdose on pictures of our pretty princess and their hunky king sunbathing or boating. Their poor spouses do inevitably look dowdy by comparison, and so by Spanish logic the two more glamorous members of the foursome are bound to be up to something. 'Admit it, our Juan Carlos is far more attractive than your Carlos [the Spanish translate names, remember] with his big ears, and his sulks. Everybody knows that the Royal couple are not happy, it is only natural she should look to the king.' It was a trainee architect who first said that to me, an avid *¡Hola!*-ist, and after a while he had cast enough doubt in my mind and I was in the queue on Thursday scouring between the lines for clues. The fact that it is all nonsense is really not very important: it is enjoyable, escapist nonsense, which is exactly what can be said about *¡Hola!*.

The relationship of the Spanish Royal family to Spain's most remarkable magazine is far more complex and subtle than that though. *¡Hola!* is given access to virtually every corner of the Royal household and there is not a single edition of the magazine which does not feature one member of the family. Occasionally they are shown in full regalia and looking suitably regal, but most of the time the tone is decidedly informal and you are more likely to see Juan Carlos with a cashmere jumper draped over his shoulders than with an ermine robe.

There has clearly been a decision by the king or his advisers, not only to allow the Royal family to be portrayed in the most popular medium of them all, but also to portray them in the most populist manner. Given Spain's recent past this is clearly a logical decision. Juan Carlos came out clearly and bravely on the side of a democratic Spain and ever since has been sure that he is seen as a democratic king, closer to the Danish model than to his autocratic ancestors, and it has worked, not just for the king but for the entire Spanish upper class. It is almost inconceivable to go to war against people whose homes you have entered on a regular basis and whom you have seen in their swimming costumes. It is also difficult to imagine many Spaniards being anything other than complimentary about their king.

Instead they are all eager to tell you the same anecdote about how Juan Carlos regularly goes out riding around Madrid at night on his motorbike with a full-face helmet so that he cannot be recognised. This, it is said, enables him to see his people without being seen. One time while out riding – so runs the more elaborate version of the story – he saw a student whose scooter had run out of petrol, so the king stopped, took him on the back of his bike to a filling station and back with fuel. Whether or not this actually happened is irrelevant. (There is no doubt though that the king certainly did dive off his Royal yacht in Majorca to save two drowning girls.) What matters is that the king is seen as a 'good guy', a slightly cheeky but always dignified king who is close to his people. And that is probably the true image anyway.

It isn't possible to gain an audience with the king, but I had now spoken to the man they sometimes call the kingmaker. My time now was being spent attempting actually to arrange the interviews with those who had responded positively to my pleading letters. That invariably seemed to involve immersing myself in the Le Carré-like lives of these intrigue-addicted people and occasionally drove me close to insanity or the first plane back to reasonable London. The rest of my energy went on trying desperately to get to bed before having breakfast. Madrid can make some things mighty difficult.

16

I couldn't say that the office I was working from was exactly typical but its oddness seemed somehow apt. On the second floor of an elaborate old apartment block off a square near the Puerta del Sol, the HQ of CSP was indicative of many of the trends occurring in Madrid. By being in the old part of town, in a nicely antiquated building, it was reversing a rush towards the new and pre-fabricated which had threatened the historic centre of so many Spanish towns. Computers and faxes, video equipment and arty English furniture sat in rooms with ornate cornices and mosaic floors, sash windows and oak-beamed ceilings. They had the latest Apple Macs and, almost unbearably, no air-conditioning. That contradiction alone was nicely Spanish.

Staffed as it was entirely by people under the age of thirty-five the whole operation was alarmingly young in a country where age still carries considerable weight and youth is only just gaining the day. And by being an independent film and television production company it was going against a tradition of corporatism and large family businesses which had been the norm in Spain for years.

CSP is the kind of place where you can drink a beer and watch a movie, or work until three in the morning, where you could see a shoot being organised in Kenya and an American car ad set up in Seville. Between the five people and one dog in the office there were at least ten languages (including Swahili) and not a single necktie. The whole thing was wildly informal, at times distractingly anarchic, and yet clearly efficient and creative. Somehow between the long lunches and late starts, between the time spent cursing the heat and playing with the dog, things got done.

The CS in the CSP was Carlos Scola whose productions these were. For not only had 'mi casa es su casa' been true, but once I was ensconced in his apartment it also became 'my office is your office'. Carlos is a Madrileño in his early thirties and an old friend who had got into film by working as a dogsbody on spaghetti westerns (which were actually paella westerns, all shot in Almería in Spain) in the late seventies. A former hippie with a huge motorbike he now wears Gucci loafers and Paul Smith suits, drives a beaten BMW and dreams of writing and directing his first feature; it is a dream which I am sure is not far off reality.

The spare room of his large attic flat up near the Retiro Park and the Ritz was now home and this office my place of work. The CSP team had also somehow become my team and the inevitably labyrinthine business of trying to organise interviews with Spaniards had become a group project, one which they adopted with remarkable gusto.

The group consisted of Lorenzo the second director and Carlos' best friend who has the gravel voice of one who has seen some serious action. This included a long period spent organising safaris in East Africa (hence the Swahili) when his hair grew down his back. Now it is short and neat and he specialises in wild-life films. His occasionally red eyes show that his own life can sometimes still get pretty wild. Pepe, who was away at the time, is an intellectual who had once been active on the political left and now comes up with ideas for films. Octavio, who is fresh out of nightclubs, plays a lot with the computers, searches for locations and runs to the shops. Pim is a Dutchman with a pony tail and a motorbike who is a demon with cameras of every kind and speaks Spanish considerably better than most people in the office.

This was the crew who helped me actually pin down those who agreed to be interviewed, who told me where and when to go in a city whose patterns were still mysterious to me,

135

and who gave me a deeper insight into the ways of the new Spanish world.

Certainly I learned the role that conversation plays in life. The time spent sitting around the office talking, chatting over lunch, discussing things over a drink in the evening was phenomenal. The Spanish are on the whole both voluble and articulate: they love to argue and time spent sitting around jawing would never be considered to be wasted time, so you spend a long time sitting around talking.

Then when you do make an appointment with somebody you may well have to spend more time sitting around waiting for them. Spaniards invariably arrange to meet you in a bar and then proceed to be late. But because sitting in a bar watching the world go by is a national hobby, they somehow think they have done you a favour by allowing you the perfect opportunity to do just that. Anyone trying to write a book about Spain should first undergo some intensive wait-training.

Once there, though, they will invariably display perfect manners. In terms of politeness and generosity the Spanish usually behave in a way which would seem almost antiquatedly correct even in England; try paying for a drink in their company and see how you get on. The Spanish *caballero* is the closest historical cousin to the English concept of the gentleman, and he is currently in far better shape.

The simple good manners of your average Spaniard (if you don't include being late as bad manners, which they don't seem to), and even of the hyped up population of Madrid, is part of the attraction of the place. Sitting talking over an elastic lunch in a restaurant opposite the office, Pim the Dutch photographer said that the general demeanour of the people was the biggest single reason he decided to make Spain his home.

'I came to Spain eight years ago, first to Barcelona which I liked, then to Madrid which I liked even more. I instantly felt right here because people have got their priorities organised correctly. The life-style is the most attractive I have seen

136

anywhere because it has the best balance; it can be kind of extreme but it is balanced.'

The views of an outsider who had made his home in Spain were interesting to me. Many foreigners have settled in Spain in the last few years, because as Pim put it, 'This has been a fascinating time to be here.' In the past the Hemingways of this world were attracted to Spain precisely because nothing changed there, because the romantic past was still tangible. But from Pino back in Barcelona on that first wild night to Pim here in Madrid a couple of years later, the outsiders I had spoken to were attracted by the fact that things were changing. They saw a new country was emerging which they could play a part in creating.

'It has been a real adventure here in the past few years, very enjoyable, I cannot think of anywhere in the world that I would rather have been. But there are still some things that I cannot get used to. We Dutch think of ourselves as very liberal but I still get wound up sometimes here. I find it difficult to accept for example that the Spanish are so inefficient. They are making a real effort to get better, because of nineteen-ninety-two and all that, but still you say everything twice and nothing happens. I put film in to be processed, say I need it urgently, come back and of course nothing has been done, it doesn't get developed for days. Have you tried getting a telephone here?'

I laughed and repeated the story about Inka and her desperate telephonic intrigues. Pim shook his head and allowed himself an ironic laugh.

'Even after eight years that kind of thing still amazes me. They are making a real push now because they know they have to and I have to say that many things have got much better, but this is terrible struggle for them, it does not come naturally.'

I then went into my 'when do they ever sleep' routine, shaking my head like a good northern European. Pim, by now reverting to his roots, joined in with incredible and censorious tales of company directors running off on some pretence or other to sneak some ZZZ's in their car in the executive car park and workers sleeping at their computer terminals. He also told me that the latest Madrid fashion was to go to the all-night clubs for an hour in the morning for a gin and tonic and a chat with friends before going to work. We were getting on well and so Pim invited me to continue the conversation that evening in a bar called Archies. It took me a while to see the irony when he said, 'I'll see you there at two.'

I doubt if Pim got too much sleep that night. Archies was rocking, crowded with clothes-horse stable-mates from some model agency party and he and I both went on from there at about five. Much of that night blurs now but I do remember him saying that the biggest worry he had about Spain now was the rise in prices for everything, but in particular for property. In an echo of Sr Cebrian he said, 'In a land where average wages still haven't grown to the standards of the north, house prices in Madrid have soared almost beyond comprehension. The apartment I live in cost four million pesetas six years ago, now it would be nearly fifty million.'

The next day I had to meet a property speculator.

The name of Celso García is known throughout Spain. If you live in a fair-sized town, chances are you had one on your high street, for the García family owned a chain of department stores. I say own*ed* because they recently sold controlling interest to St Michael through his earthbound agents Marks & Spencer. British companies have been moving into Spain in a big way in recent years, and so have the multi-national corporations, breaking into the traditional structure of Spanish commerce which was run by a few merchant families and the all-powerful banks. The banks are often the most impressive and imposing buildings in a Spanish city, stylish palaces dedicated to the power and panache of money.

Celso García is undoubtedly a powerful young man: in his early thirties, he has taken over the considerable family interests now that his parents have retired, sold the chain to the English and gone to live in the Americas. Meeting him in a Madrid bar (he was on time and I was late), it seemed somehow remarkable that he should be how he is.

When you've grown up with the idea that all wealthy Spaniards are fascist ogres, meeting a pleasant, open young man, immaculate in a monogrammed button-down shirt, slightly balding and yet not all that different from yourself, comes as something of a surprise. I don't know what I was expecting, but apart from those initials on his cuff he could have been an ordinary middle-class man from England or New England. The lesson I learned straight away is that Spanish business is now euro-business and business, as they say, is business.

'I do business now in Germany or France and it is with people of my age and my kind. In Spain the older generation has delegated and moved on, so we are all the products of the same period, we've all been to the same business schools. We Spanish are now equals in the business community and that is incredible.'

The interview was conducted, like many that I was to do, in a combination of his excellent English and my now adequate Spanish, because no matter how good Spaniards are at foreign languages there comes a time in a conversation when English will not suffice for what they are trying to say. Spanish is an expressive, resonant tongue and for a business-man Celso García was remarkably communicative. His business now is 'development' which means real estate and finance. He has benefited from a property boom which has seen prices rising at a remarkable rate of forty per cent annually. To the question of whether this is a good thing he replies, 'It is dangerous certainly, but prices had to rise to equal the rest of Europe, it was one of the many difficult transformations we have had to go through. For forty years we lived in an artificial world, we had to cross an important bridge to reality, all of us.'

Travelling back to his youth he talks without any senti-mentality about growing up privileged and protected in a country where you could leave your car-door open in the knowledge that no one would dare take anything, not just for fear of the Guardia Civil but because of an all-powerful mix of civility and servility. This had been a land where people would doff their caps to the rich kid, where ordinary people rarely talked because they knew their opinion was not valued and besides talking was dangerous. That has all changed and he was smiling when he said, 'Now of course they steal the radio from your car when everything is locked. We are not as secure and so some of the older people they look back and say it was better then. Sometimes my father will talk like that but he knows this is just nostalgia for something artificial. The problems we have today are those of the real world and we have the good things too. One thing is clear, we are living in a democracy, a society in the open air with all that means. I have travelled widely and I believe our society is the most open in Europe, our temperament, our mentality, is all there to see, this place is an open book.'

The bar we were sitting in — me drinking one of the many beers which I would get through on a typically baking Madrid day, he with mineral water — had recently undergone a major overhaul. It had been clad in a thin veneer of pale marble, a kind of ascetic Comme Des Garçons aesthetic which is threatening to cover up too many cracks in Spain right now. Even humble bars have waiters dressed in ridiculous bell-boy livery and they all appear to be doing good trade. There seemed to me to be a worrying analogy here with the booming Spanish economy. For despite the apparent wealth it is difficult to see exactly what Spain produces. Seat cars certainly, but what else exactly? Is the whole thing a show without substance?

'There is no doubt that we are better consumers than producers, the Spanish love to spend money, so shops and the retail sector are booming. Agriculture of course is important and becoming very efficient, but our real flair now is in communications and presentation. We are catching up fast in high technology too.'

The truth is *El País* and its PRISA parent is one of the most successful companies in Spain today, dealing as it does in words and images. The banks of course do well, as does fashion and design, advertising and the leisure industries – Spain never did take too enthusiastically or efficiently to mass production. Almost all heavy industry is situated in the north, in the somewhat less than Spanish Basque lands and Catalonia. The justified reputation for individualism and *mañana*-ism weighed against large-scale production throughout the rest of the country. Despite the fact that the Spanish are now working much more efficiently they are still not working in large factories making things.

Those high technology and high style concerns may well be the way of the future, with Spain taking on the role of Europe's silicon plateau, but they are understandably concentrated squarely in the big cities. Does this mean that Spain is splitting yet again into two, divided between the affluent, modern urban centres and the poor, backward rural parts?

'Certainly business is conducted in the major centres, that is inevitable and, yes, life is very different in the small towns, but that is true everywhere and there is probably more of a consensus here than in many countries. The idea of Europe and the finding of freedom has forged that consensus. And unlike, say, France we do not have just one dominant city which Paris is: there is Madrid of course, but there is also Barcelona, Seville, Bilbao, so this is spread across Spain.'

Admittedly he had a large stake in it and a very good living from it, but there was still something quite moving about hearing a man, a businessman, talk about his country with great affection and yet no hint of nationalism. Celso García was shining when he said, 'When I was fifteen I could never imagine that Spain could be as it is now, never, it is like a dream to see how far we have progressed. The future is definitely positive, this is still a passionate, strong country and we are learning to turn that to our advantage, it can be a wonderful place to live and we finally seem able to live in it together.'

It was a while yet before I heard voices to the opposite.

17

They couldn't be less alike. Both have raven-black hair and large, dark, oval eyes to match. Both are in their twenties and attractive in the kind of odd, angular way which makes you unsure, makes you look twice and then again. Both are famous abroad and deep in the spirit of the new Spain. They really aren't at all alike, but there are a few similarities.

One of which is that they both are known by versions of their real names. Sybilla is just Sybilla, a single word which has become a shorthand for a particular style, an elegance, the surname Sorondo, which actually follows it is never heard or seen: Sybilla suffices on a label perfectly. Rossy de Palma meanwhile is really Rossy something else, but like a matador she has adopted the title of her home town as her fighting name. She is Rossy from Palma Majorca, the girl who plays the underbelly of Madrid in the movies Almodóvar makes. Both of these women are, in their own very different ways, products of the pressure-cooker city and paragons of a new kind of Spanish femininity. Other than that they have nothing in common whatsoever.

Sybilla is the more established of the two. Although still strikingly young for an internationally recognised couturier, and looking even younger because of her tiny frame and elfin features, she has been part of Spain's new wave of creativity from the very moment that the sea began to swell. In the very early, turbulent years of the *movida*, the movement, which rocked Madrid in the late seventies the teenage Sybilla was the girl putting the shirts on the backs of the prime movers.

The journey from there to famed and fêted designer, winner of the Balenciaga award given by the king himself, controller of a Milan-based fashion house, and object of mass Japanese desire, has been a long one in a short time. A bit like Spain really.

Rossy de Palma ('When I write something personal I use my real name, it keeps it special') only arrived in Madrid when the *movida* was something that trendy tourists went searching for. She really was a kid when the likes of Almodóvar and the singer Alaska, the sculptor Cristobal and Sybilla, were whipping up such a storm, a kid on the holiday island of Majorca watching the mainland twist wonderful convulsions as it lurched into the new world. One thing holiday islands do have, though, is nightclubs and so she entered them, decided that she could sing and so formed an avant-garde electronic group called 'Impossible'. She was, she says, looking for a direction and having a great time looking. A bit like Spain really.

Sybilla's background is a warped story board of contemporary ways, a cosmopolitan fairy story of the new world. Born of an Argentinian magnate and a Polish fashion designer countess, she lived her early years in New York before arriving as an eight-year-old to be taught at Madrid's top private school. She is quite likely to have been the only kid there who wore a complete psychedelic Haight-Ashbury outfit, had snails woven into her hair, lived with a vast menagerie of animals and a mother who copied Picassos and inserted her daughter's head in them. Understandably she grew up a strange mix of introverted and insistent. Talking to her now in the carefully twisted calm of her Madrid headquarters she is still precisely that. So shy that she talks in a whisper, so strong that you crane to catch every word. Sybilla is also a lot like her clothes.

'When I work, I always try to operate at the two extremes. If I do something round, I do something square; if there is softness, then there is hardness too; I try to balance, but at the limits.'

The result of this delicate balancing act is an unmistakable, but almost indescribable signature which has seen Sybilla recognised as Spain's finest fashion designer since Balenciaga. At first sight the rows of clothes hanging in her shop are unremarkable, muted, almost dowdy. Then you look a little closer and you start to notice. Dresses are cut at peculiar angles, unlikely shapes combine, material drapes against the grain and the bias, pleats and tucks appear when you least expect them. Her clothes are complex, romantic and rich. If, as Mies van der Rohe insisted, 'God is in the details', then Sybilla's clothes are truly divine. For there can rarely have been clothes which reveal their surprises and their delights quite as slowly or as slyly as Sybilla's. Nothing is quite what it seems and everything floats in its own sea.

As her friend and sometime model Rossy de Palma says, 'The dresses of Sybilla remind you of when you were a child and your mother would tell you fairy stories, when you wear them it is as if you're living in those dreams.'

This dream world designed in her own image comes together in her shop up a quiet cul-de-sac in the fashionable Salamanca district of Madrid. Here her quietly wild clothes are created upstairs by the girl herself and a team of creative assistants, most of whom have been with her since the early eighties. She had already run off to New York by then to live with her architect half-brother but returned to Madrid because it felt more exciting, more creative.

'I began to realise at seventeen how different Madrid was and how special the moment that I was living in Madrid was. The city was changing so rapidly, and I found that by going out and getting involved I could be part of that, that I could help shape the changes. Every day something new was happening, there was an incredible lightness about the place. If you went away for one day you thought you were missing out on something.'

It is difficult to imagine this frail-looking girl with her perfect, accentless English and her tendency to flutter and hide at the hint of a compliment, making a stir in the vortex of Madrid in the *madrugada* in the *movida*. But it was precisely that whirling world which first saw the talents of the young seamstress, making oufits for the other nocturnal movers, most of whom were twice her age. She had begun making clothes at the age of nine, but was determined not to follow her mother into the fashion industry.

'I wanted to be an oceanographer,' she says and you believe her. 'But sometimes things just carry you along.'

Many of those early creations came from a process of de- and then reconstructing old garments found on her regular rummages through Madrid's anarchic flea-market, the Rastro. And if you're looking for analogues between the rise of the girl and her country, an obvious one presents itself here. For Spain, it could be said, did exactly the same thing: dipping continually into the rag-bag of its past and reassembling the pieces to find a way forward.

The shop and headquarters still has numerous remnants and reminders of those Rastro days when it was a squat and home for many of Madrid's young outsiders. The junk-shop antiques combine with the works of many of Spain's leading young artists to give the place a timeless, arty, but almost do-it-yourself feel. The clothes though are now sold world-wide, produced by the Milanese giant Gibo, where she replaced Jean-Paul Gaultier as their name designer. The scale of operations is enormous, the pattern of her life now dictated by the international rhythms of an industry which knows no national boundaries. The name Sybilla has become a short-hand for a certain, quirky, but gently extravagant style of women's wear which is recognised in all the fashion capitals of the world. When you remark upon how far she has travelled she says, 'Each morning of each day I am surprised and afraid. I am not sure at all that this is what I want, but it happens.'

Sybilla portrays more openly than anyone else the perpetual surprise that most Spaniards still feel at success outside their own country. When she says, 'I honestly felt that if I worked in Spain I wouldn't have to become a big designer, because, well, Spaniards didn't,' you can see the mixture of pleasure and pain in her eyes. Yet the Sybilla who symbolises all of these things is really only Spanish by accident. Her father's business interests brought him to Madrid and that's where she stayed.

'But I feel very much part of something, I am very Spanish in a way. I recognise myself walking down the street here.'

And there perhaps is the ultimate statement of the changes which Sybilla's success signals. Here is a quirky, young, cosmopolitan 'foreign' female in a land which was traditionally conservative, xenophobic, and dominated by the old and the male. And nobody, bar perhaps Sybilla, thinks that her success is so unusual.

Rossy de Palma though is obviously unusual. You would never need to insert Rossy's head into Picasso's ladies, she looks perfectly Picasso-esque anyway. Her face is unforgettable, a unique exaggeration of the classical lines of Spanish beauty which make her look like a cubist painting. The straight jet hair, framing a long, long face, the high cheekbones, the hooked Arabic nose, full lips and deep, dark almond eyes could have come straight off the master's canvas. Instead they are known from the works of a new Spanish visual maestro, Pedro Almodóvar. And nobody would ever say that Pedro, the peroxide former choirboy who began his career as a transvestite pop singer who still occasionally opts to do interviews on TV in drag, is usual.

Perhaps more than any other single individual, Almodóvar has come to represent the new Spain to the outside world. And quite what the world thinks of the Spain Almodóvar depicts is difficult to say. In movies like *Law of Desire*, *Women on the Verge of a Nervous Breakdown* and *Tie Me Up! Tie Me Down!*, he has shown Spain, or more specifically Madrid, as a place fuelled by a hungry, powerfully comic insanity. Catholicism, repressed sexuality, machismo, and the kind of amazonian maternalism of a nation in love with the Madonna figure, are all inverted in an over-vivid and viciously hilarious swathe. There is a strong streak of surrealism which draws vividly on the tradition of Buñuel, but there is also a truly unique signature. And the face of Rossy de Palma fits perfectly in all of them.

'That world is real, the movies of Almodóvar are real. Madrid is just like this, it is a jungle. There are other Madrids too, but Pedro's one certainly exists.'

Sitting in Rossy from Palma's apartment it is not difficult to believe this. Situated in one of the many working-class barrios dotted around the centre of town, on the fifth floor of a liftless building, it is a strangely shaped and peculiarly decorated jumble of kitsch. Pop and religious icons fight for space amid old clothes and movie posters, musical instruments and toys tumble over each other in an unorchestrated medley of images. Throughout the time I am there a handsome, muscular, shirtless man with a Julius Caesar crop and a strong smile sits silently in a corner. He is, I presume, a boyfriend but no introductions are ever effected. Rossy talks a lot.

She insists that we converse in English, in order to improve her second language, but at key points in sentences she slots in a Spanish word, so the interview takes on a strange and pleasing bilingual quality. For instance she says, 'Spain is a very special country. I go to Italy often and people think we are the same. This is not at all true, we are much more *fuerte* [strong or tough]. Here there is more *marcha*.' Or, 'Before we did not believe we could do anything, especially creative, we were always told things were impossible. Now things are more *desarollo* [developing, unfolding].' And best of all, 'Freedom is never normal, you must always *luchar* [struggle, fight].'

Rossy's first struggle when she arrived from Palma was to find work and somewhere to live. For a while that meant working in nightclubs and spending days wherever she could. Soon she became accepted as one of the vampires, the Madrileños who are famous only at night, and only among those who inhabit the night. 'The night is fine, the people are more relaxed, more themselves.' The most notorious of those nocturnalites was Almodóvar, and the girl from Palma simply waited for him to ask her to be in one of his films.

'I was looking for Pedro, waiting for him to come to me. I didn't court him though, that would never have worked, I just waited, then when he came, wonderful. I never knew if I could act, but when Pedro finally called before *Law of Desire* I went. Then I knew I would find out.'

That she can act is not in doubt. Even in the over-ripe milieu of Almodóvar's movies she stands out as a charismatic and magnetic screen-presence. But as with Carmen Maura and Victoria Abril, the other stars of Almodóvar's seriously female-fixated films, the big test is to prove that she can exist away from his web. To that end she has recently been making a movie in Italy and embarking on her stage début in an all-woman play. But she realises that it is a problem.

'For me it is difficult in Spain because many people do not see me as an actress, I am just the Almodóvar girl with the special face.'

That face has come to represent Madrid itself to me: not exactly beautiful but full of character, powerful and totally unique. She is also a committed Madrileña in the way that only a convert can be. Her large eyes come alive when she speaks of her chosen city.

'Madrid is a truly exciting town. It is not a comfortable place, it is hard to get around or to get anything done, it really pushes you, makes you determined. I've spent time in Rome and New York and even that is easy compared to Madrid. This is a hard place, I think that is why it is so important.'

And it is very important that the kind of Madrid Rossy de Palma represents, the kind of Madrid and the kind of Spain that she and Almodóvar inhabit, should have found so eloquent a means of expression as those wonderfully outrageous films. More than almost any other nation, Spain has to throw off a set of stereotypes and prove that there are new faces, new ways. Statements as bold and brash as those of Almodóvar need to be made to balance things out again (as with Sybilla's creations) at the extremes.

The very existence of young women of the undoubted strength and talent of Sybilla Sorondo and Rossy de Palma is of course the most important symbol; two women who have found their place in a Spain where a woman's place is no longer only in the home or the church. But what was most remarkable and most affecting to me was the way in which both of these women are so powerfully attached to their Spain, and so confident about its future. This confidence was becoming a recurrent feature of the interviews I was conducting. Rossy de Palma put it like this: 'Spain is very different. We may become more normal Europeans but we will find our own way, a Mediterranean way. When we first entered Europe everybody said we must become like Germans, "Sshh, be quiet," they said, "go early to sleep, work all the time." But it never happened, instead we are creating our own path.'

Sybilla said, 'I feel very happy here because it is a very creative place. If there is a unifying characteristic of the Spanish it is their individualism. That has always been the case and it is even more true today because we have learned to really live with that. It means there is not one Spanish style, or, if there is, that style is individualism itself.'

Rossy de Palma and Sybilla Sorondo: two Spanish individuals of great style, two remarkable women of Madrid.

18

Watching *Mr and Mrs* is something of a revelation. Having seen the staid, arthritic British version of that game show, where Darby has to guess whether Joan prefers butter to margarine, I wasn't quite prepared for the Spanish way. The male presenter is of course suitably smarmy, and there is a blonde girl (blonde girls, no matter what they look like, are held in esteem here and almost inevitably end up with jobs on game shows) wandering around to no apparent avail. The questions though are much more risqué than at home and I was shocked one day idling an evening in the apartment to hear the smarmy man ask a woman contestant, 'Would your husband ever be attracted to another man?'

I was even more amazed when she answered, 'He already has, there's this guy at his office and I have seen them flirting. I'm not sure what they get up to when I'm not there, but I'm convinced there's something going on.'

The poor husband was then dragged from his soundproof box and asked what his wife had answered. Amazingly he smiled a little embarrassed smile, said the same thing that she had and won the point.

Although it has not reached Italian standards of proliferation or titillation, Spanish television is definitely heading that way. An Italian show, dubbed into Spanish and entitled *Cor What Heat* now appears regularly on Telecinco, one of the new independent stations. Yet another game show – in this one if the contestants get the answers wrong they have to remove an item of clothing, or else nominate a euro-stripper (there is one from each of the member nations) to do the same. The questions are on little rosettes stuck on the breasts of a team of buxom hostesses who flash their assets throughout the show. The whole thing is wildly silly and somehow almost naïve in its candour.

This peculiar obsession with televised tits seems to be endemic in Spain now. There is a soft-porn movie of the *Emmanuelle* variety on most weekends, and there is also now a stripper to round off the Angel Cassas Show. Sr Cassas is a kind of bearded Terry Wogan, a famous chatshow host who gets to talk to Spanish celebrities and announce that Miguel Bose is going to sing yet again. He also gets the privilege of grilling whichever American film star happens to be in town, and usually makes a fairly good job of doing just that. But somehow after watching an excellent, intelligent interview with Martin Sheen and his son Emilio Estevez, in Spain looking for their roots, and espousing various radical issues, the switch to a girl in a blonde wig disrobing to the tune of 'Don't Smoke in Bed' was just too much to take.

Watching Inka on her TV programme was not difficult though. It felt good to know that she had been able to achieve her ambitions and that we could be friends. She had told me that she was not especially happy working inside the still suffocating structure of Spanish state television and was thinking of moving onto the other side of the camera. We were now friends which made me feel close to my old city, close to Barcelona again. Hearing a cool Catalan head can occasionally be a relief when you have to deal day in, day out with the more fiery minds of Madrid.

Discothequa de Verano can get pretty damn warm too. I had taken to wandering around the flat naked during the afternoons; I was alone and the air-conditioning for all its hum and bluster was not efficient enough to cover up the fact that Madrid is a sauna. It is a good job I was alone the first time I saw *Discotheque of Summer*.

The programme, yet another Telecinco production, goes out mid-afternoon, a prime-time slot in a land of siestas, and basically consists of a group of Madrid teenagers partying live in the studio. The latest club track is played and these kids dance as furiously and also as sexily as possible. The air-conditioning in the Telecinco studio clearly isn't too efficient either, for the girls in particular – few of them looking older than sixteen at the outside – were not wearing very much more than I was. The cameramen were obviously under orders to point their machines straight up between the legs of the Lolitas gyrating on plinths. When I first saw this I felt old and puritan; I also felt that it might be wise to go and put on some trousers.

That Spanish teenagers like to enjoy themselves wasn't exactly a surprise to me. In the major cities you can witness an oddly logical, but still peculiar, spectacle of Spanish juvenile life at about seven or eight o'clock most evenings. For it is then that you see groups of youngsters, aged from maybe twelve to seventeen, gathering on street corners, the boys in their Chipie jeans, the girls with their biggest shoulderpads and shortest skirts. The sexes tend to be separated, the most adventurous maybe meeting in the middle of the two camps to giggle and strut. Then at some secret signal they all walk together to Paradise or Performance, Trauma or Casanova.

These are discotheques, which later on in the evening will be packed with older Spaniards drinking rum and coke and quite probably doing coke in the toilets. But before midnight they open up their doors exclusively to those too young to indulge in such adult pleasures, but old enough to jump about to Janet Jackson records and snog behind the speakers. For the clubs it represents a kind of economic second front, as they take money over the door and sell soft drinks. For the kids it is a training ground for the long nights soon and sure to come, and a chance maybe to practise those steps for the day when they can secure a ticket to flash their thighs on *Discothequa de Verano*.

It is of course a highly sensible idea, but one that struck me as odd coming from Spain. For despite all the evidence to the contrary I have never been able to eradicate the notion that this is at heart a Catholic, censorious country. Even when you know things have changed it is difficult to accept sometimes that they have changed quite as much as that. So I spent much of my time in Madrid walking on the shady side of the street and looking for proof that the past is still present. It is certainly easier to see signs that the old days have been put away.

Just around the corner from Carlos' apartment in an adjunct to the famed Prado, known as the Casón del Buen Retiro, a one-time Royal ballroom and a suitably bombastic building for the kings of Madrid to twirl in, stands the most potent public symbol of the end of yesterday. For next to a room of nondescript nineteenth-century paintings, in a gallery all its own, stands the most famous Spanish painting of the twentieth century, and the most notorious image of the last bloody bout of internecine strife, Picasso's *Guernica*.

The day that *Guernica* arrived in its new Madrid home from the New York Museum of Modern Art late in 1981 was a wildly symbolic one. Before his death Picasso had decreed that this epic depiction of the bombing by Hitler's airmen (they were on loan to the nationalist forces at the time and practising the skills they would later use on London) of the sacred Basque town of Guernica could not return to Spain until liberty had also come home. So after five years of democracy it was decided that the time had come to bring back the picture.

Today it stands behind a fat sheet of bullet-proof glass, lest some necrophiliac fanatic should decide to take a pop at this famed anti-authoritarian tirade. Seeing the real thing for the first time I found it hard to imagine any of the mix of Americans and out-of-towners who filed past it alongside me getting so wound up. Picasso's *Guernica* is a little like the New York skyline, one of those famous sights which we have all seen vicariously so many times before we ever actually set eyes on the real thing. Unlike the powerful profile of the cubic city though *Guernica* failed to fill me with awe.

It has been reproduced so many times, used so often as a piece of propaganda or just as a convenient form of historical shorthand, that its ability to shock or even move has largely gone. But perhaps conversely its power as a painting has increased. Picasso's *Guernica* has been turned into a *Mona Lisa*, into an icon of the everyday which sits in its place so that tourists can add another tick to their scorecard of travellers' collectibles. It is perhaps fitting that this work, overburdened as it has been with its origins, can now be allowed to become a painting again in the same way that Spain is becoming a normal country.

If *Guernica* has come back then the eagle has definitely gone. The stern and strident-looking black eagle who nested in the middle of the Spanish flag during the dictatorship has disappeared from almost every standard now. Like so many of the relics of the General's rule they have just been allowed to fade away, as quickly and discreetly as possible. Street names throughout Spain were changed after the War: the Diagonal in Barcelona became the Avenida Generalissimo Franco; and streets and squares named after Falangist heroes like Calvo Sotelo and Primo de Rivera sprung up everywhere.

Since the return of the democracy though they have largely reverted to their former names. No one I spoke to can remember any renaming ceremony, people just started using the old names (in some cases they always had) again, and the street signs mysteriously switched. It was almost as if they had never been altered in the first place, as if you were remembering it wrong. That feeling that maybe the Civil War never happened after all was beginning to worry me.

I asked some of my new-found Madrileño mates about this apparent collective amnesia and in mock-conspiratorial tones they let me in on the *pacto de olvido*. This, they explained, is basically a tacit national agreement to forget the past, to stop harking on about the old days and, for the sake of Spain, to go forward with the new democracy no matter which side you were or are on. The 'agreement to forget' is precisely what Cebrian was talking about when he predicted that I would find few gainsayers to the current consensus. It is also perhaps one of the true reasons for the Spanish success story.

The fact that the *pacto de olvido* has been so well observed in such a divided nation is a testament to the fundamental, collective desire for it to work. The fact that my friends had let me in on the pact was a testament to their collective desire to get me to shut up about the Franco days and stop asking them stupid questions. I agreed not to bug them so much, but I still went off looking for some memories which were intact. I did though wonder whether they had a pact to forget because they hadn't quite come to terms, whether this self-willed amnesia was actually a substitute for a genuine reconciliation. Most Spaniards I believe have real trouble accepting the recent past and so they would rather dismiss it from their minds. But there is no doubt that has worked.

I was determined though to search out the remains of that past and in a crusty, dense, little shop by the Plaza Mayor I found a place where the recollections are still alive. The old part of Madrid contains numerous purveyors of relics. There are shops flogging religious regalia, another with iron-age corsets, a third with artificial limbs and yet another which sells Guardia Civil outfits, Falangist badges, flags with eagles, and ceramic busts of Franco staring sternly, or riding a white horse in his El Cid, crusader gear. Rifling through this silly paraphernalia reminded me of nothing more than the claustrophobic, pedantic hours I spent as a youth in my brief but devout period as a stamp-collector. The shopkeeper was an old, quiet man who would not have looked out of place in a library, and the only browser seemed to suit the anorak he was wearing. I certainly couldn't find the militant spirit of the old Spain here, in anything other than a pickle jar.

Another possible contender proved fairly fruitless. Opposite a porno-cinema in a run-down eastern sector of Madrid are the offices of the CNT, the anarchist trade union. I entered the building full of romance and left it with a certain sadness. I wanted heroic visions and there were certainly a few murals of square-jawed revolutionists waving black and red flags. But there was also an air of decrepitude and bygones as a few old comrades mingled with a couple of young anarcho-punks in an unlikely coalition of rebellion. There was an ageing dandy with a surrealist moustache who sold me a copy of their paper, but there was also a smell of cat's piss and distant dreams. I sipped a beer opposite in a bar full of workers and wondered.

I did stop in my tracks one day while searching the streets for echoes of the old conflicts. On a huge roadside billboard I saw the legend, writ large, *No Pasa Nada*. Was this the famous old communist slogan of defiance, 'They Shall Not Pass'? But that of course is *No Pasarán*; this was 'Nothing Passes' and as I looked closer I realised it was a slogan advertising sanitary towels, not La Pasionaria and the heroic resistance of the staunchly republican people of Madrid. Time, I realised, to go to the museum.

About two hundred yards from Carlos' flat is a museum which I walked past almost every day without giving it a second glance. Carlos though was adamant that I should go inside. 'It's great, you get the place completely to yourself, nobody ever goes there.' Exactly what everybody is missing is the shiny detritus of hundreds of years of Spanish military history as it is stored in the Army Museum. Those memories I was searching for were all in here.

Real guns and toy soldiers, endless standards and medals, muskets and mortars. Objects of death through the ages sit in glass cases in an oddly unstructured paean to the wonders of the Spanish army. There is much talk of fatherland and honour, numerous references to God and glory and a kind of polished pomposity which seems almost camp. Also there was at the time of my visit almost nobody there save a few soldier boys with savage crops standing with their backs unnaturally straight, a handful of what I would guess were ex-servicemen and their wives and a couple of the anoraked philatelists I had seen in the shop in the Plaza Mayor. The one thing that the Army Museum did provide me with though was a real sense in which the last civil war was just one chapter in a grisly national flirtation with blood-letting. A flirtation which truly and finally and thankfully seems to be over.

The Ultras though like to let it be known that they like to let some blood occasionally. The kind of hooliganism which British youths regularly unleash on the costas has never caught on with the Spanish. But like so much of mainland Europe, Spain has recently taken to the very British tradition of fighting at football. They certainly haven't adopted football hooliganism with the rigour or vigour of the Dutch and Germans, but the larger teams now have crews which very occasionally clash, and the crew which follows Real Madrid is the Ultras. And the Ultras are naturally out on the right wing.

'Patriotism, Justice and Revolution' is the most common piece of rightist sloganeering seen in Spain today. It is the slogan of the FFJ, the Falangist youth, just one of the myriad groups which exist on the now splintered far right. Occasionally in Madrid that will be accompanied by the name of the Ultras and the slogan 'White Power' (in English) which refers both to the famous white strip of Real as well as to the more obvious racist meaning.

Searching still for this elusive ghost of mine I spent a small part of an evening in a lugubrious bar in the southern suburbs of Madrid talking to a pair of sorry Ultras. Pablo and Pacquito are both in their early twenties, both supporters of Real and both self-professed fascists. That choice of word is actually very informative, for the Falange, for all their evils, were never Nazis. After a few minutes talking to these two young men I realised that I knew them and knew them well.

I had met the pair of them near the Plaza Mayor, and approached them because Pablo had the close-cropped hair and the MA1 flying-jacket uniform of the new Nazis. I asked if they were Ultras, they said yes and agreed to talk to this odd English journalist, seemingly pleased by the attention. Once I arrived at their barrio though I realised that this was a futile journey; I wanted to know about the Falangist heritage, and the authoritarian right in an age of pluralism; they wanted to cadge some beers and natter about the British 'Oi' group Screwdriver and the exploits of Leeds United's away firm.

The reason I knew them so well is that these boys were not Spanish exotica, but carbon-copy white euro-trash. Pablo and Pacquito are indicative of the kind of juvenile malcontent who is now commonplace throughout the continent. Unemployed, ill-educated and aware that their traditional working-class culture is disappearing, they have looked towards Britain's disaffected bovver boys for a role model. They even poured out some fairly standard venom against blacks, learned I guess by rote, because Spain is a country with a minuscule (although rising) black population. After a short and thoroughly depressing time I made my excuses and left.

Obviously Pablo and Pacquito are not entirely typical of every young right-wing Spaniard. There is still a bourgeois, Catholic, traditionalist movement, but it is tiny. When the media runs a scare story about the rise of the new right it is the likes of the Ultras, of those two kids who could have come from Dresden or Bruges or Barnsley, that they talk about. The fact that its fanatics are now the same as everyone else's is perhaps another perverse sign that Spain has become part of the European consensus.

Still though there are enough who care, enough to mount a march every year to the Pharaoh's tomb.

Each November, on the anniversary of the death of Francisco Franco there is a march to honour his memory, which ends up with a wreath-laying ceremony at his tomb in the Valley of the Fallen. I had first seen this peculiarly chilling but compulsive spectacle on TV back in Barcelona and Inka told me then how in 1976, one year after his demise, there were nearly two million people marching, two million people from all over Spain who would gladly have welcomed back their master. The numbers decreased rapidly, though, until now where it is down to a few thousand old die-hards and young hot-heads.

The Ultras are there, as are the more disciplined Falangist youth with their neat haircuts, Sam Browne belts and blue shirts. There are also veterans of the struggle, old nationalist soldiers who haven't completely faded away yet. Then there is the oddest group of all, the nice, middle-class families in their suits and pleated skirts who would look more at home at a flower show or a school sports day. On that day in November all of Spain is reminded that the wounds have not entirely been healed, that they may have agreed to forget, but they do not all agree. The rest of the time you wouldn't really notice. The rest of the time the Valley of the Fallen is a theme-park.

Carlos agreed to drive me out to the great monument on a dreamily steaming Madrid Sunday. It lies about forty kilometres out of town, a little past the famed Escorial. El Escorial is the vast, gaunt, pointless monument to the devout vanity of Philip II, which is part palace, part monastery and a complete monstrosity of giant proportions. This testament to the excesses of Inquisitorial Catholicism is the most famous piece of architectural extremism in Spain. Franco's folly a few kilometres up the motorway is its main competitor.

Although nominally a monument to all those who died in the Civil War, the fact that the church and its giant cross were constructed by republican prisoners, many of whom gave their lives blasting it out of the rock, is indicative of exactly which side is celebrated here. It consists of a vast cave-like basilica excavated out of a granite mountain and an impossibly tall stone cross (490 feet, in fact) on top. The cross is said to be the largest in the world and the overgrown, freakish edifice dominates the bleak, grey valley in which it sits.

That it is impressive is without doubt. The scale of the whole sorry, silly endeavour is such that when you first see it from afar you are rocked back in your seat. As a monument to death it is unsurpassed in the sheer immensity of its proportions and its inflated imagery. At the base of the cross souped-up lions and eagles sit, trying desperately to be imperial. Beneath the towering crucifix there is a monastery, dwarfed by the scale of everything around it, which houses the monks whose sole job is to attend the graves of the two famous men buried in the cavernous church. José Antonio Primo de Rivera, the founder of the Falangist movement, who was killed early in the Civil War, and Franco himself.

Comparisons with the great pyramids of Egypt are almost inevitable and the place is known by Madrileños as the Pharaoh's tomb. And in the same way that the Valley of the Kings has become a tourist attraction, so the Valley of the Fallen is now on the coach party and picnic itinerary.

During the drive to the tomb Carlos explained how there had been a raging debate about whether the whole thing should be dynamited because of the offence it caused to so many people. Obviously those on the right, especially the widows of men who had fallen for Franco, wanted the monument retained. More surprisingly though many on the left argued that it should be left to stand as a terrible testament to the horrors which occurred, a massive reminder of where dictatorships lead. It is such an ugly and repulsive edifice that they were undoubtedly right. Perhaps they also knew that it was bound to become such a trivial behemoth.

Complete with a funicular to carry you to the top of the cross, a snack bar with video games and a souvenir shop, the place now has an almost festive feel. Try as it may to be a grave grave, it has become a kind of Disneyland of death where American tourists play Frisbee in the square and sunbathe on the lions. Inside the supposedly sombre temple, the last resting place of the Generalissimo and the spiritual home of the souls of all those who perished fighting 'For God and Fatherland', I heard a fat 'yanqui' in shorts say to his wife, 'It's kinda nice here.' Death by tourism is surely a more fitting end than any explosion.

It is still said though that some of the tourists standing gawping at the stone slab which bears the name of the dictator are actually plain-clothes policemen hovering to catch anybody spitting on or attempting to deface the graves. There are always fresh flowers on Franco's tomb and when I was there, there were a couple of those nationalist widows wearing black remembering their men. But the real sign of how Spain now deals with its most recent skeleton is to be found in the souvenir shop.

There are plenty of picture postcards and ashtrays of the monument, key-rings bearing the face of Juan Carlos and various members of his family. You can purchase a holy virgin, an eagle-less flag and a valueless coin. But there is not a single trace, not a mention or murmur, about the man who commissioned the thing to act as his eternal mausoleum. In a re-write of Stalinist proportions, Franco has been edited out of the story, expunged from history and expelled even from his own bloated memorial. The whole thing has been stripped of all meaning and left to the ravages of scantily clad visitors.

When I asked the ageing superintendent of the souvenir shop why there is no Franco memorabilia on sale he simply shrugged and said it had been taken out a long time ago. Then sensing that maybe I was a fellow believer he leaned forward and whispered conspiratorially but with some pride, 'There is a little shop near the Plaza Mayor.'

19

There is also a little man who sits on Saturdays outside one of the department stores on Velázquez selling that stuff. He's got icons and badges and the like of the Generalissimo and bits of Falangist fluff laid out on a trestle-table. He's a skinny little man who must occasionally get rid of a key-ring or a cheap statuette to the middle-class families out cruising the fancy clothes shops and furniture stores in this most exlusive area of Madrid. The look on his wrinkled old face when he heard and then saw the reds coming will stay with me for ever. He didn't know at that point that they couldn't possibly see him.

I didn't know anything about the demonstration either, I was staring half-heartedly into shop windows and ambling uptown when I heard car horns blaring angrily and saw a couple of Policía Nacional officers trying to reroute the BMWs and Citroens whose drivers were not too happy about being stopped. Then I heard the chanting and saw the first red banners and placards with the logos of the two major trade unions, the communist CCOO and the socialist UGT, as the procession rounded the corner onto the broad, tree-lined Calle. It took me a while to notice amid all the colour and clamour of a political demonstration in Spain that we were actually seeing the blind leading the blind, and the lame and the crippled and even the perfectly healthy-sighted. A great job they were making of it too. The car horns were shamed into silence when they realised just who was marching. I ran up the street to catch a glimpse of the old man hawking his trinkets. I knew it would be a peach.

For this was a demonstration by the workers of ONCE, the organisation of blind people which runs a hugely successful lottery. The blind man the kiosks where the tickets are sold, and they make a percentage of the money raised. A plan to sell season-tickets to the lottery was apparently putting their commission under threat and so they had organised a national demonstration to protest about that and to push for a pension scheme for all ONCE workers. And what a demonstration they had.

At the head of the march was a blind drummer being led by his guide-dog, followed by a line of blind people in wheelchairs which stretched right across the length of the street. Behind them came roughly 30,000 demonstrators, a mass of marchers stretching way back down the Calle, where every sighted person was accompanied by one who was visually or physically handicapped. There were blind couples and groups of blind women, sighted children riding on the shoulders of blind fathers. Many of the happy, singing marchers had decorated their guide-dogs and their white canes with the stickers and ribbons of their trade union. There were also handicapped people of every kind with their crutches and their wheelchairs, some being helped by friends, others proudly making their own way, a few wearing the T-shirts of the Special Olympics to be held in Barcelona in 1992.

There were also thousands of ordinary working-class Spaniards who had come from all over the country, from Asturias and Extremadura, from La Mancha and León, to walk alongside their handicapped friends or lovers, family or workmates, holding hands and linking arms.

My amazement at seeing this slow-moving column snaking purposefully up the street was matched by the many shoppers who stopped to watch and the shop workers who poured out of their stores to witness this incredible spectacle. Choosing to march along the Madrid equivalent of Fifth Avenue when it was packed with opulent shoppers was obviously an intentional tactic, but even the immaculately heeled denizens of this district could not fail to be moved by so impressive a sight. You could see the look in their eyes change from hatred to, well to something else, as they saw thousands of severely handicapped people singing their campaign songs, and dancing, laughing and parading, many with red flowers in their hair. The skinny old man with the Falangist stall looked aghast, then looked confused, then packed up and left. I wish he had still been there when the CNT group came round the corner.

There weren't many of them, I admit, two dozen maybe with the black and red flag of their union on their shoulders, singing their rousing old tunes and appearing to enjoy themselves immensely as they took part in their huge parade. But I thought, standing there on this Saturday morning lifted by the joy and the spirit of the whole glorious event, that only in this strange and precious land could you get a group of blind anarchists marching for their rights. That was a very big day indeed.

20

One day in the office I saw this picture. There was Lorenzo, my gruff-voiced, Swahili-speaking mate looking ill at ease in a grey suit and an improbable tie, but with his usual inane grin in place, and standing next to him was none other than the tall dark man, Juan Carlos, the king. I wondered whether Lorenzo had perhaps taken part in some kind of Spanish equivalent of the Duke of Edinburgh Awards, but the thought of such a committed bon viveur hiking over moorland or tying knots in old age pensioners was a little too much to countenance. The truth though was just as unlikely.

'The king I know him well, he is a good friend of my family. We used to visit him all the time, I remember the king rolling on the floor with me as a kid, he's a lovely man.'

'Lorenzo, how come the king is a friend of the family, how come he rolls around on your floor?'

'My mother is a countess and my father was an important general in the army, we have known the Royal family for ever, they are just friends.'

'Lorenzo, does this mean that you knew Franco too?'

'Yes, of course, my father comes from a big military family and he went on to become the governor of Navarre in Franco days. I met Franco many times, but unlike the king I cannot say that I ever felt comfortable with him. He was a powerful man, but not one who made you feel at ease. I believe that may have been the reason that I did not go into the army.'

'Lorenzo, how come you didn't tell me this?'

For weeks I had been trying to find a way of entering society.

I needed to talk to somebody from the old order, somebody from 'alta sociedad' who remembered and perhaps cherished the way things were. I was also in dire need of meeting somebody who had been part of the Franco regime and could look back on those times and on the changes which have occurred since. Lorenzo, who had been invaluable in terms of making introductions and setting up interviews, had sat and discussed this with me, yet he had not mentioned the fact that his mum and dad fitted the bill perfectly on both counts.

'They are my family. You know how it is, you do not think of your own family in this way. I will arrange for you to have lunch with my mother and father. She will enjoy this.'

If I had known Lorenzo's surname I might of course have realised. Queipo de Llano is not exactly a common name in Spain, and it is not one which would go unnoticed in too many parts of this large country. In the Army Museum there is a microphone which belonged to a Queipo de Llano, and his pearl-handled pistol is there too. The microphone was used to make daily broadcasts from Radio Seville during the Civil War, the most famous and fervent nationalist voice of them all. The pearl-handled pistol was used to fight just as ferociously for that cause, and to take no doubt the lives of a large number of republicans. Depending on which side you were on, Queipo de Llano was one of the most steadfast and resolute defenders of the fatherland and the true faith, or else he was a Falangist butcher. He was also Lorenzo's grandad.

His father became, as family tradition dictated, a military man, serving after the Civil War and achieving extremely high office. As the governor-general of the province of Navarre he not only got to act as president of the famous fiesta of San Fermines with its bull run in Pamplona, he also got the dubious honour of running a province which the Basques claimed as part of their separate state. His brother, Lorenzo's uncle and also a military man, was blown away by an ETA car bomb, and as a child Lorenzo went to school in a staff car with soldiers to guard him.

Certainly Lorenzo could not be more different from anybody's image of a bulwark of conservatism. A grinning corsair of a man with impeccable manners, idiolectic English and an infectious ease he is both a libertine and a non-conformist. It was fascinating and a little confusing then to hear him tell tales of growing up surrounded by long black cars and starched uniforms, to hear stories of attending Franco's funeral, of travelling to a northern prison to visit Milans del Bosch, the most senior of the army officers incarcerated after the Tejero affair.

Milans del Bosch had been a close friend of his father and was coming to the end of a fifteen-year sentence for trying to destroy the democracy. When I asked Lorenzo about del Bosch he was admirably unwilling to criticise a family friend and talked unconvincingly about an army man simply doing his job. He did though make a telling comment concerning political scandal in this land where people seem to expect their leaders to be dubious: 'We all do bad things, we have all made those mistakes.' Catholicism, I thought, may not be the dominant religion any more but it still runs deep.

When I asked him about his father Francisco, and what he now thought about the old days, Lorenzo smiled and said, 'My father says, "That was then." He is a happy old cynic now, he watches it all and makes jokes. He knows those days are gone, that all belongs to the past.'

His mother though belongs to another world entirely. Her full title would take up a large chunk of this chapter, the bits that really matter still come to Cristina Fernandez de Villavicencio, Condez de Toreno, Marquesa de Guadiaro. In a land burdened with thousands of minor aristos, she is a major one.

Home is an apartment on Calle Velázquez, the broad, central Madrid street which plays a similar role in that city to the Avenue Foch in Paris. It consists of an endless series of large, dark rooms full of antiques and militaria and hung with tapestries and great masters. On Sundays though, the day we had agreed to meet and talk, the staff have the day off and so an arrangement was made to have lunch in a restaurant, lunch with the countess and the general.

They arrived in an old but immaculate green Bentley and looked so completely the part that no introduction was necessary. He was somewhere in his sixties, deep, leathery brown, balding, his belly just emerging over the top of his slacks. He was wearing a silk shirt open at the neck with a sports jacket on top and a pair of sunglasses which made him look like somebody big in South America. She was of a similar age, but looking younger in an immaculate white Chanel suit, a small blonde woman who had clearly once been a considerable beauty and the kind of woman who makes you rush to open doors. When I did just that as she entered the restaurant she whispered to me in firm and remarkable English, 'My husband, you must understand, does not wish to discuss politics.'

It was a bit of a blow, but not entirely unexpected. It was also an immediate indication as to who was really in charge.

The general spoke some English and seemed to understand most of what was said as his wife took the opportunity to show off her dazzling linguistic skills. She spoke an English of a kind that the English queen herself would struggle to equal, pedantically correct and precisely elocuted. Like all true Spanish aristocrats the countess had been brought up by an English nanny, presented to English society, and left with a life-long bout of Anglophilia. When she asked me what I thought about Margaret Thatcher it was as if one of the great women of Surrey were grilling you about their hero and I could do little but blab about her being a strong woman.

For a while the conversation ranged around all of the normal topics: horses, the difficulty in obtaining decent domestic staff and the crippling price rises at the Connaught. Hearing the countess describe her last visit to London was a wonderful vignette of another existence.

'My family have stayed at the Connaught and used it as their London home for so long, but the prices have become ludicrous. I told them it is now too expensive and we can no longer afford it. So before we left the last time I kissed the staff, everybody from the manager to the bellhops and wished them all a fond farewell. London will never seem quite the same again.'

The links with England were clearly important to her and there was a certain envy of the extant country homes of the landed English gentry: 'A series of civil wars and constant turbulence has meant that we do not have such great houses left. The aristocracy still has a role to play here, but it is not as clearly defined as in England.'

Despite a certain almost whimsical nostalgia for former glories, her response when I dared ask the first serious question of the afternoon came as something of a surprise. I asked them both what they felt about the changes which had occurred in Spain during the last fifteen years. Heeding the warning about politics I didn't mention the Generalissimo, but we all knew what I meant, and as usual it was the countess who answered first.

'It is better here now, not in every respect of course, you lose some things and you gain others, but we had to change, you have to be very stupid to try and stand still.'

Her husband, a man who had been at the heart of the Franco regime, nodded his head and joined in.

'I do not know if the change is for the good or the bad, but the change *is*. You cannot go back, it is impossible. It does not matter whether you want it to be or not, the past is over, those days are done.'

Even though Juan Luis Cebrian had warned me that it would be impossible to find anybody who really wished to return to the old ways I was still surprised by those answers. Francisco Queipo de Llano continued without any trace of sadness or chagrin, a wealthy man who makes his money out of gin and gives his services as head of the Spanish Red Cross, a man approaching old age and watching the world.

'This is a period of great transformation, rapid, irrevocable changes for Spain and for the whole continent. In that respect it is a time for the young, not for old men, this is an exciting time to be young, I think.'

The countess took up this point with some passion.

'It is certainly better than when I was young, life then, especially for somebody from my background, was so formal and rigid, it was incredibly suffocating.' With a suitably slight flutter of her bright, flirtatious eyes she continued, 'Do not misunderstand me, I believe in femininity, not feminism, but life is certainly far better for girls here now, all of that stupid machismo has gone.'

It is difficult to imagine even the most macho man ever giving Cristina Fernandez de Villavicencio a hard time. She bossed the waiters about mercilessly, told her husband off and put on a little-girl-lost voice every time she realised she had gone too far.

Trying desperately to elicit some serious criticisms of contemporary Spain from my most likely candidates I pressed them on what things about living in Madrid most irked them now, was it the crime, the drugs, the pollution? This time he spoke first, and a certain weary look came over his face.

'The traffic now is terrible, you cannot drive through Madrid at certain times, everybody has cars and they all use them.'

It took me a little while to see the irony when his wife took up the theme and said, 'Yes, take last night for instance at four o'clock in the morning we were stuck in a terrible traffic jam which lasted for ever. What are all those people doing out at that time of night?'

The fact that they, a couple of pensionable age, were out at that time of night surely begged the biggest question of all, but one which had obviously not occurred to the countess and one I did not deign to ask. I did think though that it spoke volumes about their innate and almost naive élitism, but also about the irrepressibility of a people who will not go to bed at a reasonable hour. It also made me like them both a little bit more which, given his manners and her charm, wasn't difficult to do despite any historical prejudices.

I wasn't going to press him about his political career. It was clear that was a distant and very different time in his life and, in fact if not in years, in the life of his country. At one point though, talking rather aimlessly about global events in general and Russia in particular, (she predictably had a Russian grandmother), I saw the general shake his head wearily and say quietly, 'Ideas are dangerous.' Down now to a whisper he repeated the line to himself, as if remembering, deep down, chastening memories, 'Ideas are dangerous.' It sent a chill.

Whether it was the ideas which fired left or right which Francisco Queipo de Llano found so worrying I don't know. My guess would be that it was both, any. The sense you get now from those who lived through the Franco years, those who supported to some degree or other the man who was seen as a bulwark against communism, is that both sides seem equally bad and thinking back is too much of a strain. They did not believe that they were wrong then, but from the viewpoint of the open, tolerant society of today it is all different and what once seemed clear and cut is dark. I'm not sure that many feel ashamed, the general certainly does not seem like a man in remorse. But they don't much like looking back.

The rest of lunch meandered through much small talk about London and Madrid and ¡Hola! – 'That silly little magazine,' said the countess with undeniable accuracy – food, wine and travel. This Sunday meal was profoundly bourgeois in the most archaic sense of the word. When lunch ended the general predictably refused to let me anywhere near the bill, she waited for doors to be opened. We said farewell in fine and formal style.

When it was all over I found many things difficult to process, to fit into the patterns of my prejudice. I wondered for example what my old left-wing mates in Barcelona would make of my lunching with the enemy, which is undoubtedly how they would view a couple like General Quiepo de Llano and his aristocratic wife. I also wasn't really sure what I really felt about the experience. I don't think I had changed my mind about anything, but I was made aware once again that things look a little different when you see them close up.

21

I don't think it was the strain of having lunch with the countess so much as the pressure of living and trying to work in a city which is so hot that the minute you dry yourself off after a shower you need another one. I had grown to love Madrid. All my inherited Catalan prejudices had evaporated and I was completely taken by the unique (if sometimes exasperating) spirit of the place and its people, but that spirit combined with that heat can wear you out and I needed a holiday.

The question though was where to go? It had to be somewhere which I could fool myself into believing was research for the book, but I didn't know where. I canvassed a few friends and the Madrileño consensus seemed to be that I should head south to Puerto Santa Maria. 'Puerto', as they call it, is a little fishing village near Cádiz on the Costa de la Luz which has become extremely fashionable among those who realise just how tacky Marbella is. But I'd already travelled extensively in Andalusia and couldn't justify another jaunt in that direction. So I decided to phone some Barcelonan friends to see where they suggested.

Inka, who was now living back in her home town and producing rather than presenting television programmes, insisted that I must go to San Sebastian, for that she said, is very definitely the most wonderful place in all the world. I took a certain pleasure in telling her that I had already arranged a trip up to the Basque lands for some interviews but that was not until a few months' time, I needed a holiday straight away. Miguel, my old poet mate waxed lyrical about the *rias* of Galicia and how it is so wonderful because it rains a lot. Even though I was burning up in Madrid I didn't relish the idea of taking a holiday in a place with weather like Manchester, so I rejected his suggestion. Then I decided that I would ask Pepo.

Pepo Sol knows good restaurants. He's the kind of Catalan sophisticate, a man in his fifties who wears his clothes and his life well, whom you would always trust to point your credit card in the right direction. For not only does Pepo know good restaurants, he enjoys all his pleasures with an undeniable *élan* which makes him both good company and a revered sage in all things desirable. So I decided to ask Pepo Sol where I should go, by asking him where he would go.

'This is no question, Robert. When I retire, which I am sure you realise will be very soon, because I am a tired man, I shall move my life and my house to Majorca, as this is the finest place in all Spain to lie down. And the finest place on the whole island is the village of Deia. I would go there, and if you wish to have a week where you feel that everything is good then you too should go to Deia.'

The problem with seeking the advice of a fellow like Pepo is that you then have to follow it. Despite trusting the man who had first introduced me to the delights of *paella negra*, rice cooked in squid's ink, I was definitely a little dubious about the prospect of a week spent on an island with the pallid and the raucous. I mean Majorca.

The very name sends shivers and conjures demons. Majorca, it is always pronounced in my mind's ear with a hard 'j' and an even harder English accent. The person mispronouncing the native Catalan name of this Balearic island is wearing an oversized sombrero, carrying a donkey and trailing a family of bad children. The place they are headed is a turbulent ocean of pink flesh and grey concrete. Everything is horrible.

I knew though that the Spanish had not been quite as profligate with their coastal beauty spots as you might imagine.

Living in Barcelona I had plenty of opportunities to explore the splendid coast-line of the Costa Brava. I realised after many days' lying-down-and-gorging in quiet blue coves like Aiguafreda and Aiguablava and superb, unhurried fishing villages like Roses and Cadaques that not everything on that snaking coastline was Lloret del Mar and teenagers like I used to be.

There is actually a misunderstanding of scale which leads the British to believe that they have wrecked everything. There's a certain warped vanity involved here too: even at our most destructive we are not that powerful. Spain, you must always remind yourself, is a very big place. Apart from the uniform disaster of the Costa del Sol, all of the various coastal stretches and islands still have large tracts left relatively untainted. These were preserved, as much as anything, for Spaniards, the wealthier of whom invariably have holiday homes that they do not wish to share with the inexcusable children of northern Europe.

As a result it is hard to find a Spaniard who is bitter about the rape of the Torremolinoses and Tossas. The Spanish are a profoundly unsentimental people and they know that all those pounds and kroner were invaluable in terms of taking their country out of its bitter place in the Third World. To them a line of concrete eyesores by the seaside was a small price to pay for a chance to join modern times. And besides, they don't go to those places.

But still I think my voice over the phone must have portrayed just a little of the apprehension I undoubtedly felt at the mention of Majorca. I was to get to know that tone of voice well.

'Trust me, Robert, it is a perfect place,' said Pepo Sol. So I phoned Hattie in England, told her to book a ticket and meet me at Palma airport. 'Majorca?' she said with that same dubious tone of voice. 'Trust me,' I said with some doubt, 'Pepo Sol knows good restaurants.'

Palma airport in the summer months is one of the busiest in the world, a place which is disconcertingly both frantic and languorous at the same time, as the hurrying climb over the waiting. The local workers do their best to maintain some sanity but Palma airport has really gone beyond. Arriving there with the packaged and the ravaged was not portentous of good times.

Young bodies are sprawled across the floor, grooving motionlessly to blaring beat-boxes. The tannoy drones in too many languages, the drunken snore and the worried scamper without sense. Palma airport in the summer is like some chaotic field hospital in the middle of a terrible war which everybody is losing. When you have been waiting for many hours at an equally fetid British airfield and suffered the smell of charter airline food this is not a place to be and I could tell that my girlfriend was far from convinced about the wisdom of this trip. The car-hire desk is like the escape committee meeting.

Soon though we were away and in the hills, with the bucket seats and flimsy skin of the cheapest Seat Marbella available for hire providing scant protection from the plummet which offered itself should there be a slip. The road wound round the mountainside picture-book perilously. The sea appeared and disappeared to our left, and I began to lose the spectre of the tattooed ghosts who had haunted my holiday plans.

Then, after a brightly indeterminate amount of time, still in the hills, the Mediterranean a long way down there but visible and darkest blue, we were in Deia. At this point we both thanked dear Pepo.

The village itself and the hills around it are a kind of primeval plaster-pink, as if one grew directly from the other. There are pines in a forest of dark green down to the water, this verdant view punctuated erratically by gashes of rock and the occasional glimpse of the Mediterranean. The air is just hot and dusty enough to remind you that this is Spain.

Curling in a skew-whiff spiral up a hill, as so many small Spanish towns do, with a church predictably at the crown, Deia has a main street that runs through its base, while the body of the settlement hangs out over the sea. Bougainvillaea drapes itself around patios, gently scrambling the lines still further with its deep cherry tones. But the overall impression is of the kind of slightly austere beauty that is typical of the best of Iberian villages. Deia feels, whatever time you approach it, wonderfully still. On that first day, after such a journey, it felt miraculous.

This is where Robert Graves most famously lived and wrote, and the air of art still hangs a little forcefully over the village. English people, some too old and paunchy for the vaguely bohemian clothes they are wearing, sit on the terrace of the local hangout with a glass of wine in hand and argue theatrically, as if this was still 1959. The Deians wander by unmoved. Certainly there is a sense here that you are on the kind of Spanish holiday people used to take when the place was a secret. Except in Deia it is not so much an anachronism as the way it has always been, and perhaps the way it could be again elsewhere.

Because Deia has that perfectly realised combination of the preserved and the improved which is such a recurring theme in this country. Any visitor would be naive in the extreme to believe that they had stumbled on some quaint peasant settlement still living delightfully in the Dark Ages. This is a highly efficient holiday-machine where the locals own BMWs and know full well the value of their very beautiful village. The balance between old-world charm and modern efficiency is so well done that you don't even notice.

Nothing too much actually occurs in Deia, of course, but it doesn't happen with a wonderful rhythm.

That week was spent by the pool reading and playing backgammon, drinking to a doze sometimes or wandering down to the rocky cove of Deia beach where a bathing platform allows you to launch yourself into the waves. I did some snorkelling, spending one afternoon in the company of a large squid who seemed to go about his business unbothered by my presence. Later on without any shame I ate one of his relatives with a few of the local clams too.

Days in Deia are bright and slow. Then in the evening

when you've bathed and dried the sun sets and the glow of the mountains all around you takes on a rich rose colour which turns slowly slate as darkness becomes complete.

It is time then for some strolling and a lazy aperitif enlivened by trying to eavesdrop on the ageing arty archetypes who are invariably sodden by this stage. Food is taken as slowly as possible because, like as not, it is good food, and anyway everything in Deia is taken slowly, except your money.

The end of each day is spent gazing at the greatness of it all or else sitting for a final drink or a coffee with the local youngsters in their bar where there is invariably a dodgy old Santana record playing. Tomorrow you do the same.

That first week in Deia I never felt inclined to leave, never really felt capable of dragging myself away, and Hattie decided that she had found nirvana. On subsequent visits to the island though I've also discovered the pleasures of Palma. By day it is a town of some stature, solid and real, by night a town of truly Spanish habits. I've also ventured into the barren and beautiful interior and to the stunning northern coast with its coves and caves. All of this is available should you so desire, but chances are you will not desire. For as Pepo Sol said, Deia is a very fine place to lie down.

Tourism, Spain's largest single industry, is currently undergoing a major crisis and resorts which were full are now crashing. In a perverse echo of the kind of economic malaise which struck Britain in the late seventies and eighties, so Spain is suffering from a kind of post-package holiday obsolescence. As the first industrialised nation Britain was over-reliant on anachronistic industries which no longer had a market. Whole towns and areas found themselves without a function as the shipyards, steel works and coal mines closed. And Spain, as the world's first tourist economy, is facing a similar plight.

The two are of course inextricably linked, as it was British working-class holidaymakers who first flocked to the Costas. Without them and their Dutch, Swedish and German counterparts, the likes of Torremolinos and Benidorm, the Spanish leisure industry equivalents of Corby and Sunderland, could soon become tourist ghost towns, left way behind in a world where holiday tastes have changed. People are no longer prepared to spend two weeks in concentration camps by the sea. So the Spanish tourist industry is attempting to change too.

One tactic on the Costa del Sol has been to replace the stained tower block hotels with gleaming white architectural confections known as luxury apartments (they are just as aesthetically offensive as the eyesores they are replacing), each with access to a golf course which may well have been designed by Sevy himself. That awful word 'executive' is now big in the Spanish holiday lexicon.

Another more rewarding response has been the selling of the Spanish interior. Vast sums of government money have been put into a campaign to alter the popular conception of Spain and push the *paradores* and castles, mountains and cities, to push in many ways the image of the country which existed before the tourist boom. The slogan 'Spain – Everything Under The Sun' accompanied by lush photographs and a Miró image has appeared in every suitably glossy magazine throughout the travelling world.

That campaign has gone some way to re-educating and diverting some visitors to the country. Tourism to the towns and to the countryside is up, as anybody who has tried to book into a *parador* recently will know. It has also been a good example of the considerable style that the Spanish today can bring to bear, especially when flogging the Spain of yesterday.

But there is still a lot more to do if Spain is not to be seen as a place where only those who are economically or spiritually struggling go on holiday. That doubting, slightly superior tone of voice which I gave Pepo when he first suggested I take a trip to Majorca has greeted me almost every time I have told people how much I adore that island. The exception is when you meet another lucky soul who has spent some time in Deia. They just wink conspiratorially and ask you not to tell too many people. Spain has to tell the world that it still has many places as perfect as Deia. Well almost.

22

It is a short hop from Majorca to Ibiza, but one which should be made with more than some trepidation. I fear for my life every time I board a plane bound for that terrible place, wondering whether my will and my constitution will be strong enough to hold out in the face of such provocation. This time the test was even tougher, for I could not afford to fall into the 'rave-chill cycle' of nights spent partying and days spent dying by the pool. I was a man on a mission. I had said goodbye to Hattie and before I could return to Madrid I had to return to a Spanish place of my youth.

Ibiza, I thought as I attempted to escape from yet another overworked island airport, would be full of great memories for me, if only I could actually remember any of them. This time though I had to know what I was doing, because what I was actually doing was interviewing the two most important men on the island.

When the summer is over Gori heads back to the Basque lands and Bazilio takes a far longer flight to his home in Rio. They need a rest by then; the season is long and hard and it takes its toll on even the most battle-hardened of campaigners. But as we sit on the terrace of their famous temple up on the hill the summer months of madness do not seem to have hurt them yet. Gori and Bazilio are partners, two men of that indeterminate age which could be forties or fifties, both of them light grey and deep brown from years of sun and profoundly cool from years of success. Gori and Bazilio are the men behind the Ku and the Ku is the club which launched a thousand hangovers.

In any list of the world's great nightclubs, Ku Ibiza would have to be right up there. A vast open air pleasure palace in the middle of the island that can hold 4000 revellers in the most technologically luxuriant surroundings imaginable. Ku is based around a swimming pool, a dance-floor and the philosophy that the long Balearic summer nights are built for abandon. This is a place of aristocrats and international fashion trash, transvestites and shopkeepers, men from Madrid and the wanton women of at least five continents, a place where few questions are asked and many liberties are taken.

The House of the Rising Sun couldn't possibly match the Ku when the time comes to count the number of poor and rich, boys and girls, that it has ruined. I know I'm one, and I am eternally thankful to the two men sitting sipping coffee, staring out over their domain. Both are wearing the kind of baggy lightweight clothes of those who rarely have to look smart, and neither looks as if he has seen socks for many years. They are undoubtedly men of stature.

The first time I went to Ibiza was the first time I went back to Spain after those brief teenage encounters, and I could barely credit that this was a stern, serious Catholic country fighting its way back to the world. Now a decade or so later, Ibiza is internationally famous for the success of its excess. It is a summer mecca for those who, in the jargon of the night, are MFI, Mad For It. Few can have been madder than I was a decade or so ago, fresh out of university and determined to get wrecked. But I never imagined that destruction could be so sweet or so complete. The first time I went to Ibiza it hurt.

When I talked about this to the two men who are perhaps most to blame they both smiled and Gori who has the slightly gruff, nicotine tones that so many Spaniards take on in middle age said, 'Even if you had gone back thirty years Ibiza was an exciting place, but at the start of the eighties it really took off and started to happen. Spain wanted to have fun, and Ibiza has always been the island of good times, you obviously caught Ibiza at a good time.'

I asked why Ku was so successful, what had carried its name way beyond the Balearics.

'I think it is because Ku is unique in Ibiza and Ibiza is unique in the world.'

As a Brazilian Bazilio is clearly free from the inferiority complex which still holds back many Spaniards, but then he's right. The surreal, pleasure-soaked world of this Iberian island is like no other. Except that any major Spanish city on a Friday night now comes close to the intensity of Ibiza. That first jaw-dropping visit of mine was like a premonition of so many nights to come in Barcelona and Madrid. When I put this to Gori his head nodded.

'You are right, what used to happen only in Ibiza is now normal throughout Spain. In terms of nightlife this place was like a blueprint for the country.'

Half an hour due west of Barcelona as the DC10 flies, Ibiza has long had an almost institutionalised role as Spain's venal colony. Even during the days when women were stoned in Andalusia for wearing bikinis, and homosexuality was seen as the work of the devil or the Comintern, Ibiza had a reputation for liberalism and licence.

The locals of this small, attractive island, Catalan by language, and easy-going by nature, have always been known as an independent and tolerant lot, who were pleased to let outsiders go about their pleasures. As a result many of those who wished to escape the moral constrictions of the mainland and head for freedom went there, either for a fortnight of debauchery or a lifetime of pleasant exile.

In the sixties its seemingly endless supply of sandy, sleepy bays acted as a perfect landing spot for those from all over Europe who wanted to drop out, and the air of peace and patchouli hung heavy over the island. As a result of all of this Ibiza, with its pretty old town overlooking the port, its streets busy with bars and cafés, was already a cosmopolitan and comparatively hedonistic place when Franco croaked his last. And then it went really wild.

The tourist boom which transformed Spain inevitably left its indelible concrete stain on the island, but only half of it. San Antonio, a dense and brutal ghetto of boxes with balconies, on the east coast of the island, fills up for the summer season with the young of all Europe in search of quick tans and cheap gratification. Here girls from Essex and Dortmund wear white mules and court boys who throw up in the sea in the morning.

Here too one evening, standing in the doorway of a chip shop, I saw a trio of young French boys bowling arm in arm in arm towards one of the numerous tawdry local discos. They should perhaps have known better than to sing in a war zone, but the sound of a Gallic voice raised in song was more than a dozen or so British lads hanging nearby could take. One of the brave young Brits stepped into the path of the three French and with a cry of 'Platini's a dickhead' proceeded to punch the nearest kid to bloody oblivion while his mates cheered. That's what San Antonio is like.

But Ibiza Town isn't and the two rarely meet. Where San An, as the English call it, is rotten and squalid, so the other side of this narrow island is exciting and charming – in an Ibizan kind of way, you understand. And the Ibizan way is way over the top.

The very worst clothes in the world are on sale in the small boutiques that line the narrow streets that burrow into the old town. And the people who buy these skimpy, spangled things don thongs and wear make-up on the beach. They sit around the bars where you are supposed to see and be seen, aching to make an impression. Then they parade in the perpetual rumba that winds around town every evening, so that many can appreciate their fringed purple cowboy boots. Some of them are German.

Others though, both young and old, adopt a more leisurely approach to their leisure. During the day there are beaches of varying degrees of nudity and hipness. Those who really want to seek solitude and a burnt bum take a boat over to the pretty little island of Formentera and lie down a lot. Or else they rent a car and drive to the rugged north coast of the island for a spot of communing with nature. The daytime in Ibiza is really made for recovering.

The evening begins as so many do with a drink, perhaps in the fine company of the cropped-haired, overt inverts, who hang out at the top of the old town, playing king of the castle and grooving to high-energy disco. Or to one of the more relaxed bars where you can sit outside and watch the preposterous nightly carnival go by. Many times this has been my route through a long journey.

Some of the participants in this jolly nightly affair are semi-professionals, the *cocos locos*, the wild local ravers employed by the clubs to keep the outrage quotient up, acting as living advertisements for a particular niterie. Others are simply very camp followers living out their fantasies for all to see. They cavort through the streets, many in drag and make-up, handing out flyers for discos and bars and making this place feel like some bizarre little Rio in carnival. Then they move onto the clubs where they will dance among the successful and the desirous, the sophisticated and the scandalous of numerous nations, until way into tomorrow. All of this occurs apparently without trouble or hurt and with an efficiency, a dedication to the business of pleasure, which is quite remarkable.

It was going for a holiday to the island in 1978 which led to the opening of Ku. Gori and Bazilio already owned a discotheque of the same name in San Sebastian, the elegant resort town on the Basque coast which had long been the summer destination for Spanish *alta sociedad*. There they had come up with the idea of a large club out of the city centre, away from neighbours and open to the usually benign elements, and it worked. Seeing that Ibiza had all the potential for taking the same idea a good few stages further, they bought a plot of scrub land on a hill above nowhere, built a small swimming pool and a tiny dance-floor. They were well on their way to owning an international nocturnal institution.

Every year now there is a three-day international music event held at Ku, filmed for Spanish TV and sold throughout the world, attracting as it does many of the best young dance-orientated acts in the world. Almost every Spanish celebrity and numerous names and faces from other countries have spent time in their roped-off star bar. But it is the fact that the ordinary visitor can go and have a great time in startling surroundings which has made the place such a continued success.

The smaller, bright-eyed Brazilian speaks this time: 'The Ku is made up of everybody from princes to pimps because so is Ibiza. We took the mixture which was on the island and made a place where they can all exist side by side, we treat them all with respect.'

I wondered, remembering that night spent in San An, whether that mixture was ever an explosive one? I was also curious to know how the authorities felt about their ever expanding monument to the night. Bazilio, like so many of the outsiders who have settled in the new Spain, many of them from the corners of the Latin world, is a passionate advocate for his adopted country: 'We have never had anything but support from the authorities, no problems at all. They recognise the job we do for the island and they know that the people who come here are good people. In ten years we have never had a fight, not one. No, Spain today is a country where you can make things happen.'

The things which happen at Ku are no different from those which occur at nightclubs the world over. But they happen on a bigger scale here, with more people spending more hours and more money, and they happen with an *élan* which makes the whole thing seem effortless.

Dancing, flirting, or just drinking and talking in the open, warm air, while the pines and palms do their stuff, makes the pleasures involved seem easier, more open. This doesn't feel like forbidden fruit, but it is rich and ripe and right. It is mature in a way that going out rarely is in England. If the relaxed and rational Spanish attitude towards pleasure is perfectly expressed anywhere, it is here in the Ku at about four in the morning. And then, of course, I go and spoil it all.

It's just that you can go on in Ibiza, on and on. Clubs like the aptly named Amnesia and the huge concrete bunker known as Space stay open and frantic until long after the good folks have been up and breakfasted and down to the beach. You can go on and on in Ibiza, and so I do.

No matter how many times I return to the island, pledging that this time I'll take it easy, there is always at least one night that extends itself into an exhausting odyssey. It was way too late to know what time it was one warm, befuddled morning when I met some remarkable and dubious fellow countrymen.

There are invariably lots of English in the Ibizan after-hours clubs. Not the chip-eating, French-punching kind of English kids who make San Antonio such a nightmare, but serious nightclub English. There has long been a strong link between the London club *cognoscenti* and the island. This is where the club-runners, the DJs and die-hards of the British capital traditionally go for a kind of souped-up busman's holiday. This is where many of the more startling trends really start.

When the acid house scene first emerged in a sweaty back street fitness centre in south London towards the end of the eighties, the DJs who spun those mesmeric, electronic dance records, DJs like Danny Rampling and Paul Oakenfeld, had both been working in Ibiza the summer before. They came clean about the genealogy of the scene and called it 'Balearic Beat'. They knew where they had first heard those sounds, first seen people trance-dancing until dawn, many of them in the open air, wearing the brightly coloured, baggy clothes of a sunny summer holiday. Knew too where they had first seen people gently floating on ecstasy.

All those vast raves in fields that threw the British tabloid press into such fits of apoplexy were actually an attempt to re-create the experience of Ibiza. These were kids who did not want their holiday to stop, who knew from their Spanish nights that you do not turn into a pumpkin if you dance after three o'clock.

So it's no surprise that more and more of those smiling, spaced out English mateys in shapeless lilac clothes and shoes which look like Cornish pasties started heading for Ibiza to feel the real thing for themselves. And it's no real surprise that others went to feed off them.

Just as the Costa del Sol in the seventies and eighties became a kind of Essex in exile, where self-made British villains retired with their money and their molls, so Ibiza could be in danger of becoming a junior nineties' version of the same. For that last long night introduced me to a group of brazen young English men, itinerant euro-criminals using Ibiza as their summer base. Some of them had even turned Dutch.

I had already done the rounds of Ku, Pacha and Amnesia and with the kind of momentum which attaches itself to that kind of night, I wound up in one of those places that simply refused to accept that night inevitably becomes day. Most of the people here were English or Spanish, the Barcelonan contingent which regularly pops over to Ibiza for a weekend rave, challenging *Los Ingleses* to an unspoken test of stamina.

I was introduced by a London boy, whom I know to say hello to in shebeens back home, to a skinny kid with a heavy Midlands accent. Without any embarrassment or boasting (and as I remember it without me asking) my new-found acquaintance told me he'd begun intercontinental blagging at Nottingham Forest away games. When his team played in Europe he financed the trip by thieving from some unsuspecting shop in Cologne or Brussels.

I knew this had been a fairly common pursuit before English clubs were banned from European competitions after Heysel. Liverpool supporters were famed for turning over jewellers' and shops selling highly prized designer sportswear every time their team had a good European Cup run. But I presumed it had stopped now that there were no games to go to.

My man explained, though, that just because the teams were banned, it didn't mean that the lads couldn't still hop on a ferry to do a spot of continental skulduggery. And besides, it was even easier when the authorities weren't expecting hordes of barbarian British in town. So easy in fact that loads of kids were doing it, a whole band of latter-day English brigands, mostly in their twenties and early thirties, many of them ex-football fans, who lived by travelling around Europe in little firms robbing from shops, trading on stolen credit cards and generally doing badness. In the end some of them simply stopped coming home altogether.

'Everyone's too wise there, there's too many people on the blag,' said my kid from Nottingham. A mate of his, a short, bony Liverpudlian with angled eyes carried on the explanation: 'In places like Austria or Switzerland they simply don't seem used to our kind, there's very little street crime there, no one checks cards, and no one expects you to walk into a jewellers', pick up a Rolex and have it on your toes. They're so bourgie it's piss easy.'

These two both lived for part of the year in Amsterdam now. It wasn't hard to shift a few drugs in nightclubs there to tide themselves over, and besides, they said, the living in that famously liberal city is all round easy. They still travel though for robbing and to all the big sporting and music events on the continent, sometimes to tout some tickets, and just to see the English kids who inevitably turn up. They also go to Ibiza every summer season, dozens of them, and I seemed on that endless night to meet them all.

Dressed in the casual clothes of all holiday-makers, many had long, almost hippie-like hair. But these boys were not especially into peace and love. They were certainly big on spending money though, flashing wedges of notes like a symbol of buccaneer success. Bottles of champagne were the standard order and they went through vast amounts in the time I was talking to them. One went on matter of factly about free-basing £1500 worth of cocaine in a night as if that were fairly normal. They also seemed remarkably unconcerned about discussing their bent business. Somehow I was down by law, I was accepted and privy to the secrets of their murky world.

They make their money while on the island by selling drugs, providing 'security' for some of the dodgier nightclubs (a group of West Ham supporters who were supposedly members of the famed Inter City Firm of football hooligans were especially big on nightclub organisation and protection) and working credit cards and cheque-books stolen from tourists, or especially shipped out from England when they are past their buy-by date back there. They remain on the island for the entire summer season turning brown and looking remarkably fit, given their levels of consumption.

'It's great here, no one seems bothered about what you do, and the old bill don't give you any grief at all,' said a man with a north London accent wider than the Holloway Road and a baggy Paul Smith shirt. He also showed me his Dutch passport.

'It's very wise to get yourself married to a Dutch girl,' he explained as if I was somehow intent on taking up the profession. 'All the boys are doing it because then you get a Dutch passport which means under EEC law that wherever you get nicked in the Community after nineteen-ninety-two, you can chose to serve your sentence in the country of which you are a national. Holland has the softest prison system in Europe, it's a doddle. You can marry a whore in Amsterdam for two hundred quid.'

Drinking yet another glass of their generously proffered champagne I thought about how Spain believes that it is well prepared for 1992 and all that, but it doesn't come close to these boys.

Then when one of them said that they were moving on to Goa in India for the winter, because there were going to be loads of English club kids going there to retrace the hippie trail, I knew that it had all gone too far. The time had finally come to head for my bed and a 'Do Not Disturb' sign. The sun can look very, very bright when you emerge from a time like that.

The night about to come in the Ku was also likely to be a tough one. The Ibiza '92 music festival, which was being organised by Pino, the Italian Barcelonan who had taken me out on my first-ever mainland night, was on the third and final night in its third year and a noisy chaos prevailed. Camera crews in tight jeans were panicking in all directions. Pressmen and PRs, DJs and pop stars were jostling to be heard over the sound-checks. On stage the silicon amazon, Brigitte Nielsen, was trying to justify her position as a headline act by unfurling her legs and attempting to remember some of the words to her one song so that she could mime them for the men in tight jeans.

The place was restless in about five languages, but the men at the centre of it were happy to take time out to talk about their new projects (Spaniards always have 'projects') in the Canary Islands, and about the land in which they have prospered.

'On Sundays the people used to go to church,' said Gori in response to my question about the apparent conflict between Catholicism and hedonism, 'but now it is difficult because they are still in the discotheques when morning mass begins. These are the new temples and that is the new ritual, when we do things we do them thoroughly.'

He was smiling just a little. But when I asked him whether he could have envisaged all of this when he was a young man back in the Basque lands in the days of the dictator, he became more serious.

'The fact that my land, the Basque country, was one of the most abused and repressed parts of Spain throughout the Franco time, meant that we always fought against this, fought against the repression. That heritage of struggle can give you visions of a better way and the will to achieve those visions. Mine have led me here to a nightclub, but the same drive has led people in many directions.'

My next direction was back to the mainland and an appointment with a swordsman.

190

23

Espartaco is the *número uno*. Some say he is the most *número uno, número uno* since Dominguin, the *figura del época*, the master of his age in a bravura era for the brave bulls and the even braver men who walk with them in the sand. Espartaco is Juan Antonio Ruiz, a powerhouse matador with a faultless sword and a cheesy smile who regularly ignites the sun, but sometimes leaves the shade a little cold. Espartaco, Spartacus, the boy from Espartinas in Andalusia, whose father was a failed torero, is the only man in Spain who earns £50,000 for forty minutes work and works over a hundred times a year. And even those who aren't entirely convinced don't doubt that he deserves it.

To begin to understand the arcane, labyrinthine and sometimes spiteful world in which Juan Antonio Ruiz has made his chosen name so exalted could take a hundred repetitive, puzzling, nothing-happening afternoons, as you inch laboriously towards the truths contained in the ritual. Or it could perhaps take thirty seconds of wonderment which can raise you out of your seat and out of yourself, thirty seconds of transcendent beauty which can make sense of it all. Then you have to spend the hundred dreary days searching again for that feeling.

The *corrida de toros*, the unique, untranslatable event which is not, as we so crassly call it, 'bullfighting' but which is essential to an understanding of Spain, particularly now, is never an easy thing, especially for those who have to go out and do it. Espartaco not only does it more often than anybody else, he does it more consistently.

Travelling to the inconsequential town of Manzanares in the relentlessly plain, plain south of Madrid, a town which for its one *corrida* of the year had hired the *número uno*, I realised I was off to talk to the boy who done good, then done it again and again. Espartaco, the most popular bullfighter in the world, deserves the colossal sums he can command because he has turned the *corrida*, the national fiesta, the most capricious, fragile and consistently frustrating event in the world, into something resembling an exact science.

Through a powerful combination of valour and stubbornness, *afición* and athleticism, Espartaco has developed a style of dancing with, and then dispatching, bulls, which despite the violent vicissitudes and the sheer unpredictability of the animals, the weather, the plaza, the crowd, the atmosphere and the fates means that, chances are, he will deliver. Espartaco is such a huge star, Espartaco demands and deserves all that money, because like almost no torero before him, he comes complete with something close to a guarantee.

And for all the people who have splashed out to see their one *corrida* of the year from the baking, blinding seats in the sun, that is a very important quality. 'But where,' say the wealthy knowing men who sit regularly in the shade, in the exalted seats low down by the action, those who look for minute details of foot movements or the line of the cape; these *aficionados* who consider themselves the keepers of the precious soul of the national fiesta murmer, 'But where does that leave art?' No one doubts that Espartaco is the number one, but nothing is ever simple in this business of the bulls.

It is probably predictable that I went to my first *corrida* carrying a predilection. I'd read, of course, all the professional Anglo-Saxon romantics who'd filled that hole they assumed they had in their northern hearts, through the gleaming spectacle in the sun. I fell from afar for the idea of an entertainment where style is the only judgement, where grace is the goal and where death is both the enemy and the aim. I wanted to like, for all my ignorant love of Spain, the pride of its manhood clad in the glittering suit of lights, engaging in the struggle to create beauty with the beast. I was pretty corny.

I wanted to like, and in the first afternoon in the Plaza de Toros de Monumental in Barcelona, I did. Thankfully I also knew that, as Kenneth Tynan said, 'No public spectacle in the world is more technical, offers less to the untaught observer, than a bullfight.' Or else I might have wondered why I was also confused and lost and sometimes bored by what was happening. I was, though, entranced enough to set about learning.

To the first-time observer, sitting high up probably, in the cheap seats, surrounded by a noisy, restless crowd, the shape of the event is almost indecipherable, as it kaleidoscopes along in a glare of brilliant colours and a blare of badly played trumpets, in strange rites and deeply buried mores. From the opening procession of all those involved in the proceedings (bar the most important ones, the ones the posters always describe as the *seis toros bravos seis*, the six brave bulls), to the time when the last of those animals has been dragged from the blood-stained arena (which is simply the Spanish word for sand) all is running to a pre-ordained and tightly regulated pattern. If this chapter is to make any sense and, I believe, if Spain is really to make any sense, it is a pattern which must, briefly, be explained.

Each *corrida* comprises six bulls, usually all of them from the same bloodline or *ganadería*, and most usually of three matadors, who are to face two bulls each. The bulls must be at least four years old, and must never have seen a man on foot before they run into the ring. (A bull which has seen the shape of a man would know not to keep lunging for the cloth.) Which matador meets which bulls is determined by a drawing of lots which takes place on the morning of the *corrida*, but the order of appearance is determined by the seniority of the toreros involved.

At the blow of a trumpet, the sound which prefaces every act of this tragedy, the first matador and his *cuadrilla*, or team, of three footmen – *banderilleros* – and two horsemen –

picadores – will see for the first time the animal they have to work with. The first time you see this animal you will gasp. The *toro de lidia*, the Iberian fighting bull, is a beast so unlike the domestic bull as to be an entirely different species. Rising to the shoulder of a man, weighing anywhere between five hundred and seven hundred kilos it is a lithe, muscular, flowing animal, fast and beautiful. When the Spanish talk of the *corrida* they say, 'I am going to see the bulls,' and when you too have watched one of these awesome, handsome animals come charging out of the main gate and across the golden ring you will know why. You and the matador have now seen the bull, it is time to begin the reason for its being.

At first the matador and his footmen – *peones* – lure the bull around the ring using the large magenta cape known as the *capote*, judging all the time its idiosyncrasies, its dangers and its possibilities. Then the matador will begin to use that cape to make a series of ornate, flowing passes, bringing the bull nearer and nearer to his body. The bull, unable to distinguish between man and cloth, will continue to follow this lure, attempting to sink his horns into the air behind the *capote*, learning though all the time. A trumpet blows.

This announces the introduction of the picadors on their padded battle horses. Their job is to use long lances – *picas* – which are inserted into the shoulder of the bull as it charges. The *suerte de varas*, or trial of the *picas*, is done both to test the courage and strength of the bull and to weaken its neck muscle, so as to lower its head and enable the matador to perform his fatal final dance. Between each charge, each matador must perform a *quite*, leading the bull away from the horse and out into the centre of the ring. Here he will execute more of the long, dramatic passes, twirling the large cape around him before leaving the bull in the best position to take the next charge. Usually this happens three times before the president, the man in charge of proceedings in his box on high, signals the end of the trial and the trumpet blows for the next act.

The horses leave the ring and the *banderilleros* take up

their pairs of long wooden sticks tipped with a barb and decorated with coloured paper ribbons. Three pairs of these banderillas are placed into the back of the bull in a variety of ways which basically involve running at the bull and leaning into it. This displays a different skill with the bull, allows it a little rest after the extreme exertions of the horse and also brings it to the condition where the matador can create the last great act, the *faena*. For the final time the trumpet blows.

The matador will then remove his peculiar, almost comic, black hat known as a *montera*, and if he believes there is a good *faena* to be had with the bull he will dedicate the animal to somebody, maybe the president, maybe a pretty girl, maybe to the entire crowd. Then he will walk forward alone into the arena, with a smaller red cape – the *muleta* – and begin to create the series of passes, the movement of man and bull for which the afternoon will hopefully be remembered. Each particular pass has a name, each movement a purpose, but essentially the matador is wrapping the bull around his body in such a way that both become almost as one. The slower and more graceful the movements, the more deliberate and artistic the movements, the more dangerous and enthralling the movements, the more powerful and elevating the *faena* is. Until finally the matador, realising that the animal has given its all, will reach for his sword.

This ultimate, decisive act of the *corrida* involves the matador positioning the bull, stilled now by the hypnosis of the cloth, directly in front of him. Then using the *muleta* in one hand he must bring the bull forward, ensuring that its head goes down as he aims his horns one last time at the phantom target. At that point the matador leaps over the horns and sinks his sword into a small, fleshy gap between the shoulder blades of the animal and into his heart. This is the pre-ordained end, no options.

If he has been good, the matador will be applauded, he will take a lap of honour and perhaps be awarded one or even two of the ears of the animal. If the bull has performed well, it will also receive a rousing ovation as it is dragged by horses from the ring. For everyone here will know that no matador can ever be good if the bull is not also good, the relationship between the two is the essence of the art.

Six times this will happen in an afternoon, the whole process taking about twenty minutes for each bull. This is the order of things, this is how it always is and how it must be. This is the structure of the *corrida de toros* as it takes place throughout the season from March to October, throughout Spain. You must understand these never-changing bones before you can begin to understand. But you must see, and you must see one day blessed with greatness, before you can begin to feel.

Most likely though the play won't run to parts. One of the great misconceptions about 'bullfighting' (that name doesn't help here) is that it is a sport. Any event as formalised and rigid, and most importantly where the 'result' is always the same, could not possibly be construed as a contest. There can only ever be one 'winner', it is not meant to be fair. The matador and the bull are playing out their predetermined roles, but then no one told the bull that, and at times it seems like the matador didn't remember either. So things can go awry.

The absolute unpredictability of a theatrical production involving a genuinely wild and ferocious animal is what gives the *corrida* its uniqueness, it also means it can go wrong. It can be funny, it can be dull and all too often it can be terrible. Podgy little *banderilleros* colliding slapstick style in a frenzy of fear, or a hesitant, fading matador stepping on his cape while attempting to prance like a lithe young hero; these will be greeted with howls of laughter and derision by a voluble crowd which has come to be entertained. There is a comic romantic interlude which punctuates many *corridas* when a bull which has been judged unfit (most commonly because it has a problem with its legs, you cannot *torear* a bull which keeps falling over) has to be enticed out of the ring by the introduction of a small herd of bovine beauties, clanging bells and all.

Humour undoubtedly has its place in the spectacle, which veers like so much in Spain from the rococo to the reserved, the grandiose to the economical, and it is part of the Spaniard's ease with the whole thing that he or she can laugh at so sanguine an event. But when it is just plain bad no one is laughing, when it's bad you see the blood.

If the communion between man and animal fails to occur, if instead of honesty and excellence all you get is pretence and vanity from a matador who has instructed his picador to screw the lance deep into the bull's back to weaken it or who chops a few grubby passes at the bull, keeping it as far away from his body as possible, complaining all the while that the animal is bad, then you see the blood. You see the cheap plimsolls of the horse-handlers splashing about in pools of it in the sand. You see the bull coughing and spluttering the stuff up, and the incompetent or dishonest torero wiping it off his cape and his sword. Worst of all, if the kill is done incorrectly and it all ends in a dismal orgy of stabbing and gouging, then the whole thing becomes horribly, indefensibly ugly.

Spaniards go the *corrida* for many different reasons. The class divisions in Spanish society do not, as in England, create separate cultures, they mean that people separate inside the same cultures. At football the upper classes sit in the upper tiers while the urchins stand below. In bullfighting this is institutionalised as the divide between the *sol y sombra*, the seats in the sun and the shade, the two sections supposedly watching different events. The sun, it is said, goes for the sheer spectacle and an afternoon of high and gaudy drama. While the *sombra* houses the true *afición*, those looking for what Lorca called 'the last serious thing in the modern world'. (Though, truth be told, many of those in the best and most excruciatingly expensive seats are there solely for the social cachet of an event which is seen as akin to opera.) Nobody, though, whatever their social standing or their taste in entertainment, goes to see ugliness. Squalor is all too common in Spain to pay money to watch it.

When you see a bad *corrida*, and there are so many that those who follow the bulls talk of having their *afición* 'tested', as religious men have their faith tested, then you begin to understand, in an odd, negative, nagging way, what the whole thing really means. The feeling at the end of a dull or messy *corrida*, where no one involved has been able to lift themselves up from the bloody morass of mundanity, is one of hollow distaste. There has been no catharsis, no release of all your excitement and emotional investment, but worst of all is the horrid, disillusioning doubt that this could ever be beautiful.

For what the *corrida* actually represents is the struggle to create order and beauty, to create civilisation and finally art out of the chaos of nature. In burning Spain, a land where the forces of nature have rarely been benign, and especially in Andalusia, the hardest, most unforgiving terrain in Europe, the relentless everyday battle with the sun and the soil is symbolised by this ritual duel between the most powerful, the most magnificent champion that nature can offer and a man in a fancy suit armed with a piece of cloth. The fact that it is so difficult and dangerous to do is what makes the art of the matador so breathtaking, so emotionally uplifting when it is done well.

The process of taming the bull, bringing it under your dominion and then performing this precise delicate ballet together, before finally confirming that man is the master by consigning this great animal to its fate, is a rich and potent metaphor. And when that doesn't happen, when the men out there cannot achieve that harmony and poetry, then there has been no affirmation of our ability to rise above, no sign that we are more than the beasts. And that kind of doubt can gnaw away at your very spirit.

If all of this sounds impossibly romantic and baroque, then that is how it is, because that is how Spain is. Every summer's day it sends young men out there to risk their lives in order to prove that just as her artists can produce great paintings and sculptures, her architects wonderful cities, her writers great words and her musicians superb music, so her fêted and famed young toreros can take the elemental power of a bull and turn it into a ballet of stillness and rectitude. Scores of serious books are published on the subject every year. Magazines of *toreo* flourish, every newspaper devotes pages from its culture section to discuss and debate taurine affairs. Television programmes analyse every detail of the latest *corrida* and noted *aficionados* are broadcast discussing the purity or poetry of one matador's style over another. *Tertulias* of the great *aficionados* from Spain and abroad are organised regularly to further the art of taurine debate. All of this in a language which would seem florid, archaic, hyperbolic, downright ridiculous in almost any other context. But then, when you've been touched by one of the great days, when you've felt the collective silence of 15,000 people moved to stillness by the movement of man and animal slowed to a dream, then it makes sense.

For a while though it looked as if it was all about to stop making sense, as if it were about to stop. There is currently a great shortage of toreros in Spain between the ages of roughly twenty-one and twenty-seven, for that is the lost generation. For a time straddling the end of Francoism and the beginning of the democracy, nobody it seemed wanted to go out to face the bulls and fewer and fewer people wanted to watch them do it. The main reason was the kind of blight by association which affected so many of the definitively 'Spanish' cultural forms. Franco loved having his picture taken alongside El Cordobes, and the whole thing was smeared with an ugly patina of nationalism and isolationism. Understandably therefore most of the young with their urges towards the new and the European weren't too enthusiastic.

There were also the much publicised abuses, the horn shaving, the manipulation of the draw, the open bribery of the taurine press, all of which still occur to various degrees. Bullfighting, like boxing, has a smoky underworld surrounding it where fat men with cigars make fortunes out of rising stars, and falling fall-guys, where manipulation and money go hand in hand. In the late seventies though this had reached a nadir where overweight, ageing toreros went through the motions with dodgy bulls in front of a crowd of confused tourists and lard-arsed old Francoists. But then, as with so many things in Spain in the early eighties, it began to change, to progress by looking backwards.

One sign was the emergence of a couple of toreros dedicated to reviving the most exacting traditions of the *corrida*. Headed by a poet and trained architect, Luis Francisco Espla, their aim was to re-establish the national fiesta as a rich and honourable event. They did so by fighting in a rigidly classical manner, dragging up ancient passes and customs which had long been forgotten in an age when El Cordobes, 'the Spanish Beatle', with his long hair and ugly pop-star antics had dominated.

Even more importantly a group of very young matadors, an entirely different generation from those tainted by the patronage of the Generalissimo, began to appear as *novilleros*, trainee matadors, and started to cause a fuss. These teenagers, some of them sons of former toreros, others graduates of the taurine schools which were becoming increasingly established, were wholly of the new Spain. Their attitude was both thoroughly professional, but also rich in *afición*, in the love of the bulls, and it spread. Some of the older toreros responded to the challenge of these youngsters while others faded away. The crowds though kept going and growing.

Suddenly it seemed the *corrida* was fashionable again. High society was attending, especially at the great *ferias*, or festivals. The king showed his *afición* by acting as president at important *corridas* in Madrid, the intellectuals began again to see the richness of the allegory and perhaps most importantly the young, who had looked like turning their backs on the ancient institution, began, just as they had with flamenco, to embrace it. When I first arrived in Barcelona to live, the friends I made, the friends of Inka – arty young Catalan intellectuals who ten years before, would have dismissed the bulls as a bloody, Spanish anachronism – were eager *aficion-ados*. A true high time for the national fiesta was beginning.

At the beginning of my *afición*, at that first confusing *corrida*, the man who they had come to see was none other than Espartaco. His period as *número uno* had not yet really begun, but he had certainly established himself as a *figura*, a name who could attract people to the plazas. I don't remember too much of what he did that day, except that he walked the walk, the dramatic, theatrical step towards the bull with toes pointed, leading leg outstretched, chest expanded, head thrown back with disdain, the cape draping nonchalantly by his side.

The very feminine aspect of this man in an overtight suit encrusted with jewels, in pink stockings and ballet shoes, struck me then as a wonderfully androgynous contradiction. Here was the ultimate in Spanish machismo prancing like the most camp of dancers. And when at the end he killed well and won an ear, the crowd threw him flowers which he carried with pride in his lap of honour, smiling all the time that too cheesy smile. The whole scene was so elaborate, the notions of maleness so buried in a powdered and perfumed past that only a society as easy with its contradictions as Spain could possibly continue to devote itself to such a spectacle.

Intoxicated, I continued to go to bulls. Sundays during the season became highly ritualised with a walk to the *Plaza de Toros* timed to arrive an hour early, long enough to secure a ticket and then sit in one of the cafés around the ring and drink it in. Barcelona is not a town with great *afición*, but those who care, many of them expatriate Andalusians with bad teeth and fine white shirts, gather in the taurine cafés to smoke copiously, gaze up at old black and white photographs of the maestri and dissect the merits of the current matadors (who are never of course fit to tie the leggings of those who went before).

Here and in the fights which followed I began to pick up some of the wisdoms of this world which is as tightly wrapped and as complex as any intestine (and at times just as full of shit). I learned for instance which *ganadería* to fear the most: it's the Miuras, the bulls of death bred by don Eduardo Miura. I learned the many superstitions, how the colour yellow is never to be worn to a plaza, how a *montera* falling the wrong way up on the arena is a portent of disaster. I also gained knowledge of the solemn and sentimental rituals, the hugs from a senior matador when a young *novillero* takes his *alternativa* to join the senior ranks. And the tears when a matador retires in the ring by cutting the *coleta*, the pony tail which marks all who walk the sand. I also learned that horns are still sometimes shaved, that bulls can be carefully selected, that critics can be paid and crowds conned by crafty toreros who know every trick.

I learned too why some doubted this new sensation, this Espartaco, as they spat the word *tremendista* at me. *Tremendismo* is the style of bullfighting where the dangerous, the exciting, the flash, is preferred to the controlled, the profound, the artistic. *Arte* and *tremendismo* stand at opposite extremes in *toreo* and Espartaco, they said, spent too long showing off on his knees or with his back to the bull ever really to achieve art. I believed then and still do that Espartaco was no *tremendista*, but a true *dominador*, a man capable of imposing his will on almost any animal. I was now embroiled in the kind of debate to which lifetimes are dedicated.

I also knew that I had to travel outside the taurine backwater of Barcelona to see what this was all about, so I began to travel. It was on a day in Madrid in San Isidro that I came close to one of the constant truths contained in the *corrida*, too close. San Isidro is the holy saint of Madrid, and so his week is the time of the capital's top taurine festival. This, along with the *feria de abril* in Seville, is the most important week of bullfighting in Spain. Tickets on the days when the greatest *figuras* are appearing can change hands on the black market for hundreds of pounds, and on this day I had queued up at seven in the morning to secure a seat to see a bill which included a particular favourite of mine, little Joselito.

Like Espartaco, Joselito had become a full matador at the remarkable age of sixteen, taking the name of one of the greatest Andalusian toreros of the classical age and then attempting to live up to it. A Madrileño, he was appearing here in his home ring of Las Ventas, in San Isidro, and the pressure would obviously be on him to achieve something special. I was ensconced in a good seat, low down by the *barrera* which divides the crowd from the ring, and it was a perfect May day with the sun shining but not yet raging. And as Joselito shaped up to meet his first bull my heart was pounding and my muscles taut with expectation. Joselito's must have been a hundred times worse, he knew what the draw had decided he must now face.

A 696-kilogram bull is a giant even by the standards of this magnificent animal, and the 696 kilos of jet black muscle which came racing out of the *toril* on that afternoon was the largest and most terrifying *toro* I have ever seen, taller than the skinny Madrileño kid about to try to play it. The gasp from Las Ventas, the largest plaza in Spain, when it first saw that bull was tangible, you could feel the expulsion of air as Joselito shaped up to do his best. A few passes with the *capote* went well, but you could see that he was nervous, his movements not quite assured enough, the vital rhythm not quite there.

Perhaps it was that nervousness which made the young torero try too hard, but he performed a series of difficult passes with the cape before this enormous bull had even been *picad*. Then standing a few feet in front of me he attempted a pass known as a *farol*, an ancient and rarely seen movement with the *capote*, where it is swirled above the head of the matador and the bull passes by him high up. As the magenta cape rose up, so did the bull, but the timing was off and a horn hooked straight into the neck of the young Madrileño, who for one awful moment was hanging by the throat off the terrible weapon of that animal.

I'd seen gorings before of course, matadors bumped and bashed and occasionally bleeding from the thigh or arm, that is all part of the test. But this was different, a terrible injury that the entire crowd instantly realised could be fatal, a horrific wound to a young man who was carried straight to the infirmary amid a kind of shocked murmur. The *corrida* is not like a Grand Prix, people do not go to see the crashes, and the entire crowd was shocked and nervous and down. A blanched hush continued as we realised that one of the other matadors now had to take over that murderous bull, tame it, pass it and finally kill it, knowing that Joselito was possibly dying a few metres away.

Curro Vazquez, the senior matador that day, ironically notorious for his frequent displays of cowardice in the ring, stepped forward to do just that. Without any apparent signs of fear he brought that bull under his dominion, using the cloth to entrance the beast, and finally create a *faena* of some beauty and enormous valour. He was awarded a richly deserved ear, but despite the pounding excitement the atmosphere of the day was sober, intense but muted. For we had all been made all too aware of one of the truths of the *corrida*, the simple fact that in the ring, as in all life, death and calamity are only ever a few millimetres away. Those same couple of millimetres actually saved Joselito whose neck was entered fifteen centimetres by a horn which was a hair's breadth from his jugular vein and certain death. The scar which now runs the length of his neck and up to his chin is a reminder that we almost lost little Joselito that day.

The proximity of death on that afternoon was a potent reminder to us all. The idea that death is a part of life, an everyday occurrence, is another of the powerful lessons of the *corrida*. The bulls will of course die every time, as all bulls bred by man must. After the six *toros* have been killed they are skinned and butchered in a special room beneath the ring, hanging as white and sinewy carcasses for all who wish to see. The slaughterhouse is a fact of life in every society, but in Spain through the ritual of the national fiesta it is open, the facts of death are not hidden away, but accepted, even saluted.

The realisation and acceptance of the inevitability of life and death, the notion that between the two it is possible to create something valid, maybe even something lasting, is perhaps the ultimate lesson of the *corrida*. A lesson which thankfully Joselito did not have to pay the ultimate price to teach us that day. That though is a lesson which those of us who live in societies where truths are hidden away, where squeamishness and hypocrisy are endemic, and where we are further removed from both death and life, could do well to heed.

This I came to feel from beginning to know the bulls and beginning to understand their place. The Spanish are not a cruel people, but they are intensely honest. It is perhaps cruel that we breed animals to eat them, but no more so that we give the bull, who has lived a fine life to the age of four or five, a chance to end that life in honour in the sunlight. Honour is still hugely respected here and so is the bull. Riding to Manzanares in the plain, plain south of Madrid, I was going to see a small community reaffirm its ties to the soil and pay its respects to the power of the brave bulls and to the men who can master them. I was going to see the *número uno*. It felt odd to see him eating lunch.

The arrangement was to meet in the *parador* on the edge of town where Espartaco and his team were encamped for the day. During the season a successful matador's life consists of driving up and down the motorways of Spain (and these days France too; the *corrida* is growing massively in the south west and in Provence centred around Arles and Nîmes) and indeed the large Mercedes estate car, the traditional symbol of taurine success, was parked in the drive outside.

That car became notorious a few years back when a female French journalist name of Denise Beaulieu embarked on a peculiar assignment, to sleep with some of the top matadors in order to ascertain for her magazine, *Le Globe* of Paris, whether their famed machismo extended outside of the ring. In the case of Espartaco she caused a great and much loved scandal by claiming that they made love in the back of his

Mercedes, but that it was extremely disappointing because he cared more about keeping his leather upholstery pristine than he did about satisfying her. Thankfully as I am neither French nor female his manager seemed to have no qualms about an interview with me, this foreign writer.

Bullfight managers or *apoderados* are famously oily men with large cigars and sweat stains on their crumpled light-weight suits. But the man who met me in the lobby of the hotel was too young, too clean and too clever to fit into that fedora-wearing photo-fit. A former taurine writer, he had taken over the management of the young star quite recently and unlike the old-style *apoderados* with their stables of men, had only this one matador on his books. He led me into the dining room where Juan Antonio Ruiz was finishing his lunch. It felt odd to see him wearing a tracksuit.

The first impression on meeting the twenty-eight-year-old torero was that I was looking at an athlete whose expertise could have been on the football field or the running track. A muscular, clearly very fit man whose features are a little too square and coarse to be really handsome, he moved with the easy almost languorous grace of those who are perfectly tuned, climbing the stairs to his room in leaps that were hard to keep up with. He didn't though seem like a man involved in a poetry.

Walking into the flawless, faceless and profoundly ordinary hotel room it was hard to tie all this in with the vivid, bloody proceedings of the plaza, with the wealth and fame of this young man, or the prospect of the *corrida* which was just three hours away. Here I was talking to Juan Antonio who had a glutinous Andalusian accent and a none too propitious taste in sportswear.

Sitting on the bed he explained how it had taken him twelve difficult and frustrating years to achieve this level of success, the early years spent desperately trying to gain a chance to risk his life for next to no money in some God-forsaken little ring. The small plazas which are scattered around rural Spain, with no medical facilities, miles from the nearest hospital, are known as the *plazas de mal muerte*, the places of bad death. Knowing that, it must take some serious dedication to serve your bloody and usually pointless apprenticeship in them. Some are driven by absolute poverty, for Espartaco it was the chance to succeed where his father had failed which drove him on.

'He is the reason I was so determined to succeed, he had no luck as a matador and I was determined to make up for that. I grew up in a house where everything was related to bullfighting. Every day from the time I was born I saw the suit of lights and the cape and I fell under their spell.'

I too saw the cape, a *capote* draped over a chair waiting to be unfurled that afternoon, and beneath it the glittering arm of the white suit of lights, the white suit which is his favourite and most famous outfit and the one he was to wear that day. I saw too his small array of talismans, the Virgin Mary and the crucifix, the rosary and the photo of his girlfriend laid out neatly on the dressing table. And the magic of those charms and of the suit worked, he became for me then Espartaco, a torero I have grown to care for more than some. And this Espartaco talked like he fought.

I have seen the man they are calling the *figura del época*, the figure of his age, many times now in different plazas on different days, seen him often enough to know that he is not a *tremendista*, but he can be. Espartaco is a scrupulously honest torero who has learnt that to succeed you must give the crowd what they want. So in the smaller rings, or even in a large one like Barcelona where the *afición* is not so great, he will pull out the tricks, play to the gallery, cut ears by providing genuine if sometimes superficial excitement. In the more important, more serious rings his style is more sober, more classical, with an attempt to do everything as correctly as the purists desire.

The very fact that he has such control as to be able to do both is a sign of his remarkable skill with the bulls, the sign of a true *dominador*. The fact that he always bothers to try to please is a sign of his integrity in a world so often shamed by deceit. The fact that he does not have *duende*, is never likely to send you home from a *corrida* with a heart truly overflowing, is not his fault. His personality is too straight, too uncomplicated for that. He is a remarkably brave, technically expert man who answered, I believe, all of my questions with absolute honesty. He also said exactly what I expected.

For instance when I asked about the relationship between himself and the bulls he gave the standard answer. 'The bull is my friend,' he said as I waited for him to say just that. But then there's no doubt that he meant just that. As he explained, the relationship between the torero and the *toro* is a complex, symbiotic one.

'If it was not for the bull we would not be doing this interview, I would not be where I am, neither I nor my family would enjoy wealth. Without the bull you cannot have the triumphs, so the bull is my best friend, I owe everything to him. Also though without the fiesta *brava* the bulls would not exist. The fighting bull would perish as a species, it would be extinct, there is no other reason for that great animal to be bred. We rely for our very existence on each other and I try to respect that.'

That of course is the text-book answer, but then in many ways Espartaco is a text-book torero, an unfailing if unsurprising paragon; it is also undeniably true. And when he says, 'I always try to kill well because the bull deserves to die well, it is a noble animal which deserves a decent end,' then you know that not only does he mean it, but that he does it. Espartaco's swordsmanship is so great that he kills more consistently than almost any matador before him. He lives out his words as he deals out death.

There is also no doubt that he was being scrupulously truthful when I asked him about his relationship with fear. This hero who struts across the sand with that exaggerated, boastful walk said, 'It is constant, every hour, every day, it never goes away. That is your real enemy, that is what you are fighting, not the bull, you fight fear but it is difficult. The public and the bull are gone after the show, but the fear is always there day and night.'

I certainly couldn't detect any fear in his easy eyes, on this day when he was due to face death yet again, but there was a certain flicker of something when I mentioned the word art. Through long seasons of incredible consistency he has earned that position of number one, cast aside all the doubters. But that word art still caused a stir, it is the one word the detractors dangle at him like some kind of negative charm. So when I asked him if he thought the *corrida* was an art form, he gave an answer which speaks volumes about his *toreo*.

'This is showbusiness, it is a spectacle, but it is a great show in which art is necessary, the art comes from risking your life. Everything here is very real, the bull is real and when it gores you, believe me, that is very real. This is not a movie, it is more captivating because it is so genuine, at least it is if you understand it. I think I understand bullfighting and what people enjoy, I understand why it is important, and that includes art but it is not just art.'

That is not the answer you would get from the great exponents of *arte*, the unpredictable, histrionic toreros with their *gitano* blood, who are just as likely to leave the ring under a hail of angry cushions as on the shoulders of ecstatic *aficionados*. They can perhaps provide the most precious, the most soaring moments to be gained in a plaza but all too often they give nothing. That is though a square appraisal of the way Espartaco approaches his chosen profession, and the new level of professionalism which he has brought to it. And the rewards it has brought to him are enormous.

In classic style he has invested, as almost all successful toreros do, in a *finca*, a ranch where he can breed bulls and maintain the tradition which he has served and which has served him so well. That's where he will retire to when the day comes to face the bulls for the last time, and to cut the *coleta* from the back of his head. How, though, will he know when the time has come? So many go on too long, shadows

209

who've been shot but can't see it, living on the strength of former triumphs.

'I will not be around for too long, as soon as I see my standards going down I will retire, it has taken a lot to get to this position and I would not want to spoil it. Right now I still have mistakes to correct, still have things to learn. I want to do things that no one has done before.'

I almost believed him. And at six o'clock that afternoon, in the small, affluent, whitewashed town of Manzanares, in his own straight and steady way, he did just that. There were no dramatic new passes invented, no breathtaking innovations to make you sing. But there was a perfect understanding of the bulls and the people who had paid to see them. I watched him work his two animals with dignity and honesty, taking them perfectly through the stages of the classic drama that they were born to play their part in. For doing just that he was awarded the ears of the animals and the applause of the crowd. He was also given flowers from a man who called him maestro. But what was truly unique about this Espartaco was the knowledge that tomorrow afternoon in some other ring in some other town he would probably do exactly the same thing again.

My afternoon with the *número uno* did little to alter my *afición*. It showed me that away from the ring there is a less romantic, more prosaic side to the people involved. Yet those rings where the bulls run and the men sparkle and strut, remain for me places which have the power to transform, places of the most potent alchemy. They, perhaps more than any other single thing, will pull me always back to Spain.

24

And then I go and spoil it all by doing something stupid like going to Malpica.

It is probably not surprising that the Spanish Tourist Board has never chosen to promote the name of the coast which runs along the very north western corner of their country. Long before the Costa Blanca and the Costa del Sol became international shorthand for mass package-trip tourism, the ragged, jagged coastline of northern Galicia was known as *la costa de la muerte*, the coast of death. When you arrive in a town like Malpica you can smell the decay in the air.

The coast of death was so called because its fierce Atlantic waves and needle-point rocks regularly claimed the lives of sailors who left those shores to hunt the seas. Now it feels like the place itself is dying. Malpica, a one-time whaling port, looks like a dishevelled and distressed old woman, who can no longer keep herself clean, an embarrassment to her family with their posh new ways, who has been left to rot quietly in a forgotten and forlorn corner. Nobody, it seems, is bothering to save the whalers.

When you have spent months convincing yourself that Spain is the coming country of Europe, the great success story, the brilliant new land, it can come as something of a come-down to find yourself in a broken place like Malpica. There are no colours there, it is a town bereft of tones, where a perpetual putty-grey hangs over the sea and shore, blurring the lines between the two, and where the wafts of rotting vegetation and pungent chemicals provide a constant, nauseating backbeat. The detritus of a few failed developments lying here and there, breeze-blocks and plastic tubing left to fester by the roadside, only serves to add to the profound sadness which hangs over the place. Everyone is hunched in Malpica.

Gallegans, the people of Galicia, are famous for being melancholy souls, and when you see a sorry little town like Malpica drowning in its own, onerous void, it isn't hard to see why. They are also famous for going away. Gallegans are the great emigrants who for hundreds of years have left the many disconsolate little fishing towns along the *costa de la muerte* to head for better, richer lands, so there are more of them in Buenos Aires alone than in the whole of Galicia. Despite the fact that I felt a writer's need to look and understand I left Malpica pretty quickly too.

When they are away though, these small dark people, earning their fortunes in other countries, they are all said to develop something called *morriña*, a tugging, gnawing homesickness for their misty and magical homeland. That took me a little longer to understand.

I honestly believe that I first met the Gallegan thousands of miles away in Havana, Cuba. Long before I had ever travelled north from Madrid to their rocky, Celtic homeland with its excess of dolmens and crosses, and a language closer to Portuguese than Spanish, I had come upon these people. Throughout South America the term *Gallego* has come to mean one who is of a melancholic and sombre disposition, and Cuba is full of them. For all the strident African spirit of the place with its *santería* and its rumba and its mambo, there is a serious, devout, austere air about the Cubans and their surprisingly straight-backed capital. Rather than being a result of the strictures of centralist socialism I believe that rigid system was made possible and is perpetuated by the sombre spirit of the Gallegans. Angel Castro left a little town like Malpica to make a new life in Cuba, where he became a successful land owner and gave birth to a son named Fidel. And Fidel created a country in the image of a homeland he'd never seen. You have to have something to think about when you are sitting (albeit briefly) in the one bleak bar in a one-time whaling port.

Along with the fine lace, wonderful oysters and acidic wine, Galicia is known for producing devout and authoritarian leaders. El Cid, the greatest of the Spanish warrior chiefs was a Gallegan. So was the General of this book title, Francisco Franco himself, and it was partly a desire to see his homeland which made me choose this lost and lonesome corner. As you drive through this austere, granite landscape, where the light seems to come through a perpetual filter of haze, it all makes sense.

Posters line the walls of the small, steeply arcaded coastal towns exhorting those who follow the true faith to go out to South America and become missionaries. The poverty and toughness of the land is obvious, families live on and off tiny pockets of stony soil which are barely more than allotments, where you see old women in short socks, draped in black or in the bright synthetic colours of contemporary poverty, bent double wielding scythes or carrying ragged bundles on their heads. Oxen still drag carts and old trucks spewing thick, rancid fumes roll by from time to time like so many Eastern European convoys. Indeed the whole scene could come from Poland or Czechoslovakia and it doesn't seem remotely like Spain. Galicia, certainly in its poorest, most backward northern region known as the *Rias Altas* feels like it's been left behind, as if it is peripheral not just to Spain, but to the whole continent.

And that's how it has always been. Galicia has always been poor, always been devout, always been different. Its soul lies in the magnificent, brooding town of Santiago de Compostela, the ancient pilgrim city which supposedly keeps the remains of St James in its most holy cathedral. This is a handsome, moving, perfectly preserved town where the affecting sobriety of the architecture mirrors the nature of its people and seeps into the visitor like so much spiritual rising damp. Even though it has so many visitors and a large young student population Santiago speaks more quietly, goes to bed earlier and works harder than other great Spanish cities. The vast, gaunt Jesuit seminary on the edge of town is perfectly placed.

Apart from Santiago, and unlike the rest of Spain, Galicia is not famous for its urban flair. There are few beautiful towns and little in the way of excitement. Most people live in tiny villages strung out along ill-laid roads in a selection of jerry-built homes. In the south this has been tempered by the recent growth of tourism. The *rias*, or estuaries, which bite deep into this filigree coastline are lined with long fine sandy beaches where many of my friends from Barcelona and Madrid go annually to absorb the attractive dampness and easy, soporific pace of resorts like Bayona and Cambados.

Tourism has brought a new-found affluence and lightness to the parts of the region which are touched by travelling big-city money. But even outside the holiday areas you will suddenly see a beacon of investment blazing in all its terrible taste out of the relentless grey. An opulent ranch-style bungalow complete with computerised satellite aerials, long cars and security fences sticks out like an overdressed adult in a crowd of scruffy schoolkids in this region. And you see quite a few of them. And it can only mean one of two things.

The first is that the owner has actually found that fortune he or she went searching the world for. Those who have emigrated and made money abroad traditionally return to their homeland to erect grand homes as a testament to their success. The gaudy bungalows of these *Americanos* no doubt act as a continued spur to the young, taunting them with tales of easy riches in distant lands. There is though another equally dubious example for the young Gallegan to follow. That big new house could belong to one of the *narco-traficantes*.

Apart from fishing and farming, the other traditional craft of the area is smuggling. It would be difficult to imagine a coastline more perfectly tailored for bringing in contraband. The *rias* have cut intricate paths deep inland, with numerous coves and deserted off-shore islands which are a godsend for anybody attempting to import, store and distribute illegal goods without being detected. Galicia is perfect for smuggling, so there has always been smuggling. But now the cargo of the *contrabandistas* has changed.

In the sixties and seventies the trafficking was in cigarettes, the common addiction of almost every Spaniard and a vital currency. Tobacco smuggling was an accepted, almost respected, part of Galician life with whole villages involved in operations to import thousands of cases of Marlboro or Winston at a time from motor boats driven deep into the *rias*. From there they were distributed throughout Spain on a long-established network that ended up with them being sold in bars and on street corners in every part of the country. Throughout the dictatorship the authorities turned a severely myopic eye to these activities, tobacco smuggling was no more than a civic offence, and this was seen as a way of providing some sort of income to a profoundly poor region.

But the democracy could not be dealing with such obvious anomalies, and in the early eighties there was a huge crackdown. Tobacco trafficking was made a crime, motor launches were banned and many of the Galician tobacco barons were arrested (though never brought to court). That, they say, is when the Spanish connection began.

My connection here was a girl named Angela, a friend of a Catalan friend, who I had phoned up in Barcelona to see if he knew anybody who knew anything about Galicia. In between raving about the latest new designer bar in town and taunting me for living in Madrid, he suggested that I should meet this girl who would know a little about the business of the *narcotraficantes*.

Walking through her home town of Pontevedra, a pretty, drowsy old seaside town with a surfeit of shoe shops, there were far too many scruffy, leaden-eyed kids hanging out. I had arranged to meet her in a bar which she had suggested and I soon began to feel a little uneasy about the venue. Some of those kids with hollow eyes were looking a little desperate and I didn't fancy hanging around for hours until somebody decided to mug me for the price of some drugs. By Spanish standards Angela was remarkably prompt though and I didn't have to wait long before she arrived to settle my nerves.

'Don't worry they will not cause any trouble, I brought you here to show you.'

Angela is in her early twenties, Gallegan, the daughter of a middle-class family, her father is a dentist, and she is a recent graduate of the university in Santiago. The reason she knows a bit about the *narco-traficantes* is that her brother is part of the chain, the part at the end that hurts. Her brother is a junkie.

'He is a heroin addict. The drug which is smuggled here is not heroin but cocaine, this is the major drop-off point for all of Europe from Colombia, the whole network starts here. But there has developed a culture of drugs among many of the young people here, which has led in the case of some, a few mind you, but a growing few, to the kind of condition you see outside.'

Perhaps it's her scientific training (she was studying to be a biochemist) or perhaps it's the fact that Spaniards in general have a pretty relaxed attitude towards drugs, but Angela didn't seem too wound up by the situation. She admitted that in common with most people of her age she had taken *coca* a few times at parties and saw no problem with that.

'I do not think that the major problem here is drugs, it is boredom, lack of opportunities. I believe we have a drug problem here for the same reason that we have the highest illegitimacy rate in Spain, a mixture of poverty which leads to ignorance, and the sheer fact that life leaves us behind. The big dependency is not on drugs, but on smuggling.'

She went on to explain how there was a real duplicity in the attitude of ordinary people to the big smugglers. For years when they concentrated on tobacco they had been seen as Robin Hood figures, colourful characters known and often idolised in a community which also benefited from the money they brought to the area. Now that the effects of the drug trade are all too visible some (but by no means all) are standing out against them. There have been some major busts, including a former Colombian bullfighter who was living in the region, but others soon step in to fill the places of those who are arrested. There are local organisations like Arise, formed by the parents of kids like Angela's brother who are trying to bring pressure to bear. But the big slogan of the area which you can see scrawled on walls is, 'Drugs No – Tobacco Yes.'

'What they cannot see is that our reliance on smuggling has really fucked everybody up, the whole economy of the area, it is so ingrained that we cannot live without it. Yet it means that we do not bring real investment, do not pull ourselves up, when your whole economy is black you can never really improve yourselves.'

Angela's response to all this is that like so many before her she is planning to leave. She was smiling when she said, 'Before my people used to go to South America, but there is little point in that any more, they have even worse problems than us. But there is nothing for me in Galicia. So I will look for work in Europe, I have a skill which I can use anywhere.'

I asked her if she thinks she will suffer from *morriña* like so many Gallegans before her.

'Probably, I like it here. I also know that things can seem pretty romantic from a long way away.'

25

There are seven hundred reasons not to feel like that, but
there is still a certain power, a romance maybe which can
turn your head and twitch those nerves tied to your sentimental soul. It's all inside your head of course but even though
you know that, the incantation, the history as a magic potion
still begins to work. Sitting in the main square in Guernica
watching excitable schoolkids kick a ball around during the
siesta I had to remind myself that the blood now flows the
other way, had to remind myself of the dying families at the
Hipercor.

If you didn't know the stories, Guernica would be an
unremarkable, unattractive little town. The power isn't in
the buildings or the sights but in the web of truth and myth
which has wound itself round the town which has become a
totem. In the land of the Basques, the high and separate land
of these dark and different people, Guernica is more than just
a squat little city in a valley by the motorway, it is a symbol
of continuity of a destiny as yet unfulfilled. The dense,
troubled magic of Guernica is the reason that seven hundred
people have died since 1961, is the reason why eighteen died
so terribly in the Hipercor supermarket in Barcelona on that
black Friday. I had to remember the looks on the faces of their
families to stop the magic of Guernica working on me.

The mythology of Guernica goes back way beyond the day
in April 1936 when the bombs of the Condor Legion blew
away nearly 1500 Basques out shopping on market day. Apart
from the sheer revulsion at the world's first taste of blitzkrieg,

the reason that the attack on Guernica was seen as so terrible was because it was an attack upon an idea. The reason that Guernica was singled out for such punishment by the nationalists was because it was the concrete incarnation of the very concept of Basqueness.

Here was the town which represented the remarkable notion that these people with their dark hair and blue eyes, their unique, unfathomable language full of Xs, Zs and Ks and their strange games of strength and speed are the only surviving aboriginal Europeans. They call their language Euskara and their land, now in Spain and France, where that language is spoken, Euskadi. ETA stands for *Euskadi Ta Askatasuna*, Euskadi And Freedom, and freedom for the Euskadi is symbolised by a tree which grows in the town of Guernica. That's why the place has its magic.

The bit about the Basques being Europe's sole surviving aboriginals may sound like precisely the kind of mythology made to sustain terrorist groups, but it isn't only the angry young militants of ETA who believe it. Most scholars now seem to accept that their language (which sounds half way between a smoker's cough and a stutter) is the only one on our continent to pre-date the Indo-European influx from the east three thousand years ago. That their blood type with its unique preponderance of Rhesus-negative points to the same conclusion, as does a marked difference in cranial shape and a complete lack of migration mythology. Basically it seems that the Basques, secure in their impenetrable redoubt, surrounded by wooded mountains and hugging the Atlantic, are indeed very different from their French and Spanish neighbours and from any other peoples anywhere.

And that tree in Guernica (the one there now is actually son of tree) marks the spot where their forefathers have traditionally come together from the corners of their inaccessible land to practise a rudimentary form of democracy, distinct and apart from the rule of any other nation states. It was that which was under attack that day in 1936, that which was so severely repressed by Franco for forty years. And realising

219

all that can make you start to understand the motivation of the few hundred young militants who are still out there, hiding in safe houses, dodging the authorities and planting bombs and firing Kalashnikovs. But it cannot possibly condone it, that's what I had to keep reminding myself.

ETA began their violent history relatively recently, starting out in the early sixties as a student group dedicated to the preservation of their outlawed language. But they soon developed into a full-scale terrorist organisation with a thick but rather translucent patina of Marxist-Leninism for ideological colour. Traditionally the Basques were a profoundly conservative people, deeply Catholic, and only finding themselves supporting the republican side in the Civil War because of the centralism of the Francoists. At heart their struggle has always been a nationalist one, led by the sons and daughters of the most remote rural areas who are trying to establish some kind of purist, almost pre-industrial Basque idyll.

The industrial revolution was clearly a long and bloody one in the Basque lands and the battle lines are still etched deep into a countryside scarred and soured by the blows of heavy production. The deep green of the mountainsides where farmers live in Alpine-looking chalets called *caserios* is punctuated by brooding, belching towns, as stridently ugly as the countryside is beautiful. Among the most unlovely of them is Bilbao, the largest industrial centre in Spain and the biggest Basque town by far.

The most imposing building in town is La Catedral, the home of athletic club of Bilbao, whose vast crest looms over the city below. The stadium is known as the cathedral because it is a shrine to Basque separatism, and no non-Basques have ever played for the club. Given the hatred of Spaniards by some in these parts, I'm amazed they even deign to play in the same league as the enemy while the war is still going on.

In this grimy, not poor, but undeniably tough town, it is easy to see how the rhetoric of revolutionism has worked its way into the fabric of ordinary people's lives, smothering them in an impenetrable fog of politics. The perpetual graffiti forms a street language of its own baffling complexity. The initials of this and that party and tendency running into the slogans of some splinter group or other. The kind of giant, full-colour murals which provide the only real colour to the streets of Belfast are also emblazoned on numerous walls here, singing the praises of some dead or imprisoned martyr to the all-consuming cause. Comparisons between those two blighted communities are inevitable; Bilbao is not a divided city, but it is, like the drear Ulster capital, a place where history clearly matters too much and where the future looks a long way off.

Another link between the two towns is the fact that the initials of the Irish Republican Army seem to appear almost as regularly as those of Euskadi Ta Askatasuna. These people, who consider themselves to be so different to those all around them, look for some kind of companionship among those who also stand outside. They believe no doubt in a brother-hood of struggle, in a perceived, poetic unity of the oppressed. But walking around the barrio in the evening, roving from bar to bar, I felt that they were actually stuck fast in a mire of their own creation.

Everything about the twisting drinking quarter of Bilbao is gaunt. Compared to most Spanish cities this tenderloin looks unloved and unlit, a dingy warren of streets where kids with black clothes and even darker stares seem to lurk on every corner. All of the signs of a large junkie population are apparent wherever you look and the place feels heavy and sad. Some say that ETA wages war against the drug dealers, others that they are the drug dealers, using the money raised from heroin to finance the war. I have no idea which of those is true, possibly it's both. ETA is fractured into numerous factions who sometimes seem to hate each other as much as they do the Spanish, and somebody is certainly pushing, and pushing hard.

The style of the young things trying their best to look menacing is decidedly spiky, an aggressive, militaristic and incredibly dated combination of Doc Marten boots, fatigues and black leather. It's as if they are stuck, every one of them, in a sad depressive period at the end of the British punk era, a period which all but a few die-hards and dinosaurs have passed through in the rest of Europe. And when you walk into a bar like FSLN, the sense of being adrift in a strange, unsettling time-warp world grows even stronger.

The student bar at the LSE looked a bit like this when I first went there at the end of the seventies, but even that haven of carefully studied radicalism didn't boast a large framed photo of Vladimir Ilich Lenin behind the bar. Named after the Nicaraguan guerilla movement, FSLN is perhaps the most strident of half a dozen bars within a couple of streets which flaunt their affiliations for all to see. In the FSLN, Identikit punky young men in their twenties sat around cradling glasses of cider, drinking in the torpor, making sure their scowls were in place and their leanings in view.

One corner of the FSLN is given over to a bookshop and news-stand where piles of tracts from all the trouble spots lay dry and curly like so many stale old pub sandwiches. There are papers extolling the wonders of Libya and North Korea, of the Red Army Faction and the Shining Path and others supporting liberation movements in countries I didn't know needed liberating. Most of these were in Spanish, the language of the oppressor, and when a young man in a stripy Dennis The Menace jumper tried to sell me a paper with a front page story about the Intifada I asked him why it was not in Euskara he said, 'Euskara is very difficult to learn, those who were not brought up in it have great trouble.'

What he meant was that only something like twenty per cent of the Basques can actually speak their own language, and to learn to do so from scratch is a mammoth task, so even the struggle takes place in the hated Spanish language. When I asked him a little more about 'the problems' he became understandably coy. At that time about five hundred ETA activists were in Spanish prisons and the whole thing is profoundly clandestine. It is also the deadly business of a very small minority, no more than seventeen per cent regularly supporting Herri Batasuna, the political wing of ETA.

Yet what the militants have succeeded in doing is creating a culture of violence and perpetual struggle which in Bilbao at least looks introverted and directionless and means that the place is full of people wallowing in a self-imposed, masochistic sense of oppression which no longer makes any sense. In Guernica I could feel the power of the myth, in Bilbao I just saw its consequences for the everyday life of that city and they were not pretty. Time, I thought, to move to somewhere that is.

If contrasts and contradictions have been the recurring theme of this book, if they are what make Spain so special, then the most spectacular contrast to be found in Spain is the one between Bilbao and San Sebastian just a hundred kilometres away. If Bilbao is the physical embodiment of the blackened side of the Basque history and culture, then San Sebastian is its shining pearl.

In terms of natural beauty I have yet to see anywhere in Europe which can compete with the huge oyster-shaped bay around which San Sebastian is built. Two implausibly long and fine beaches of genuine gold curl round to the sugar-loaf mountains which sit at each end, while a third verdant hill rises from the Atlantic as if placed there specifically to curb the wind and waves and create a scene of exquisite calm. And the city that the Basques have built to accompany these abundant riches is itself a splendid testament to a high and sophisticated civilisation.

It is a resort town of elegant white promenades lined with tamarind trees and atmospheric squares the equal of any on the peninsula. It is a town too covered in graffiti screaming of hunger strikes and demonstrations. In Euskara the city is known as Donostia and this town with two names has a decidedly split personality. As the cultural capital of the Basques it is also the centre of ETA's command structure, but the culture can certainly make you forget. I had come here to meet two of the cultural icons of contemporary Basqueness.

223

My guide through the decidedly strange ways of these people and their finest town was one Rafael Aguirre, a writer, rower and representative of the tourist trade in this thriving resort. San Sebastian is a casino and a race-track town, it has jazz and film festivals of the highest calibre and the most exalted hotel in Spain. The first place Rafael took me through was the *parte vieja*, the mesmeric old quarter of San Sebastian which, he pointed out with a smile on his face, is not as old as it might have been.

He explained how in 1813 a bunch of prototype English hooligans attacked a mob of Napoleon's boys who were holed up there, raping and pillaging a bit before burning the place to the ground. Little was saved bar a couple of elaborate rococo churches, but the townsfolk decided to begin again and, obviously anticipating more benign tourism to come, what they built is bars and restaurants. The *parte vieja* is basically a living buffet, a marvellous testament to the greatest Basque art form of them all, cooking. Now Rafael was to give me a guided tour of the mysterious gastronomic societies before taking me to meet the great chef.

In the cobbled streets and alleys of the old town many of the doors which appear to lead to yet another restaurant have the word *privada* above them, telling members of the public that they are not allowed to enter these portals. Rafael, as a well-known face about town, could walk into all of them and be welcomed, he was of course also a man. For the gastronomic societies are clubs dedicated to the excellence and enjoyment of Basque cuisine, as long as that cuisine is cooked and eaten by men.

'There are well over a hundred of these clubs, each with a couple of hundred members and they go back a very long time,' explained Rafael. He did offer to give me the book that he'd written on the subject, but seeing as it was in Euskara I wasn't sure that it would help too much. I thought it was better to let him tell me.

'Each of the members takes it in turns to cook for a group of his friends, taking great care to make the most exciting dishes from the most secret recipes. These men who would never dream of cooking at home are wonderful chefs here, it is a tradition, a sign of your manhood. The societies are also about forgetting class differences, everyone is equal in these clubs, so they come here once or twice a week to cook and eat and enjoy themselves. Of course some people now say that it is wrong to exclude women but I say that it is a very special tradition which we would be foolish to lose.'

Walking on Friday night from society to society I couldn't help agreeing with him. The fact that I was greeted with marvellous hospitality from these singing, laughing men of all ages was certainly a factor. Here were fishermen and factory workers, businessmen and hoteliers welcoming a stranger into their clubs and what's more making him drink their pungent, fruity cider and eat their incredible food. That might also have swayed me. Miguel for example was preparing a feast of baby squids in their own ink, followed by hake in a green sauce of parsley with clams, food as good and expert as any I've ever tasted. Miguel is a lift engineer. On the wall of Kanoietan, one of the oldest and most respected societies, were a line of busts of obviously honoured men, many of them wearing the exaggerated Basque berets. 'Are these perhaps great Basque poets or nationalists?' I asked one of our hosts. 'No,' he said, 'they are famous eaters.' Next I had to see the most famous cook.

The name of Juan Marie Arzak is made to make mouths water. He is the most famous chef in the country, owner of the most famous restaurant with the most stars. Basically the rule in Spain is that the further north you travel the better the food gets. Both Catalan and Gallegan cuisines are highly rated, but it is Basque cuisine which is considered to be the greatest, and it is in San Sebastian that Basque cuisine reaches its zenith. The expertise and expectations engendered by the gastronomic societies have led to a preposterous number of great restaurants. In a town the size of Brighton there are six places with Michelin stars including two with two and one that has received the ultimate accolade of three stars. That's the one called Arzak. When you tell people you are going to eat at Arzak the look on their faces is almost as good as the food to follow.

Just out of town in a rather nondescript-looking site, there has been a restaurant called Arzak here for three generations. Juan Marie's grandfather founded the place and it has become a Basque institution almost as exalted as that tree. Those going to pay homage there are going to have to pay highly for it and sitting in the reception waiting to be seated is to see the high bourgeoisie of the Basque lands with their Rolexes and their Chanel, their overdressed children and their ease with places like this. Señor Arzak seems to know many of them personally and they are clearly very happy about that fact.

When he sits down beside you to go through the menu it is easy to see why, if he were British, Arzak would have a television programme of his own. He is a character, a small avuncular stocky man, in his fifties perhaps, who carouses you with talk of food, a voluble, likable man who makes everything sound wonderful. Then, when you eat it, it is. Arzak was recently included high in a list of the world's top ten chefs, they must have eaten his cheese ice cream, they couldn't have helped but eat his fish.

'We are a race of fishermen and so our cooking is based on fish. The average Frenchman eats something like eleven or twelve kilos of fish a year, the Spaniard about twenty-two, while the Basques eat forty-three kilos.'

Sitting by the bar with Juan Marie Arzak after the meal he is explaining the importance of *pescado* in the Basque culinary canon. The things he does with the beasts of the sea are remarkable to see and even better to eat. The style of the cooking is nouvelle, but it is nouvelle Basque, within, or perhaps at the front of, the tradition so gloriously maintained at the societies. Echoing a sentiment which I had heard so many times in so many different contexts he said, 'You cannot have new things of any value without the depth of tradition to draw on. The reason that Basque cooking is so important and so forward looking now is because we have such a perfect base and one which accepts new ideas.'

When I asked him what role the culinary societies played in all this he said instantly, 'They are the basis of it all. The culinary societies have created a culture of food which means that ordinary people are remarkably sophisticated about every aspect of cuisine, there is a popular understanding. They realise how much good food costs, and they are prepared to support high-class restaurants, they are also not prepared to accept anything but the best. This means that all of the restaurants have to maintain a remarkably high standard and that competition keeps you at your best and keeps you trying new things.'

The next time Juan Marie Arzak tries something new I want to be there.

If the sophistication of Basque culture is best seen in the food in their great city, then the ancient, the aboriginal, is to be found in a little lost town high in the hills on sports day. Sports are the other great obsession of the Basques who have a bet-on-anything reputation. Their approach to football is both fanatical and puritanical (Real Sociedad, the San Sebastian team, also won't allow 'Spaniards' to play for them, but they do have three Englishmen), but the big urban Basque sport is *jai alai*, or pelota. Pelota is a way of hitting a ball against a wall which makes squash look like croquet.

Rafael had also written a book about *jai alai*, but trying to follow it live was difficult enough. He was trying to explain the three different varieties of the game, which basically depend on whether you hit the rock-hard little ball with a huge basket, a leather glove or your bare flesh. The true heroes, he explained, are those who play with just their hands, which must be because they can't have hands for very long. The players in *jai alai* have to wear crash helmets because if the ball hits them on the temple they will die. *Jai alai* is said to be the fastest game in the world and having watched it in deep and daft amazement for half an hour I won't argue with that. The Basques watch through a cloud of cigar smoke and then bet on every rapid rally. Bets are placed in hollowed out tennis balls which fly up and down from the punters to the bookies by the side of the court in a baffling blur of moving money. It is all great fun and completely incomprehensible.

'Now,' said Rafael, 'you must see some of the other sports like cutting the grass and pulling stones.'

The cleaving of a new motorway through the spectacular rock of the Basque lands was said to be the most expensive road-building scheme per metre ever undertaken when it was started in the late seventies. It has certainly increased access to the small towns high in the interior, but it doesn't as yet seem to have altered them very much. Going to one of the small mountain towns to watch a day of traditional sports is a bit like seeing how things might perhaps have been.

People look different up there, they all look the same. Here the notion of a short, stocky, muscular race of men all with dark hair and blue eyes, all of them remarkably hirsute and yet somehow fine featured, confronts you every time you look at somebody. I wouldn't look at anybody too closely. It is said (by Basques admittedly) that the strongest man in the world is from these parts. He is the champion of the Basque games, a sort of Highland games without the skirts or the subtleties, a series of sports which must have seemed pretty basic when the Romans were running scared of this mob.

The true rural version of the Basque games does indeed include cutting the grass, where the wielding of scythes is turned into a sweepstake and another where they bet on which bullock can pull a heavy lump of stone fastest or farthest (I never worked out which) across a farmyard. But the upmarket high-tech version I saw consists of two villages competing in a day-long series of events such as bouncing great weights off your chest, chopping up lumps of wood and throwing sticks into the waste-paper basket. There is even one where you drag that lump of stone across a cobbled yard like a bullock. When I asked my guide what the Euskara is for hernia he didn't even laugh.

And the good folk of this tiny mountain town sat there all

day, in their little concrete town square, the men in their berets, the girls in their stone-washed jeans, watching their young and hairy heroes take on the ne'er-do-wells from another probably equally odd little town a valley or two away. When it was all over they retired to the one bar and indulged in the other Basque sport of staring at the Englishman. Here they were definitely staring in Euskara.

Back in San Sebastian that evening they were also talking their own language, but the words were altogether more intense. I'd arranged to meet Rafael in Constitution Square for a taste of the wonderful local tapas and a glass of cider. When I got there the place was burning.

In one corner of that peaceful, powerfully symmetrical plaza a stage had been erected and banners bearing slogans in angry-looking Euskara were flying overhead. A crowd of a few hundred was watching a troop of costumed boys dance a kind of Highland fling to a tape of a monotonous, droning music. I suspected that it might be some kind of folk event, and I suppose that in a way it was. It's just that the folk were here to honour a prodigal son, one J. M. Zubiaurtre, who had come home that day after an absence of ten years. He'd been in a Spanish prison.

An ETA activist, Sr Zubiaurtre was being welcomed back to his native city by those who still carried the flame. The dancers were followed by a priest in full regalia who made a speech about the 'theology of independence', a stern, serious priest with white hair whom Rafael referred to as 'a lover of lost causes'. Next came a couple of men in early middle age with button-down shirts and pullovers draped over their shoulders on this warm late summer evening. These were singers in the traditional style who improvised unaccompanied verse about the struggle, making a strangely compelling sound out of their consonant-cluttered tongue.

Then the man himself was introduced on stage to applause which was warm but restrained, and to hugs from the priest. At this point the two singers slid into a warbling, melancholic tune which Rafael told me was the Euskadi national anthem.

Suddenly the voodoo which which had taken hold of me in Guernica started to work again, and when the crowd burst into a shout of 'Askatasuna' – freedom, the power of that word, potent in any language, became almost too much to bear.

Rafael though brought me back down, 'I was moved ten years ago, but there are other democratic ways now. If some people need this to sustain themselves then that is OK, but it is not my business.'

In the rest of Constitution Square little girls played leapfrog, lovers canoodled and many were eating and drinking, going about their pleasure as this serious, sentimental, dangerous business was going on behind them. The two it seems could not, or had learned not to, see each other.

San Sebastian lives with the problems in quite a remarkable way, never seeming to deny that they exist, yet never allowing them to drown out the attractions of this splendid town. The Basques are far too proud of their pearl to allow it to become subsumed by the swamp of the struggle. In many ways the refinements, the splendours, the sheer civility of San Sebastian act as the most powerful advertisement for the Basque cause, a beacon of an ancient civilisation which has achieved a great cultural maturity. If San Sebastian is a symbol of the sophistication of Basqueness, then Eduardo Chillida is the living symbol of San Sebastian. I was more excited about this meeting than any other this book had made possible.

Since the deaths of Dali and Miró, the two great names in Spanish art have been the Catalan painter Antoni Tàpies and the Basque sculptor Eduardo Chillida. Tàpies, whose wrenching, angular abstracts with their obsession with the crucifix and their combative, sorrowful imagery born of his memories of the Civil War, has just been honoured by the opening of the Fundacio Tàpies, a museum in Barcelona dedicated solely to his work. Eduardo Chillida doesn't have such an edifice, his monuments are open to the elements, his great monuments live in the Basque lands.

One of them is in Vitoria, the small town in the mountains which is now the capital of the autonomous province of País Vasco. A second is in Guernica, a moving but somehow uplifting, even optimistic piece created to mark the fiftieth anniversary of the bloody day the bombs fell. The third work, the most famous work, known as the *Combs of the Wind* sits on a ferocious, elemental outcrop of rock facing the Atlantic directly beneath his house in his home town of San Sebastian. Eduardo Chillida is recognised throughout the world as one of the most important sculptors of our age, winner of many of the great international prizes, including the ultimate 'Omnagio' from the Venice Biennale. But Eduardo Chillida is not recognised anywhere like he is recognised in San Sebastian.

That is perhaps accounted for partly by his decision to return to his home town in the early 1950s when it was still suffering under the yoke of the dictatorship. After studying architecture in Madrid, he turned to sculpture and moved, as so many of his artistic contemporaries did, to Paris. But after a few years working there and beginning to gain an international reputation he decided suddenly to come home: 'I discovered the importance of being a Basque.' He then set about assuring his artistic independence and successfully avoiding political interference. That fact, that he was now being recognised as a major international talent, perhaps gave him a certain artistic immunity. Certainly his success must have acted as an example to his countrymen who were also struggling in their many ways to attain a certain independence. Soon he was showing major works throughout the world, but the monuments to his homeland were yet to come.

Chillida's great public works, executed since the death of Franco, are on a truly gargantuan scale; vast, enveloping structures in iron and stone where shapes within shapes play with our perceptions of space and light and where the artificial and the natural compete and combine. The *Combs of the Wind*, originally planned in 1952 but not realised until three years after Franco's death, consists of a series of terraces laid into the natural rock which act as a platform for three vast, sinuous, wrought-iron structures protruding from the rockfaces themselves. The terracing has a number of holes bored into it which act as conduits for the waves which come rhythmically rushing through them, creating a roar and a spray of foam. The combs resemble giant, rusted anchors twisted and weathered by the waves, yet proudly defying them.

Standing by this great piece, especially when the elements have whipped themselves up a storm, the salt is rushing through the tubes and the waves are lashing the iron fingers, is to become part of a hugely symbolic and enormously physical representation of this city and its people. Iron-mining and production formed the basis of the Basque wealth, and huge iron anchors were a great speciality. Also the Basques are a sea-faring people, the first man actually to circumnavigate the world, Juan Sebastian El Cano, came from this shoreline, and the relationship of man and the sea is still vividly part of their everyday existence. San Sebastian is above all a seaside town and it has come to be represented by that powerful sea-shaped image created by Eduardo Chillida. And every day the people of the city walk out to feel its power.

The *Combs* have become the emblem of the city and Eduardo Chillida has become the greatest living symbol of Basque pride and aspirations, a kind of Vaclav Havel for his people who is instantly recognised as he strolls around his home town. He even used to be their goalie.

'Playing in goal is the most sculptural position, it is all about spatial relationships, about distances and angles.'

Eduardo Chillida is smiling a wry old smile as he talks about his former job as goalkeeper for Real Sociedad. Now in his sixties, he still has the fit and lean looks of a former athlete, a tanned, handsome man who exudes an easy but imposing stature. He is sitting in the living room of his remarkable house which oozes a cool aesthetic rectitude perched high on the side of a hill overlooking the bay. This is a serene, clean room with huge windows which frame that wonderful view, and works of art which are enough to make a boy nervous. There are a few of his own small pieces, intricately worked blocks of white marble and cast iron. There is a Picasso or two alongside his own paintings, a few American abstracts worth a mint, and on one wall a Miró so large and so fine that it takes the breath away to see it as part of somebody's house, part of their life.

'I do miss Miró, he was a great friend, a wonderful artist.'

Chillida is in many ways one of the last links to that generation of Spanish artists who were so influential in shaping their age, and to hear him talk of Miró and Picasso is to be transported to the time not so long ago when Spain was seen as the very centre of European creativity. Yet the way in which Chillida is so respected in his home now also shows the heightened role, the truly popular esteem that the visual arts still have in Spain today.

'The *Combs* were my homage to my city, and a homage to the wind and the sea which have done so much to shape that city.'

He talks in a considered, almost poetically wayward English which is accompanied by a gentle, self-mocking smile. His wife Pili, an elegant woman in white in middle age, sits watching her husband as he talks.

'I do my work as I do because I am as I am, and I am from here. I believe that man belongs to a place, to the specific and to belong to a place, to a people, is important to everybody, not just Basques, but that question of identity has been especially important to us. I am a Basque and I understand things in a Basque way which I believe is a special way, this informs the way I see, my ideas of strength, force, materials, many things, this is natural.'

Chillida is a very intellectual artist but some of the themes which seem to me to occur in his work are fundamental, physical in what they have to say about man and nature. Nature is seen in typically Iberian fashion as a powerful, bold, but not always benign force which must be confronted,

233

though can never be defeated. Gravity in particular, that which brings everything down, is seemingly tempted by much of Chillida's work with its hugeness of scale yet elegance and finesse of line. With the *Combs* it is the sea and the wind which will one day literally bring down his work as it is attacked by them every day.

'The rocks there are the result of the sea working upon them, the result of a fight and the same now happens to the *Combs*. I did not chose the place in so much as I was chosen by the place, the place came first. In relation to the city, the island, the geology, it all pointed here. The sea is the father of San Sebastian and it is my master too, I have learned so much from it. The laws of the movement of the sea, its discipline, its patterns, these are vital to my evolution as a sculptor and you have to respect them.'

Sitting listening to this fascinating and wise man, I knew that I was in the presence of a master, a gentle man whose power is universally recognised. His name has become synonymous with his city, his community, surely one of the greatest accolades any of us can wish for. When I asked him about this his smile grew even more self-deprecatory.

'I am proud certainly but my name is really not so special. I belong to the city like everybody and this is a very democratic town. It is a very civilised town too.'

As we walked into his lovely garden where sculptures sat among the trees and the fresh sea air swirled around, so one of his small grandchildren came rushing up to hug her grandfather who swept her off her feet and held her in his big goalkeeper's, sculptor's hands as he smiled that smile and said goodbye. A civilised man in his place is good to see. I knew as I left that I would feel that afternoon for ever.

26

And I knew walking along the Ramblas that I was back in my place. I'd been to one capital, two islands, three autonomous regions with four languages and dozens of towns, some forsaken by God, others blessed. My Spanish steps had carried me down and round this big country to bring me back to the point of my beginning, the place of my first love. I was in love now though not just with Barcelona, the city of the Catalans, but with Barcelona, the city of the Catalans in the country of the Spanish. I felt that I knew a little this land first glimpsed in thirsty teenage.

Down there though among the whores and the bootblacks where the city meets the sea I could see the changes which were now speeding. The tumult was still in place and still enthralling but so much was being altered, being made anew at a pace emblazoned by the threat and promise of the Olympic torch. The new and the clean, the designed, the planned, the functional were eating deep into the cherished chaos of the barrio Chino and the artful neglect of the Gotico. It was now three years since I had lived in this town, years of frenzied refurbishment, of scaffolding and burrowing which had left ghosts to wander without haunts. I felt a sadness then for my Barcelona and knew I was wrong.

I was falling foul of the selfishness which wishes to shackle a place in time. That's what Franco had and what all those haughty Hispanophiles with their sobbing love of a precious past have. The changes occurring everywhere in Barcelona were so obviously analogous to Spain as a whole that I could but celebrate them.

There were though certain danger signs. The anarchic parking which had struck me so typically Catalan was under attack from the dreaded clamps which had blighted the rest of Europe. A line of wonderful old restaurants along the waterfront which were famous for their seafood and their barkers, who stood in the street to pull in custom, were about to be closed due to the fact that they had never gained planning permission. There was also talk of a police clampdown on the more uproarious late-night clubs. Barcelona was getting a spot of pre-Olympic jitters and imposing an entirely alien puritanism so that the world would see a well-behaved city for a month in 1992.

I stood in the once-crumbling old Plaza Real where the junkies and *gitanos* had hung out, driven out now, I guess, to see that the formerly derelict apartments were being trendified by the rich and chic and looking great again. Every face was being lifted, every profile polished and the good god of design worshipped in a hundred startling new temples.

There is no doubt that some good things, some ugly, dangerous, lovely old things were disappearing in the wake of this wave of new wonders, but the city was in glory again. There must have been those, I thought, who moaned and made bad of the work of the modernists, of Gaudí and Domènech i Montaner, when they were so dramatically reinventing their town. It is too soon, before even the scaffolds have come down, to judge the merit of much of the work being done throughout Barcelona in preparation for the Olympics. But the very fact that it is being done, that Barcelona is again the most modern, the most forward-looking city in Europe, is sufficient to celebrate. Of all the designer icons currently springing up in Barcelona the one which is most everywhere, the one which is rapidly becoming the universal symbol of this most visually sophisticated city is a cat with a crooked smile.

Cobi is the mascot for the Olympic games, a cheeky cartoon

cat who seems to be emblazoned on every shirt, poster and hoarding, every plate, pen and picture-book in town. There are also thousands of plastic Cobi dolls in the poses and outfits of all the major Olympic events. Best of all there are aluminium designer Cobis sitting in the windows of all the most studiously serious shops, just waiting for the *cognoscenti* to hand over a fortune for the pleasure of owning such a trendy cat. Cobi the omnipresent cat is the invention of a man named Mariscal, and this man Mariscal is painting on the face of the new Spain. He was the reason I was back in my town.

When I first went to Barcelona, Mariscal was a name in the air, and now that I was back he was in danger of becoming an internationally acclaimed artist, a kind of Spanish equivalent of his big mate Philippe Stark. The similarities between the 'terrible child' of Parisian design and architecture and the Catalan cartoonist-turned-maker of so many things are many. Both have stamped their identity on their respective cities, both have worked in almost every medium imaginable and both have gone from being thought of as playful dilettanti to being hailed as stars in the exalted world of the visual arts. Both of them have a visibly wicked sense of humour.

Mariscal's exuberant, waggish sense of fun can literally be seen all over Barcelona. Down by the waterfront it exists in the form of a chic dockside bar adorned with a giant grinning twenty-foot-long metal Mariscal prawn which seems to be mocking the oh-so-serious statue of Columbus at the other end of the promenade. In the municipal science museum it can be seen in the Mariscal-designed children's area where the entrance is so low that adults cannot enter without crawling on their hands and knees. It can be seen in his cartoon carpets which hang with pride in grave furniture shops, or in his award-winning chair which looks remarkably like Minnie Mouse. Mariscal is lucky that he lives in the one city in the world where that kind of fun can be taken seriously.

Where Milan has risen to international prominence on the

sumptuous, broad-shouldered back of its fashion-design industry and the streamlined sophistication of its motor cars, so Barcelona has done the same through the medium of interior, graphic and furniture design, and Javier Mariscal, a funny-looking little man in his early forties, is its Armani, Versace and Maserati rolled into one.

The reasons why Barcelona should have such a design obsession are many and complex. Partly of course it is tradition; the city of Gaudí and Miró is steeped in the visually remarkable and design has always been an everyday experience. It is also a reflection of the fact that Barcelona is a major city without an industrial base, no raw materials and little heavy production, so it relies instead on arts and crafts. But under Franco the arts and especially design took on a new meaning. Where most intellectual and political life was severely controlled, design, which was viewed by the ruling right as of little importance, could get away with being radical, even revolutionary without attracting the censorship of the General.

Consequently the design schools of Barcelona became a magnet for those who wished to explore alternative avenues, for the creative and the keen. During the dictatorship you could get away with dangerous ideas discussed as aesthetics or graphics which would never have been allowed in the philosophy faculty. In the sixties a group emerged from these schools who became known as the *gauche divin*, the divine left, a bunch of architects and designers led by Oriol Bohigas and Ricardo Bofill, who represented a kind of post-Marxist intellectual avant-garde dedicated to perpetuating Barcelona's radical visual traditions. In this respect design was seen as a way of stressing a separate and distinct Catalanism, as a cultural and political tool in a world where politics was still impossible.

By the eighties, though, with thoughts of the bad old days fast receding, design and architecture took on a vital new role both in Catalonia and throughout Spain. Now the government were the providers rather than the stiflers, commissioning designers to redraw the public face of their country. It was on a poster commissioned by Mayor Maragall to sing the praises of the city that I first saw the work of Javier Mariscal.

The two most striking aspects of the Barcelona design boom of the eighties were the marvellously bright and clever municipal poster campaigns which emanated from the mayor's office and the *bares de diseño* which came from somewhere else. The designer bars of Barcelona now rank alongside the *Sagrada Familia* and the Picasso museum as tourist attractions, probably more so among the many young design *aficionados* who have flocked to the city since it became fashionable. You can always spot them, they're the ones in the black clothes with their mouths wide open.

Overdressed bars have always played a major part in the social and creative life of the city. The most famous of these, the Quatre Gats, was a fantasy of *Modernismo* where Picasso and Dali sat and argued theatrically for all to see. Then in the early seventies the *gauche divin* hung out in their hipsters in Flash Flash, a neon-bright recreation of Swinging London owned by the architect Bohigas. That tradition of bars which are there to be seen in reflowered in the eighties with an almost psychotic fury.

Seemingly each week a new bar, more elaborate, more expensive, and more emphatically 'designed' than the last, would open up to great excitement: KGB, Universal, Celeste, Zig-Zag, Nick Habanna, Amarcord, Si Si Si, Network, Velvet, Snooker, El Gambrinus, 33 . . . The trend went from austere minimalism, through a twisted high-tech modernism, where the films *Brazil* and *Blade Runner* were clearly a strong reference point, to an almost impossibly lush and totally unique new Barcelonan style known as Modernist Baroque where Edgar Allan Poe meets Richard Rodgers somewhere in a David Lynch movie.

The men who designed these fantastic spaces, like Eduardo Samso and Alfredo Arribas, 'interior architects' in their early thirties, became stars in their own right who were soon shipped off to Tokyo to make designer *doppelgängers* of these

239

surreal film-set watering holes. Quite why so much effort should be put into bars is in itself a complex question. Partly it is the all-important notion of *la marcha*, and the need to be in the happening place. That respect for the night was vital in that it is not seen as a waste to put so much into a bar because half of your life takes place in them. It was also the fact that the hip young hordes were largely poor young hordes who for the most part could not afford to own expensive pieces of design, but they could in some ways rent them for an evening by buying a drink in one of the *bares de diseño*. And to do so was a way of saying 'I am part of this movement, part of the modern world.' Partly of course it was the simple fact that the Catalans had yet again found a way of showing that they were the best in the world at doing something. And the very best interiors had an input from Mariscal.

He was actually born in 1950 in Valencia, the big Catalan-speaking town south of Barcelona, one of eleven children of a doctor. He arrived in Barcelona at the beginning of the seventies with long hair, a pair of Levis and a place at the famed Escuela Elisava to study graphic design, a place he fairly quickly dropped out of. Within a year he was drawing and publishing his own comics and forming a creative collective called the Royal Masquerade with a group of like-minded young artists who all lived together in a huge, tumbledown old house in Eixample. Perhaps he was re-creating the kind of noisy chaos he must have felt at home with all those children. Feeling the pressure of censorship though, they moved like so many of their young countrymen to Ibiza, where all the rules were more relaxed. When he returned in 1977 Mariscal was ready for his first exhibition, I don't suppose too many others were ready for it.

For the young man who had a local reputation for creating jokey, underground, hippie-ish comics put on a show which involved sculptures, ceramics, clothes, paintings, glass and video as well as his cartoons. He is now famous for the almost hysterical speed at which he works. His whole style is sketchy, apparently untutored, seemingly intuitive, and he has boasted that he can create an entire exhibition of paintings in two weeks. This though was the first glimpse of the wavy world of Mariscal, a fantasy universe in primary colours where anything is possible, and everything has the stamp of delighted, wide-eyed sophistication. Then came the chance to redesign his adopted town.

'When Franco died there was a whole new civic life which needed a completely new image and somebody had to do it, this was perfect for my generation, we just had to wake up and say hello here we are.'

I am sitting in Mariscal's plush new design studio out in Poble Nou, a once-derelict dockside area which is to be the home of the new Olympic village. It is also the home of a remarkable creative factory where teams of artists who have gathered together under the leadership of Mariscal are all working together. To call it a factory with the inevitable Warholian connotations may sound contrived, but it is the only term to use for the veritable production line which sees a dozen or so young artists collaborating on the numerous Mariscal projects and products.

'This place is new and a new challenge. For a long time I worked alone, now the aim is to work with people, to explain your ideas, to organise, to find a way to enable them to help me realise things. Now I have to be a businessman and a teacher, at times I feel as if I am doing nothing, working with this many people there is inevitably a great confusion, but I like that, a certain chaos is essential for Spaniards, it gives us energy.'

It is difficult to see the chaos though in this ordered, friendly environment which Mariscal wanders around, hovers in and over, looking indeed like some kind of benign but slightly mad schoolmaster. Checking on work, making jokes, scolding in a gentle, playful way. In this bright, light, glass building the team is creating everything from T-shirts to tables but, most noticeably when I was there, they were working away on *Cobi Discovers The Lost Planet*, a twenty-six-part animated television series starring that famous cat.

'I like cartoons and I like television, I had no idea how to make an animated film, so that seemed a good reason to do one. All the time I am trying new things that I have no idea how to do and people pay me to learn, it is very nice.'

The man talking to me is a small, stocky jumble of a fellow with a mess of dark curly hair and a face that could itself be a cartoon. His expression ranges from baleful to bemused, his movements are languorous, almost ponderous, but his mind flies around with a ping-pong velocity and a playful, jumping logic that is at times difficult to keep up with. With his recollections taking him back to the early, exciting days of Barcelona's rebirth, those basset-hound eyes almost light up.

It was Mariscal who trisected the name of the town, breaking it down into the three component parts: *Bar* (meaning bar) *Cel* (meaning sky) and *Ona* (meaning wave), each of these graphically displayed, in such a way that it soon became the Catalan equivalent of 'I love-heart New York'. Much of Mariscal's work then seemed to want to capture the essences of his city, so all the architectural landmarks were included along with lots of speeding scooters and cars and cartoon youths scurrying around their busy seaside town. If there was any one person responsible for redrawing the image of this great, resurfacing Mediterranean city it was Mariscal.

'Cities now are like enterprises, they need a corporate image, they have to sell themselves. To create a graphic, an image for Barcelona, was wonderful and easy, this is a city with a rich past, but at that time a blank sheet. That fantastic heritage of Gaudí and *Modernismo* was important but so was the geography. If you go up to the mountains you can see the reality, the shape of this city, it is all so defined. That clear picture of Barcelona helps me and it helps everybody who lives here, they have inside themselves a clear image of their own identity.'

The image of Mariscal sitting up on Tibidabo looking down at his town and sketching his quirky, naive little sketches which then become the emblems of Barcelona is even funnier because that is exactly what happened.

'That period back then, it all seemed very natural and very simple. It was a very positive thing that there was so little contemporary culture because it meant we could start afresh and start with no competition. If you live in Paris, London or Milan and you want to start a magazine it is hard because there are already so many established and people's minds are already set. Here it was all new, all exciting and it all seemed easy, we thought anything was possible because we had nothing to say otherwise and we learned by doing it which is the best way.'

The things Mariscal learned to do continued to grow as he was invited to contribute some furniture to the famed Memphis group in Milan – he designed his first and still famous piece, the *Duplex Stool* in a matter of minutes and was heard to remark, 'Heavens, this furniture-making business is a piece of cake.' Then he worked on his first bars and shops in conjunction with an architect, Alfredo Arribas, who was fresh out of college, showed his first exhibition of paintings and yet continued to draw comics and make jokes.

One of the most important themes in Mariscal's work and one of the common elements of much contemporary Spanish culture is the refusal to make any distinction between the populist and the high, between the street and the salon. This comes partly from the fact that Spanish culture has never really been divided in those terms, partly because many of the one-time lowly forms such as flamenco and bullfighting are now so exalted and because after the Franco years the only real living culture came from the streets and the night-clubs, places which even the most successful are still reluctant to leave. That's why architects are happy to design bars and why Mariscal insists on continuing with such a broad swathe.

'For me all good art is pop art and when I make a comic or a carpet it is the same as a painting, it is the same language and a body of work which you should not divide up. I love image, that is my medium, but for me that can take on any form, it just flows through different channels. If you are working for industry with mass production this is one way, another is with galleries and public places, but the vision is always the same and no one is more important.'

To show all this off he organised an exhibition of the entire works entitled '100 Years With Mariscal', a remarkable wodge of a show which premiered in his native Valencia and then moved on to a huge merchant ship anchored off the bay of Barcelona where it was open deep into the night. Those who saw it would indeed have seen a vast selection of work, but all of it clearly from a single, powerfully creative source. Although he has been influenced from many sides, by Disney and Hockney, by Lichtenstein and Rauchenberg and maybe even by his New York contemporaries Jean Michel Basquiat and Keith Haring, there is also something undeniably but indefinably Spanish about everything he does. When I ask him about this he looks even more surprised than usual: 'I think I am very Mediterranean, I feel very much part of this part of the world. Sometimes when I think about Spanish history I realise we have been here a very long time and we have a peculiar way of seeing things. We have a very particular kind of light of course and that affects and feeds you. When I see Velázquez or Goya I feel very close.'

Those links to the past have been apparent in much of the best of new Spanish design where an elegant red-backed chair will be named after Manolete and another will take the organic lines of Gaudí and reproduce them in plastic. Irony, conceit, subversion, allusion, kitsch, all of the tools and tenets of post-modernism have been apparent in Spanish design, but without the weary sense of reaction for its own sake, the cloying self-consciousness of so much eighties' design elsewhere. Everything was new to them and it showed.

The newest Mariscal project was about to be unveiled on the very night of the day that I spent at his studio and as we finished talking he invited me to the opening of the Torres de Avila.

'It is a new club we have just done, I think you will like it.'

The Torres de Avila is in Pueblo Español, a 1920s folly near the Mies van der Rohe pavilion at the foot of the pleasure mountain of Montjuích. Pueblo Español, Spanish village, is a kind of architectural Disneyland designed to show the various types of Iberian settlement in a life-sized model which has sat largely dormant apart from a few curious tourists wandering half-heartedly around. As part of the civic rebuild though the plan was to open up this ageing playground to yet more bars and clubs, so Javier Mariscal and his architect comrade Alfredo Arribas were given the Torres, a real-life mock castle, to play with.

As I approached shortly after midnight I could see that all the requisite trendy trappings of a first night were in place. The floodlighting, the queue and the long-legged, short-skirted girls checking the embossed invitations; I expected all of that but I wasn't prepared for what came next.

As I walked up to the closed, heavy wooden doors of the castle they suddenly shot open and a blinding flashlight went off as if I had just been photographed for some sinister records. This was the first jolt on a fantastic little journey, a wonderful monument to fun. The whole place is a medieval kind of twenty-first century, a dazzling, bizarre concoction of symbols and tricks, a hedonist's wonderland where many things are not quite as they seem, but others, even more remarkably, are.

In the circular room the bar, toilets, even the pool table, are a perfect round, the lift is a metal platform which whisks you to the next floor as soon as you stand on it, the roof is topped by a crystal pyramid, the walls of one room revolve, the floors of another seem to slope disastrously. The tables are made from rough-hewn marble, the sumptuous drapes from suede, it has the feel of a fantasy court with thrones and daises and parapets. Throughout, the whole thing is encrusted with a baffling, invented visual nonsense language of telluric and Masonic symbols which extend from the crazy heraldry in the high-tech subterranean loos to the cartoon sun and moon which top the twin towers of the castle.

The whole thing is an elaborate, lavish laugh, a neo-rococo so thorough and so far out as to be an entirely new language, a ludicrous tongue which could only be talked in and understood in this town. Through all of this I wandered marvelling and giggling, drinking rum and wondering just as I did when I first saw the Gaudís, not how he did it, but why they let him do it, and why they paid for it to be done. Finally I made my way onto the roof where you can stand between the towers, watch the revelries below through the glass pyramid or the city across the rooftops, away through the dark clear blue of a Mediterranean night.

There up on the roof, sitting in one of the chairs he designed, chairs made from heavy slabs of granite so that the wind cannot whip them away, sits Javier Mariscal drinking and gazing at his work through those big cartoon canine eyes. He must have known at that point that he had made the bar to top all bars. In the Torres de Avila, Mariscal and Arribas have played what must surely be the last glorious shot in a great game which has captivated and transformed a city.

We talked for a while about the bar and he accepted my compliments with a slow smile. Then he looked out over the city and said, 'I feel very close to Barcelona and very happy here. For me this is the perfect combination, a northern city in a southern country, we have the sense of joy that you get from the sun, but you can actually get things done.'

Mariscal has certainly done some of those things, but sitting there with him atop his castle I knew that it went further than that, further than we could see. What he said about Barcelona as it spread out before us no longer applies just to his city but to his country too. In so many parts of Spain a fine, sometimes extravagant, but always enjoyable balance has been achieved. There is an equilibrium in the lives of the people which allows them to enjoy the advantages of their beautiful, brilliant place in the sun, but which also enables them to be creative, successful, efficient Europeans, the true success story of the Continent. In Spain now the going is good and so is the doing.

Before returning to Madrid to try to make sense of it all I had some old friends to see.

The End

The cathedral in San Sebastian is an imposing, skyward-bound stone building turned a deep tobacco colour over the years. Set in this elegant, affluent, seaside town it doesn't have the wrath-like glare of the great, grim Spanish churches, but its grace and authority are still intact. On a bright, sunshiny Sunday I watched the neat, middle-class Basque families dressed in their best, emerging from the church after an early evening service.

The women were bunched together, their shoulderpads bumping, heels clicking on the stone steps. The men stood alone smoking, or in pairs, their hands clasped behind their backs as they swaggered lightly, their chests puffed up with the pride *caballeros* universally wear on such occasions. The children who had just been confirmed in the Catholic faith were looking ill at ease and fussy in their finery, the boys especially, seemed trussed by frills and neckties in the blue heat.

Then out of the crowd emerged two young girls, both with shoulder-length dark hair, both in the lacy, wedding-dress-white gowns which accompany a confirmation. Holding hands, they seemed to float away from the mêlée in front of the cathedral portals, moving rhythmically, dancing majestically, effortlessly towards the sea.

Looking close, believing perhaps that the religious experience had somehow enabled them to levitate, it took me a time to blink and realise that beneath the abundant bows and folds of their confirmation gowns, both girls were wearing roller-skates.

A few months later, sitting hiding from the heat in a dark Madrid café, I was drinking beer and reading a novel of Camilo Jose Cela, the most famous living Spanish writer, who had just been awarded the Nobel Prize. Quoting from Nietzsche it ran, 'Happiness . . . of whatever kind gives us air, light, and freedom of movement.' And I thought of those two girls. But most of all I thought of Spain today.

Index